auto body

repairing and repainting

by

Bill Toboldt

Author of Goodheart-Willcox Automotive Encyclopedia;
Diesel, Fundamentals, Service, Repair; Fix Your Ford;
Fix Your Chevrolet; Member, Society of Automotive
Engineers; Associate Member, Automotive Engine Re-
builders Association; Associate Member, Association of
Diesel Specialists

South Holland, Illinois
THE GOODHEART-WILLCOX COMPANY, INC.
Publishers

IMPORTANT SAFETY NOTICE

Work procedures and shop practices described in this book are effective methods of performing service operations. Some require the use
of tools and equipment specially designed for the purpose and should
be used as recommended. This book contains various safety procedures and cautions which should be carefully followed to minimize
the risk of personal injury or the possibility that improper service
methods may damage components or render the vehicle unsafe. Note,
too, that these cautions are not exhaustive. Those performing a given
service procedure or using a particular tool or piece of equipment must
first satisfy themselves that neither their safety, the safety of others,
nor the condition of the vehicle will be jeopardized by the service
method selected.

Library of Congress Cataloging in Publication Data

Toboldt, William King,
  Auto body repairing and repainting.

  Includes index.
  1. Automobiles—Bodies—Maintenance and repair.
2. Automobiles—Painting.   I. Title.
TL255.T58 1982   629.2'6'0288   82—14320
ISBN 0—87006—423—1

INTRODUCTION

In the automotive field, the repairing and repainting of car bodies is growing faster than any other service branch. In addition, the design of some car bodies is being radically changed so that new repair procedures have become necessary.

Each year, there are more cars on the road. As a result, there are more collisions, more wrecked bodies, more damaged fenders. This means plenty of work at top pay for those who have the know-how required to do quality work. Therefore, a chapter on career opportunities has been included to give information on the various areas of service in this growing field.

AUTO BODY REPAIRING AND REPAINTING covers all phases of body repairing, including new methods made necessary by the introduction of the General Motors X style cars and variations of the Mac-Pherson strut construction. In addition, refinishing procedures required by the introduction of water-based paints and clear coats are discussed. All such innovations, together with methods used in conventional designs and the use of modern, specialized equipment and materials, are given in detail.

A chapter on customizing and using fiber glass to build auto bodies is included. Also featured are chapters on using special fillers in the repair of dents and rusted areas and the use of modern adhesives in the installation of body moldings and ornaments.

AUTO BODY REPAIRING AND REPAINTING is an authorative text for students and apprentices who need a substantial background in fundamentals. The text is organized so that the contents are presented in a logical order. It is well suited for those now engaged in auto body repairing who want to increase their skills, and for owners who wish to do repair jobs that do not involve heavy structural members.

Bill Toboldt

CONTENTS

The Pontiac Fiero (top) is a mid-engine, rear-wheel drive vehicle built on a "space frame" (bottom) and a 93.4 in. (2 372 mm) wheelbase. The frame is assembled from separate stampings, then machined in a special operation that mills and drills 39 mounting pads within a tolerance of .020 in. (0.50 mm). This provides a precision structure to locate and support the plastic body panels.

Fig. 1-1. Typical unitized body construction.

Chapter 1

AUTO BODY
CONSTRUCTION

Today there are two principal types of auto body construction:

A. The unitized body construction.

B. The body and frame construction.

In the unitized body construction, Fig. 1-1, individual metal parts are welded together to make up the body assembly and provide overall body rigidity through an integral all steel welded construction.

The attachment provisions for the power train and suspension systems are provided by the underbody area, Fig. 1-2, which also contributes to the strength of the vehicle. The floor pan, Fig. 1-2, and related sections become an integral part of the frame thus eliminating the conventional separate body and frame. This is accomplished through the welded combination of boxed sections

Fig. 1-2. Underbody of unitized body.

(rocker panel areas and frame rails) and the floor pan.

The separate frame and body construction is a type of construction that has been in use for many years and continues to be used in full size cars.

Late model frames are shown in Figs. 1-3 and 1-4. Fig. 1-5 points out various trim moldings installed on a compact vehicle.

BODY DESIGN DETAILS

In working in auto body repairing and repainting, it is important to learn the names of the different parts of the automobile

SAFETY IN THE AUTO BODY SHOP

AN IMPORTANT PART OF YOUR EXPERIENCE IN THE AUTO BODY SHOP WILL BE LEARNING TO FOLLOW SAFE PRACTICES AND PROCEDURES THAT WILL PREVENT INJURIES TO YOURSELF AND TO OTHERS.

IT IS IMPORTANT AT THIS TIME, FOR YOU TO STUDY AND TO BECOME THOROUGHLY FAMILIAR WITH BASIC RULES OF SAFETY, AS DISCUSSED IN CHAPTER 34, PAGE 241.

Fig. 1-3. Perimeter type chassis frame on which the body is mounted.

Fig. 1-4. Front-wheel drive vehicle uses unitized construction with sub-frame rails.
(Chrysler Corporation)

Fig. 1-5. Modern automobile with typical trim features. A—Roof drip molding. B—Windshield reveal molding. C—Front door window frame molding. D—Front fender side molding. E—Front door side molding. F—Rear door side molding. G—Door edge guard trim. H—Bumper molding. I—Rear window reveal molding. (Ford)

Fig. 1-6. Individual parts that make a modern auto body. (Chrysler-Plymouth Div., Chrysler Corp.)

body, and also the methods used in assembling the various parts.

Typical bodies with various panels indentified are shown in Figs. 1-6 and 1-7. Note the names of the different panels and the location of the seams where they are joined to the other body panels or sections. Such seams vary with different makes and models of

1. Panel Assembly. 2. Moulding Assembly. 3. Plate Assembly. 4. Bolt. 5. Bolt. 6. Skirt. 7. Fender. 8. Moulding Unit. 9. Moulding Unit. 10. Nut. 11. Emblem. 12. Nut. 13. Extension. 14. Extension. 15. Shield. 16. Skirt. 17. Bolt. 18. Shroud Assembly. 19. Cap Assembly. 20. Core. 21. Bar Assembly. 22. Support Assembly. 23. Extension. 24. Bolt. 25. Screw. 26. Bumper. 27. Nut. 28. Spring. 29. Catch Assembly. 30. Pin. 31. Extension. 32. Extension. 33. Nut. 34. Bumper. 35. Brace. 36. Reinforcement. 37. Bolt. 38. Reinforcement Assembly. 39. Bolt. 40. Hinge Assembly. 41. Spring. 42. Nut. 43. Moulding Unit.

Fig. 1-7. Sheet metalwork of front end:

Fig. 1-8. Details of energy absorbing bumper and related parts installed on late model Chevrolet cars. Other General Motors' installations are similar.

Fig. 1-9. Rear protective strips used on Chevelle and Monte Carlo.

Fig. 1-10. Installation drawing of front fender.

bodies, but the illustrations are typical and can be used as a general guide when ordering replacement panels.

Details of front and rear bumper construction and method of mounting are shown in Figs. 1-8 and 1-9. A method used in attaching front fenders is shown in Figs. 1-10 and 1-11. Fig. 1-12 shows details of head and taillight construction.

Fig. 1-11. Dodge front fender mounting is detailed.

Fig. 1-12. Study parts of typical head and taillight assemblies. (AMC)

Fig. 1-13. *Exterior moldings and method of attachment on a typical Ford station wagon.*

Fig. 1-14. *One method of removing moulding clip.*

There are many different methods of attaching moldings. Typical methods are illustrated in Fig. 1-13 and methods of removal and installation of the attaching clips for such molding are illustrated in Figs. 1-14 and 1-15. Further details on removal and installation of trim and hardware are given in later chapters.

Before straightening any damaged body, it

Fig. 1-15. Removing moulding clip with plier-type tool.

of construction. In the case of the frame-body type of design, it is necessary to first straighten the frame, if that is damaged. In the case of the unitized body, the car is treated as a single unit.

QUIZ - Chapter 1

1. How many basic types of body construction are in common use?
   One.
   Two.
   Three.
   Four.
2. Does the unitized body construction provide overall body rigidity?
   Yes.
   No.
3. Where is the rocker panel located?
   Below the rear deck.
   Below the doors.
   Below the radiator.
   Above the rear quarter panel.

is necessary to determine the type of construction: That is, whether the body is of the unitized type, or whether the car has a conventional frame and body. This is necessary as the repair procedure will vary with the type of construction. Naturally in the case of minor damage, such as a dented panel, the procedure is the same regardless of the type

Note body components that receive corrosion protection on this late model, small car.
(Chrysler-Plymouth)

Chapter 2
BASIC HAND TOOLS
FOR BODY SHOP MECHANICS

Before attempting to remove dents from a damaged panel, you should become thoroughly familiar with the different types of tools usually used, and under what conditions each should be used. The basic hand tools used in a body shop are:

1. Assorted hammers.
2. Assorted dollies.
3. Pick tools.
4. Adjustable file holder.
5. Solder paddle.
6. Vise grip pliers.
7. Fender beading tools.
8. Assorted wrenches.
9. Assorted screwdrivers.
10. Cold chisels.

HAMMERS

Probably the most frequently used tool in the body shop is some form of dinging hammer, A, Fig. 2-1. These hammers, used together with a dolly block, B, Fig. 2-1, are used to remove dents from sheet metal. In A, Fig. 2-1, the hammer on the left is known as a combination or pick hammer. Next is a conventional dinging hammer with a long reach. Next is a dinging hammer with a shorter reach. The one on the right in Fig. 2-1, is another utility or pick hammer. While there is some difference in opinion as to names which should be used to identify different types of hammers, the ones given are accepted by most authorities.

The face of the dinging hammer may be round or square. The round-face hammer is used for general dinging, while the square-face is used for working close to a bead or other ornamentation. Also the face of the hammer may be flat or have a slight crown.

The overall length of the head of a dinging hammer may vary from 4 to 6 in. This variation in "reach" is needed because working spaces vary considerably: Some fenders are crowned more than others; also the space available for swinging the hammer varies.

The combination hammer, (any hammer with a pointed end) is used to remove small dents, which would be difficult to remove with a conventional hammer and dolly block. Such hammers are available in varying weights and point sharpness and are known as "pick" hammers.

In addition to the hammers listed, heavy roughing hammers are also available. Such hammers vary in design but are much heavier than any of those illustrated.

Hammers resembling a conventional dinging hammer, but with a corrugated face, are also used for shrinking metal. (See Chapter on Shrinking.)

Conventional ball peen or mechanic hammers are used with cold chisels and for similar work.

Under certain conditions, some mechanics prefer to use a mallet with a rubber head, for preliminary straightening and rough work. But in general such practice is discouraged in favor of other methods as explained in the chapter on the use of hand tools.

DOLLY BLOCKS

These are basically anvils and a variety of different shapes and sizes are available. Three popular shapes are shown in B, Fig. 2-1, additional shapes are shown in Fig. 2-2. These are held on one side of the dented sheet metal, while the other side of the dent is struck with the dinging hammer. It will be

Fig. 2-1. Basic hand tools for the body mechanic. A—Dinging hammer, B—Assorted dolly blocks, C—Assorted spoons, D—Assorted pick tools, E—File and file holder, F—Solder paddle, G—Vise-grip pliers, H—Cold Chisels.

Fig. 2-2. Assortment of dolly blocks. Upper, heel and utility dollies. Center, general purpose and mushroom dollies. Lower, wedge and toe dollies.

noted in B, Fig. 2-2, that the surfaces of the dollies are finished in different radii. This is done so that the dolly will conform to the curve of the panel being straightened.

SPOONS

These multi-purpose tools, shown in C, Fig. 2-1, are used as pry bars to pry the metal back into position, and are also used as dolly blocks when the area to be straightened cannot be reached with a conventional dolly block. Additional types are shown in Fig. 2-3. For example, dents in doors or deck lids can often be backed up with a spoon inserted through openings in the reenforcing on the back side of the door. Spoons are also used to distribute the hammer blows over wider areas. In such cases the spoon is placed on the ridge or damaged area and then struck

Fig. 2-3. Various types of spoons. Upper, short elbow and curved spoons. Center, offset straight and long elbow spoons. Lower, curved flat and flat top spoons.

with the hammer. Not only is the hammer blow distributed over a wider area in this manner, but also more important, the paint is not marred. Spoons are also used at times as "slappers," that is, the dented metal is slapped with the spoon in order to remove the dent.

PICK TOOLS

These are specialized pry bars, shown in D, Fig. 2-1, and are designed to reach behind brackets and reenforcing bars in order to pry the metal. They are also used as spoons. The pointed end of the pick tool is so designed that it can be placed at the high point of a dent which is then forced out. Most, but not all, pick tools have pointed ends; some are flattened.

FILE HOLDER

This important tool holds the flexible file for filing body panels. Illustrated in E, Fig.

2-1, is an unadjustable type. Adjustable types are also available as shown in Fig. 2-4. By

Fig. 2-4. Body file with flexible handle.

means of the adjustment the file is bent to conform to the curvature of the panel being repaired. The adjustment is made by turning the turnbuckle, Fig. 2-4. By filing the surface of the damaged panel, after dinging work, the high spots are quickly shown so that further work with dolly block and hammer can be performed.

SOLDER PADDLE

This tool is made of close-grained maple, and is designed for spreading the solder over the surface of the panel. A special body worker's solder which is kept in plastic condition by means of a torch, is used to fill low spots in the panel. A typical solder paddle is shown in F, Fig. 2-1. Paddles in various shapes are available.

VISE-GRIP PLIERS

The vise-grip plier G, Fig. 2-1, has many uses in the body shop. The most frequent use is to hold two adjoining pieces of sheet metal together so that they are in proper alignment while being welded.

PRY BARS

There are various types and sizes of pry bars which are used for bending fender brackets, door hinges, and other parts. Some have forked ends; others are flat.

Tools described in preceding paragraphs of this chapter may be considered as basic tools, by the body repairman. In addition to these, specialized auto body mechanic's kits of tools (general purpose tools) such as shown in Fig. 2-5, are also needed to disassemble

Fig. 2-5. Wrenches and other hand tools for disassembling body parts.

parts of the vehicle to permit replacement or repair of panels.

In addition, every mechanic should have metric wrenches. Certain late model U.S. cars and engines are being built to metric dimensions, as are nearly 2,000,000 foreign cars registered in the U.S. each year.

QUIZ – Chapter 2

1. How many basic hand tools are used in a body shop?
    Five.
    Seven.
    Eight.
    Ten.
    Fifteen.
2. A combination or pick hammer is
    Flat on both faces.
    Pointed on both faces.
    Flat on one face and pointed on the other.
3. The overall length of the head on a dinging hammer is approximately how long?
    Ranges from 4 to 6 in.
    Ranges from 8 to 10 in.
    Ranges from 2 to 3 in.
4. The surfaces of the dolly blocks are all of the same radii.
    True.
    False.
5. Spoons are a single purpose tool.
    True.
    False.
6. How are file holders adjusted to different arcs?
    By means of a setscrew.
    By means of a turnbuckle.
7. The file holder is adjusted so that the file is bent to conform to the _____ of the panel being repaired.

A few specialized tools of the body mechanic. (Kansas Jack)

Chapter 3
HOW TO
USE HAND TOOLS

USING THE HAMMER AND DOLLY

The most frequently used tools in the mechanic repairman's kit are the dinging hammer and the dolly block. As previously pointed out, the dolly is held in one hand and acts as an anvil. It is held against the damaged area while the other side of the area is struck with the dinging hammer, Fig. 3-1. Care should be taken when selecting the dolly and

Fig. 3-1. The dolly is held on one side of the panel where it acts as an anvil, while the other side of the panel is struck with the hammer.

the hammer to be used for the job at hand. First the curve of the dolly should conform approximately to the curve or crown of the panel being straightened, Fig. 3-2. In other words, never use a flat surface of a dolly on a crowned panel. The curve of the dolly should always be the same or have a smaller radius

than the curve of the panel being straightened. Similarly, when selecting a dinging hammer for work on a specific panel, the radius of the face of the hammer should always be less than the curve of the panel. A flat face of a

Fig. 3-2. The arc of the dolly block should coincide with the contour of the body panel.

hammer used on a concave surface would produce a lot of nicks which would have to be filled before refinishing. The curved face of the hammer, as shown in Fig. 3-3, should be used on concave surfaces, and the flat face

Fig. 3-3. Use the curved face of the hammer on a concave surface as shown, to avoid making small dents and nicks in the surface.

on convex. Fig. 3-4, shows the dinging operation in its simplest form. The dolly is held against one side of the dent, while the hammer blows are directed against the rim of the dent. Note that the radius of the dolly face is less than the basic curve of the panel. Also note that the hammer face for this surface is flat. If the dolly had been held on the upper surface and the hammer blows on the lower, a flat-faced dolly and a curved-face hammer should have been used.

The condition illustrated in Fig. 3-5, is

Fig. 3-4. *Simplest form of ding work. Note that radius of the dolly block face is less than the basic curve of the body.*

mer blows are directed against the rim of the dent. Note that the radius of the dolly face is less than the basic curve of the panel. Also note that the hammer face for this surface is flat. If the dolly had been held on the upper surface and the hammer blows on the lower, a flat-faced dolly and a curved-face hammer should have been used.

The condition illustrated in Fig. 3-5, is

Fig. 3-5. *Dinging OFF the dolly. Note that the dolly is directly under the dent, while the hammer blows are directed against the edge of the dent.*

known as dinging OFF the dolly. In this case, the hammer is driving one area down while the reaction of the dolly is driving an adjacent area upward. When the dolly is held directly under the area being struck by the hammer, as shown in Fig. 3-6, it is known as dinging ON the dolly. The result is that the dented metal is ironed smooth between the working faces of the dolly and the hammer. Each blow of the hammer forms a smooth spot about 1/4-in. to 3/8-in. in diameter, depending on the amount of crown of the hammer. As the dolly is moved along the surface of the panel, the succeeding hammer blows will leave a series of overlapping spots on the panel. Then another row is dinged next to the original row until the panel is straightened. As a result the area will be covered with parallel rows of spots made by the dinging hammer.

Fig. 3-6. *When the dolly is held directly under the area being struck by the hammer, it is known as dinging ON the dolly.*

USING THE DINGING HAMMER

Considerable care must be taken when using the dinging hammer. First of all, heavy blows will tend to make the metal of the body panel thinner, spreading it out and stretching it. This will cause it to have a greater area than it had originally. The face of the hammer must strike the panel squarely. Should the edge of the hammer strike the panel, a nick will be made which later will have to be filled in order to have a smooth surface.

When driving a nail with a hammer, considerable force is used with what is known as follow-through so that the nail is driven into the wood. When using a dinging hammer, no follow-through is used. Instead, it has more of a slapping action. In that way the metal is not thinned so much and stretching is kept to a minimum.

The hammer is not gripped tightly, but rather loosely, and it is held close to the end of the handle, Fig. 3-7. It is swung with more of a wrist action, rather than the full arm swing. Usually a body repairman strikes

Fig. 3-8. One method of using a spoon is as a pry bar. It can also be used as a dolly in restricted areas where a conventional dolly cannot be used.

the curve of a dolly be less than the curve of the panel. Dollies with a straight edge are used along the edge of straight molding.

USING THE SPOON

Heavy type spoons are often used as pry bars, Fig. 3-8. They are particularly helpful in prying out sheet metal on doors or trunk lids where the damaged metal is backed up by strengthening braces and panels. The heavier type spoons are also used as dollies when the design permits reaching into areas too small for the conventional dolly, Fig. 3-9.

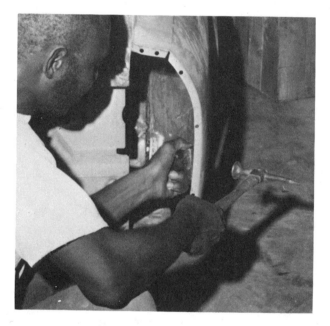

Fig. 3-7. Dolly must be held firmly against the surface of the metal.

about 100 blows per minute in doing ding work. However, this varies with different men and the character of the straightening job.

USING THE DOLLY

The dolly block is pressed firmly against the opposite side of the panel, Fig. 3-7. As a dented area is struck with a dinging hammer, the dolly block will rebound from the panel, but will return immediately, due to the pressure of the mechanic's hand. As previously pointed out, a dolly is selected so that the surface conforms to the curve of the panel being straightened. In no case should

Fig. 3-9. Spoons are also used in the same manner as a dolly when space is limited.

In such cases, one end of the spoon is held by the mechanic, while the other end backs up the damaged area of the panel. The lighter type spoons are designed to hammer over a wider area. In such cases they are placed on top of the ridge of the damaged area and struck with the dinging hammer. In that way a larger area receives the hammer blow, and at the same time there is a reduced possibility of marring the painted surface.

Do not take a firm grip on the spoon, unless it is being used as a lever. Under normal conditions it should be held loosely, the hand acting as a guide and as a positioner.

exercised concerning the weight of the blow used with the hammer, otherwise too much metal will be raised.

USING PICK TOOLS

The pick tool, Fig. 2-1, is a lever-type tool, and is used primarily to push out small

Fig. 3-10. Using a pick hammer to remove small dents.

USING THE PICK HAMMER

A pick hammer is used to raise a low spot or small dent which has been disclosed after the surface has been filed, Fig. 3-10. A fine-pointed end of a pick hammer is used on small dents, and more rounded ends on larger dents. In some cases the mechanic will place the point of the hammer on the high point of the dent, and then strike the head of the pick hammer with another hammer. In other cases the mechanics will strike the dent with the point of the pick hammer, using the hammer in the conventional manner. Care must be

Fig. 3-11. Using a pick tool.

dents in areas where normal hammer and dolly work cannot be performed, Fig. 3-11. Doors are a good example. In such cases, by working through one of the access holes in the rear face of the door, the tool can be used to force out dents on the outside panel of the door. Another method of removing such dents is by means of pull rods, as described in another chapter.

TIPS ON FILING

The fender file is used mostly to locate high and how spots, rather than to remove metal. It must be remembered that the sheet metal of which auto bodies are made is approximately 1/32-in. thick, and a file will quickly cut through it. There are adjustable file holders, Fig. 3-12, also nonadjustable file holders available. When using a body file it is pushed forward at an angle and not straight forward, Fig. 3-12. Pushing it straight forward will tend to cut a groove in the panel. Only light pressure should be

Fig. 3-12. *When using a body file it should be pushed forward at an angle.*

placed on the file as it is placed forward. Heavy pressure will tend to make the file teeth dig into the metal rather than cut it. However, sufficient pressure must be used to prevent chattering.

At the start of the cut, the teeth at the forward end of the file are doing the cutting. Then as the stroke progresses, the teeth which are actually doing the cutting, progress toward the heel or rear of the file. In that way, at the end of the stroke, all the file teeth from the front to the rear have been used. Strokes should be long and regular, not short and choppy.

If the file holder is of the flexible or adjustable type, it may be adjusted to conform approximately to the contour of the panel being filed. However, care must be exercised that the file is not flexed too far as there is always a possibility of breaking the file.

After the low and high spots which are located by the file have been removed by means of the dolly block and hammer, the file or disc sander is again used to remove scratches and tool marks.

QUIZ - Chapter 3

1. Which are the most frequently used tools in the auto body repairman's kit?
    Screwdriver.
    Welding torch.
    Dinging hammer and dolly block.
    File.
2. How is the dolly used?
    As a hammer.
    As an anvil.
    In the same manner as a pry bar.
3. The flat face of the hammer is used on concave surfaces.
    True.
    False.
4. The radius of the dolly face should be greater or less than the basic curve of the dent being straightened.
    Greater.
    Less.
    The same.
5. When using a dinging hammer it should be used in the same manner as when driving a nail.
    True.
    False.
6. Describe the manner in which a dinging hammer should be used.
7. The dolly block is held loosely against the surface of the metal.
    True.
    False.
8. Is a fender file used mostly to remove metal or to locate high and low spots?
    Remove metal.
    Locate high and low spots.
9. When using a fender file it should be pushed.
    Straight forward.
    Forward at an angle.
10. After the dents have been removed by means of the dolly block and hammer, what tool is used to remove tool marks and other slight imperfections?
    Pick hammer.
    Adjustable file.
    Power sander.

Chapter 4
SIMPLIFIED
METAL STRAIGHTENING

FUNDAMENTALS

Straightening a damaged panel on an automobile is not as difficult as it would seem from the appearance of the panel. First, carefully study the damaged area to determine the best procedure to follow in removing the damage. If the wrong procedure is used first, additional work will often be required to complete the straightening operation. If the correct method is followed, much of the damaged area will automatically flex back into shape, and the total time for complete restoration is reduced.

Before starting any panel straightening operation, it is therefore important to examine the damage carefully to ascertain the best method of straightening. Basically the procedure is to remove the damage in reverse of the way it occurred.

The uninformed body mechanic will usually seize a rubber mallet or hammer and start the job by striking at the center of the damaged area. While this will force a large area of the sheet metal back into approximately its original position, actually additional damage is being created. In fact this roughing out procedure has not corrected any of the basic damage. That is still there and in most cases some marks of the roughing hammer or mallet plus some stretched metal have been added to the original damage. Extra time is, therefore, required to restore the panel.

STARTING THE JOB RIGHT

To keep the work of straightening to a minimum, the damage must be removed in the reverse order to which it was created.

The damage caused by a collision does not occur instantaneously, but progresses from the instant of impact until the vehicle comes to rest. In other words a panel is first pushed in, and as the force continues, damage spreads further in a series of ridges. These ridges become deeper and more sharply bent, the farther they are from the point of initial contact.

Therefore, the first job of the repairman is to analyze the damage to determine where the panel was struck first and which ridges were formed last. It is these last formed ridges which must be removed first. As they are removed, the metal that is merely flexed out of position must spring back without any work being done directly on it by the mechanic.

The point of initial impact, that is the point where the damage started, can usually be

Fig. 4-1. The simplest form of dent is made when a panel is struck a direct blow.

recognized by the fact that the paint is deeply scratched, and in severe cases the metal may be torn.

The simplest form of damage occurs when a part is struck a direct blow by another vehicle. An example of such damage is seen in Fig. 4-1. More complicated damage occurs if the moving vehicle strikes a parked car on an angle so that the metal will be pushed into a series of ridges, Fig. 4-2.

is that the straightening process should start at the farthest edge of the damage, not at the center. The ridges are removed in reverse order to which they were formed.

The complete procedure for removing a simple dent, such as is illustrated in Fig. 4-1, is as follows: First, remove all dust and undercoating from the damaged area. Then using a dolly and dinging hammer, place the dolly under the spot A, Fig. 4-1, strike

Fig. 4-2. When the body is struck at an angle a more complicated series of dents and wrinkles is formed.

The most complicated damage results when a vehicle is struck a series of blows so that one set of wrinkles and dents is superimposed on another. Such a condition would result when a car is rolled over and over, Fig. 4-3.

Obviously, the damage illustrated in Fig. 4-1 was caused by a direct push from a bumper and bumper guard of another vehicle, with the force centering at B. The deepest ridge is at A. This is farthest from B, therefore, A should be removed first. As the ridge at A is removed, the entire area of damage will tend to spring back into place. On the other hand, if the mechanic works first on the area B, the ridge at A will still be there. C-D is not termed as a ridge but as a crease put in the metal by the bumper bar.

Actually the damaged area may be considered as a wheel, with its center at B, and the points A, C, E and D forming the rim of the wheel. Removing the ridges at A and E will permit the rest of the area to flex back into shape. The important point to remember

the outer surface of the panel with the dinging hammer. Keep working around that area until the panel tends to spring back into position. Then follow through with the dolly and hammer to point C, D and E. The panel should now be virtually smooth. Run the palm of a hand over the surface panel in an effort to locate any low spots by feel. Low spots can

Fig. 4-3. When a car is rolled, the most complicated series of dents are formed.

also be located by changing the position of trouble lights. Then when the panel appears to be perfectly smooth, use the body workers file. Draw it lightly over the surface, and any areas that are not touched by the file are obviously low, and will have to be raised by additional work with the dolly and dinging hammer. The areas that have been filed are high and will have to be hammered down. When the low and high spots are small in area, more like dimples, some mechanics will use a pick hammer to remove them. Both sharp and blunt-pointed pick hammers are available. The dent can be removed by using the pick hammer as a hammer, or the pointed end can be placed against the dent, and the other end struck with another hammer. Proceed in that manner until no further low or high spots are revealed by the use of the fender file. Following the initial filing, the surface should be smoothed by means of a power sander.

In order to understand how to remove the dents from a body panel, it is important to understand what happens to a piece of sheet metal (such as is used in an auto body) when it is damaged. A careful study of Fig. 4-1, shows that the damage consists of both ridges A and E, and the V-channels, C-D. In addition, in cases of more severe damage, the metal will be stretched and in some cases torn.

In the simplest type of damage, where the metal is pushed in without the formation of any ridges, or V-channels, a condition exists such as is shown in Fig. 4-4. By releasing the

Fig. 4-4. When there is no sharp ridge, the panel will spring back into position when stress is released.

strain, the panel will automatically spring back into its original shape. The metal has not been severely stressed. If the metal does not spring back, then it has been stressed beyond its elastic limit. Every material has the property of elasticity up to a certain point,

which is called its elastic limit. When stressed beyond that point, it will not return to its original shape and form.

Fig. 4-5, shows metal that has been bent into a sharp ridge. Simply pulling each end of the metal, Fig. 4-6, will not remove the ridge as it has been stressed beyond its elastic limit. Whenever metal is bent beyond its elastic limit and takes a permanent set, the metal becomes work hardened and is actually

Fig. 4-5. Illustration of metal bent into a sharp edge.

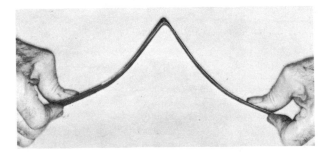

Fig. 4-6. Simply pulling on the ends of such a ridge will not remove the damage.

Fig. 4-7. Force must be applied at the bend area to remove the sharp ridge.

stiffer at the area of the bend than it was originally.

Restoring damaged panels to their original shape is largely a problem of removing the V-channels and ridges.

If an attempt is made to straighten the sheet metal, Fig. 4-5, by simply bending up the ends, Fig. 4-6, the ridge has not been changed, but two bends have been added. That is what happens when an attempt is made to straighten a damaged panel by working at the point of original impact.

However, if force is applied at the bent area, or ridge, Fig. 4-7, the metal will go back to its original shape without any difficulty.

QUIZ - Chapter 4

1. When removing a dent from an auto body panel where should the work be started?

At the center of the dent.

At the area farthest from the center of the dent.

2. To keep the work of straightening at a minimum, the damage must be removed in the same order in which it was created.

True.

False.

3. It is not necessary to remove dirt and undercoating before removing any dents.

True.

False.

4. When removing dents, should the straightening process proceed directly toward the center, or should it proceed in a circular manner toward the center.

Directly.

In a circular manner.

5. When metal is stressed beyond its elastic limit, it will spring back to its original shape when the strain is released.

True.

False.

Hand operated equipment is being used in a simple pushing operation to straighten door pillar. (Hein-Werner)

Fig. 5-1. Typical disk-type portable sander.

Chapter 5

HOW TO USE SANDERS

There are three main types of sanders used in the auto body repair work:

A. Rotary or Disk.

B. Oscillating.

C. Belt.

Disk sanders are available in portable models, Fig. 5-1, and flexible shaft models. The portable type of disk sander and grinder is used by virtually all auto body shops. It is available from several power tool manufacturers in 7 in. and 9 in. sizes. A 7 in. tool is one that can be fitted with 7 in. diameter abrasive disks; a 9 in. grinder uses 9 in. diameter disks. The usual grinder-sander used in auto body shops operates on a 110 V, 60 cycle current. Such tools are also available to operate at higher voltages. Pneumatic (air-operated) tools are also available.

Fig. 5-2. Feather edging with a disk sander.

SAFETY PRECAUTIONS

Before attempting to use a sander, or any other electrical tool, there are certain precautions that must be observed.

Make sure that any extension cables are of adequate size to carry the current being used. For example, if an extension cable of 50 ft. is being used, and a grinder or other electrical tool draws 5 amp., the extension cable must be of at least 18 gauge. The size cable for other currents and cable length is as given in the following table:

Based on current equivalent to 150 per cent of full load of tool and a loss in voltage of not over 5 volts. This table for 115-volt tools. For 220-volt tools use wire size corresponding to an extension length of one-half the contemplated length.

Full-load ampere rating (on nameplate)	0–2.00	2.10–3.4	3.5–5.00	5.10–7.0	7.10–12	12.1–16.0
Ext. Cable Length	Wire size (B & S gauge)					
25 ft.	18	18	18	18	16	14
50 ft.	18	18	18	16	14	12
75 ft.	18	18	16	14	12	10
100 ft.	18	16	14	12	10	8
200 ft.	16	14	12	10	8	6
300 ft.	14	12	10	8	6	4
400 ft.	12	10	8	6	4	4
500 ft.	12	10	8	6	4	2
600 ft.	10	8	6	4	2	2
800 ft.	10	8	6	4	2	1
1000 ft.	8	6	4	2	1	0

Note—If voltage is already low at the source (outlet), have voltage increased to standard, or use a much larger cable than listed in order to prevent any further loss in voltage.

Make sure every electrical tool is grounded. This is an important safety precaution and is an underwriters' requirement. Electrical tools should have a three conductor cable and a three blade grounding type attachment plug cap. This is used with the proper type wall receptacle.

If the shop does not have the proper type wall receptacle or outlet, special adaptor plugs are available. Such plugs, which will fit a two-prong outlet and receive the three-prong connector on the end of the electrical grinder cable, are also provided with a short ground wire which is then connected to the cover screw on the outlet box.

Electric tools should never be used by an operator standing on a wet floor, or with wet hands.

If arcing is noted at the motor brushes, the electrical tool should be repaired, as arcing will start a fire in areas where lacquers are being sprayed.

In addition to the electrical safety precautions, operators of grinding or sanding equipment should always wear safety goggles, Fig. 5-2, or a face mask. A respirator is also advisable because of the dust, paint and metal particles that are produced.

USING DISK SANDER

When using a disk sander, the tool should be held firmly but without undue pressure of the tool against the auto body. Heavy pressure will slow cutting action, and reduce the life of the abrasive disk.

The rotary sander should be used with a long sweeping motion, back and forth to produce smooth continuous coverage. The sander should not be operated in one spot, as this will tend to burn the metal. Neither should a circular motion be used. If the angle of the tool is too great, only a small area of the disk will contact the surface of the panel and a rough cut surface will be obtained. If the disk is placed flat against the work surface, the cutting action will be irregular and bumpy. In addition, it will be difficult to control the motion of the tool. For best results, the sander should be tipped with just enough pressure to bend the disk, as shown in Fig. 5-3.

Disk sanders are used to remove paint and

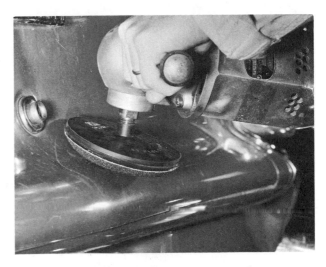

Fig. 5-3. Illustrating the correct and wrong way of using an electric sander.

to locate low spots in panels. The low spots disclosed by means of a sander are clearly shown in Fig. 5-2. When used for grinding, the disk sander is normally moved from left to right, and to remove grinding marks is moved at right angles to the grind marks.

Fig. 5-4. A cone-shaped mandrel with abrasive is used to sand sharp curved surfaces.

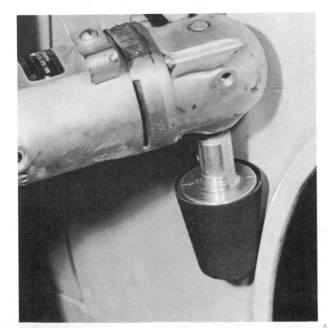

On most surfaces, the conventional flat disk is used with the sander-grinder. However, on curved surfaces, cone shaped mandrels and abrasives, Fig. 5-4, and curved pads with disk abrasives, Fig. 5-5, are available.

Fig. 5-5. Here a curved disk and abrasive is being used to sand a panel that is moderately curved.

OSCILLATING AND ORBITAL SANDERS

These sanders, which are used primarily for finish sanding of the metal and paint surface, are available in electrical and pneumatic types, Fig. 5-6. Some of these sanders

Fig. 5-6. For finish sanding of metal and paint surfaces, a sander with a reciprocating or orbital motion may be used.

have a straight reciprocating motion, while others, known as the orbital type, have a slight rotary motion.

Such sanders are used primarily for removing scratches left by the grinding operation. Many mechanics also use them for featheredging, that is the paint surrounding the damaged area is tapered back, so that there will be no sharp edge or ridge between the original paint and the area which is to be refinished.

Power sanding of this type is preferable to hand sanding methods which are time consuming. Only slight pressure should be applied when using the reciprocating or orbital type of sander. Sanders of this type can be used for either wet or dry sanding.

The pneumatic types operate at normal shop air pressure of approximately 75 psi, and are normally used for featheredging with abrasive paper of No. 60, 80 or 120 grit. The most popular is No. 80.

BELT SANDERS

A belt sander may also be used to remove paint, sand, solder and plastic and for finished sanding. As shown in Fig. 5-7, it will produce a flat surface, and can also be used on sharp curved surfaces by using just the "toe" of the tool. Abrasive belts of various grits are available. One of the major advantages of the

belt sander is that it is equipped with a dust collector which greatly improves working conditions for the body mechanic, Fig. 5-7.

When using a belt sander, it is moved back and forth across the surface of the work. Care must be taken that the sander is kept moving and not held in one position, as that would tend to burn the metal. Also when locating high and low spots on a panel be sure to keep the strokes of the sander parallel. Then after further dinging, cross sand in opposite direction from the first sanding to recheck for high and low spots.

SELECTING THE CORRECT ABRASIVE

In order to keep the time required to repair an auto body to a minimum and at the same time turn out high quality work, it is important that the correct abrasive be used at each stage of the reconditioning procedure.

Coated abrasives is a general term for all abrasives used in refinishing automobiles. In their various forms they may be known as sandpaper, waterproof paper, grinding disks, grinding combs, grinding belts, and many others.

The quality of the final finish is largely de-

Fig. 5-7. Belt sanders can be used on either flat or curved surfaces and have the added advantage that a vacuum attachment will carry away the dust.

pendent upon the proper selection and use of these coated abrasives. Although there are many types of coated abrasives, all are a combination of minerals, backing and bonds.

While the term sandpaper is still frequently used, it is not correct, as sand is not used. Of the five different minerals used as cutting agents in coated abrasives, three are natural, being mined or quarried, and two are artificially produced in electrical furnaces.

Flint quartz, commonly called "flint" is generally off-white when seen on the finished sheet of paper. Flint paper is commonly sold in hardware stores, but has almost no use in industry and auto body repair shops as other grains are far superior.

Emery consists of crystals of natural aluminum oxide, a good cutting agent, imbedded in iron oxide, which has no abrasive quality. Emery has been largely superceded by other types of abrasives.

Garnet of the same name as a semi-precious jewel and coming from the same source is sharp and hard. This is largely used in wood finishing.

Crocus is basically not an abrasive but a polishing agent of iron oxide.

Aluminum oxide is reddish brown in color, and is made in electric furnaces by fusing the mineral bauxite at extremely high temperatures. This comes from the electric furnace in large lumps, which are then crushed and separated for size. Special adhesives and processes are then used to secure the abrasive crystals.

Silicon carbide also is an electric furnace product and is produced by high temperature fusing of silica sand and coke. The result is a crystalline abrasive which is very hard and sharp.

Aluminum oxide and silicon carbide abrasive materials are the ones commonly used in auto body reconditioning and refinishing. Some authorities recommend the silicon carbide abrasive particularly for finishing primer-surfacer coats, as the crystals keep fracturing and thus continually provide a sharp cutting area to the work surface. On the other hand, aluminum oxide is extremely tough with a high resistance to fracturing, and, therefore, is capable of penetrating the surface. Because of such qualities some

authorities recommend it particularly for metal finishing.

The two most frequently used materials for bonding the abrasive to the backing material are glue and resin. In general, glue bonds are not waterproof and less resistant to heat than resin.

Paper, cloth, fiber and combinations are the usual materials used for backing. Combinations either paper and cloth, or fiber and cloth are frequently used.

SELECTING SANDING DISKS

Basically there are two broad types of sanding disks used in the auto body reconditioning field:

1. Open-grain abrasive disks.
2. Closed-grain abrasive disks.

On the open-grain disk, as the name implies, the grains of abrasive are separated so that there is appreciable space between the individual grains. The backing is only fifty to seventy percent covered with abrasive grains, leaving open space between grains. Such grits are available from 16 to 120 grit. The 16 grit has very coarse heavy grains of abrasive which are widely separated. The 120 grit disks are made up of much finer abrasive particles more closely spaced. The open-grained disks are designed for paint removal, and for cutting down welds and solder and other coarse material, which would tend to adhere to the abrasive particles on the disk, and in that way tend to reduce their cutting qualities.

The closed-grain abrasive disks are designed for work where the ground off particles are very fine and there is no tendency for these particles to adhere to the disk. On closed-grain disks, the abrasive particles are as close together as possible and there are no open areas which are not covered with abrasives. Closed grain abrasives are available in grains from 16, very coarse, to 320, extremely fine.

The grit of abrasive papers is marked on the back. Abrasive paper of various grits are shown full size in Figs. 5-8, 5-9, and 5-10.

Coarse grades remove more materials faster and fine grades produce smoother surfaces. In automobile body repair work to re-

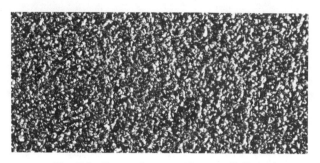

Fig. 5-8. Twenty-four grit abrasive (full size).

move paint, and the tool marks made during the straightening operation, a coarse grade, open-grain disk is used first. Then after the paint has been removed, the contour restored, and the heavy tool marks removed, a closed-grain fine grade disk should be used to provide surface smoothness. A still finer disk, usually 80 to 320 grit, is then used for feather-edging and final smoothing. Undercoats and finished lacquer, and occasionally synthetic enamel coats are sanded to produce the desired smooth surface. Such sanding may be done either dry or with water or gasoline. Dry sanding will produce a smooth surface more quickly, but wet sanding produces a smoother surface. Abrasive paper for sanding undercoats and lacquer is available in types designed specifically for wet or dry sanding. In addition, some abrasive paper manufacturers produce a single paper which can be used for either wet or dry sanding.

Abrasive paper for wet sanding is usually available in grits ranging from 60 to 180, while 60, 80 and 100 grit paper is available for dry sanding.

GRIT TO USE

There is some difference in opinion among auto body men regarding the use of specific grits for the various phases in auto body reconditioning. Some favor coarse grits, while others insist on using fine grits. It must be remembered that coarse grits, while cutting faster also produce deeper scratches which have to be removed before the actual painting; otherwise the scratches will show through the primer and color coats.

The accompanying tables show recommendations made by abrasive manufacturers for grits to be used in preparing the metal for painting, and also those to be used during the painting operation.

TABLE OF ABRASIVE GRITS
USED IN METAL PREPARATION

REFINISHING OPERATION	TYPE OF ABRASIVE	RECOMMENDED GRIT WET	DRY
Removing rust, scale, old paint, etc.	Open coat	..	16 or 24
	Closed coat	..	16 or 24
Removing welds	Open coat	..	16 or 24
	Closed coat	..	16 or 24
	Fabric abrasive wheel	..	24
Grinding Solder	Open coat	..	24
	Closed coat	..	24
Metal conditioning first step	Closed coat	..	24 or 36
Metal conditioning second step	Closed coat	..	50 or 60
Featheredging primary	Open coat	..	80 or 100
Featheredging final	Closed coat	220 or 320	220 or 320
	Open coat	..	220 or 320
Sanding primer coat	Closed coat	280 or 320	..
	Open coat	..	280 or 320

TYPE OF FINISH	TYPE OF WORK	HAND SANDING		RECIPROCATING SANDER		DISK SANDER	
		WET	DRY	WET	DRY	WET	DRY
Enamel	Quality	320	240	320	280	..	240
	Fast	280	220	280	220	..	220
Nitro Cellulose Lacquer	Quality	360	320	400	400	..	280
	Fast	320	280	320	280	..	220
Acrylic Lacquer	Quality	400	320	500	400	..	320

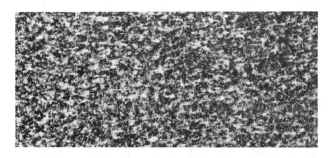

Fig. 5-9. Forty grit abrasive (full size).

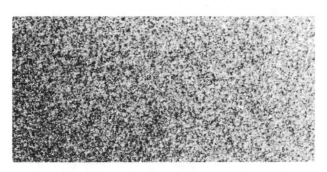

Fig. 5-10. Eighty grit abrasive (full size).

INSTALLING ABRASIVE DISK

In some designs the abrasive disk is attached to the soft backing by means of a screw, which passes through to the motor driven plate. In another design the soft backing is coated on both sides with pressure sensitive adhesive, so that the abrasive disk will adhere to it, and the soft backing in turn will stick to the motor driven plate. The disk type sander is used for virtually all types of sanding, from heavy sanding required to cut down welds, to featheredging. The soft backing, plus the fact that it is a rotating disk, permits its use on many different types of contoured surfaces. As previously pointed out, open-grain disks are used for cutting down welds, solder, and for sanding of paint. However, even the open-grain disk will at times load up or become impacted with lead. The condition can usually be overcome by stopping the sander from time to time and striking the disk a few sharp blows with a metal bar or other tool. This will usually loosen the lead adhering to the abrasive grains so that they will again cut.

When using a rotary disk sander, it is the outer edge of the abrasive disk that becomes worn and will no longer cut. However, the remainder of the disk will generally still be in good condition. To avoid throwing the disk away, the outer used edge can be trimmed from the disk which is then mounted on a smaller sander pad. By first using a 9 in. abrasive disk, then cutting to 7 in., then to 5 in., considerable savings will result. The sander pad should always be the same size as the abrasive disk. Special machines for cutting the disks are shown in Fig. 5-11.

Fig. 5-11. After considerable use, the outer edge of the abrasive disk can be cut off, and the remainder of the disk installed on a smaller pad.

FIRST　　　SECOND　　　THIRD

Fig. 5-12. Attaching grinding disk on one type of sander.

When disk sanding close to a bead, there is a possibility of the disk cutting into the bead. To avoid that possibility, it is advisable to sand such areas by hand.

Burned spots will result if the disk grinder is held in one spot too long. They will also result if too much pressure is used on the grinder, or by using a worn or glazed disk. Burned spots can be avoided by a faster working rhythm, lighter pressure, better timed strokes, and the use of proper grits in good condition.

Loose metal or dirt on the sanding area will cause scratches. A worn or filled disk will also cause scratches. Failure to cross grind, especially when changing from a coarse to a finer grit is another cause of troublesome scratches.

Cross grinding especially under strong direct light will help the mechanic to see that the entire surface is uniformly finished.

ATTACHING GRINDING DISK

While the procedure for attaching the grinding disk to the spindle of the grinder may vary slightly with different makes of grinders, the usual procedure is as follows: As shown in Fig. 5-12, first attach the flexible backing pad by threading the metal nut on the sander, spindle A. Do not thread by running the motor, but spin and tighten by hand.

Second, attach the sanding disk by laying disk B on the backing pad A, Fig. 5-12. Place the clamp nut C on the spindle, with the flange out. Give the clamp nut a turn or two into the backing pad hub.

Third, tighten the assembly by holding the backing pad with one hand and the sanding disk with the other. Turn the disk clockwise until the clamp nut draws up tight (the clamp nut will turn with the sanding disk due to the

adhesive stripping action on the nut). A spanner available as an accessory can also be used for tightening or removing the sanding disk.

SANDING PITS, DENTS AND HAMMER MARKS

While it has been repeatedly emphasized that all dents, pits, sand and hammer marks should be removed before applying primer to the panel, there are occasions when this is virtually impossible. However, such areas must still be sanded before any paint is applied, otherwise there will be poor paint adherence.

Such areas can be sanded by using an octagonal shaped disk. Such disks, Fig. 5-13, will remove paint, rust, tar, from such low

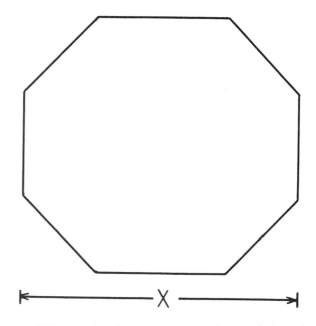

Fig. 5-13. Template for use in cutting abrasive disks to be used on rough surfaces. Dimension X is 5-1/2 in. for 7-in. disks, and 7 in. for 9-in. disks.

spots and inside curves without any difficulty. Octagonal disks are made by cutting up worn 7-in. and 9-in. disks. A pattern, such as shown in Fig. 5-13, can be made from sheet metal. In addition some of the abrasive companies will supply octagonal shaped disks on request.

RUBBING COMPOUNDS AND POLISHES

Rubbing compounds are usually in paste form and contain a fine abrasive, such as pumice. In general, if the abrasive is relatively coarse, the material is known as a rubbing compound, and if the abrasive is of fine material it is known as a polish.

Rubbing compounds are used to eliminate fine scratches around a repair area and to smooth and bring out the gloss and luster in lacquer top coats. In addition, in some instances it is also used to "dress" acrylic enamel finishes which are to be finished with acrylic lacquer.

Compounding, like polishing, can be done either by hand or by machine. Small areas are usually done by hand. In such cases fold a soft cloth into a pad and apply a small quantity of rubbing compound to either the pad or the surface of the vehicle. Rub the area with the pad and compound in straight back and forth strokes.

In the case of larger areas, the operation is usually done by machine. Apply the rubbing compound to the surface and compound using a compounding pad on the machine polisher. Confine the operation to a small area at a time. Sand scratches around a feathered edge should be compounded until eliminated. A lacquer top coat should not be compounded until completely dry and the operation is completed when the desired luster is attained.

QUIZ - Chapter 5

1. How many types of sanders are commonly used in auto body repair work?
    Three.
    Four.
    Five.
    Seven.
2. What gauge wire should be used in an extension cable 50 ft. long, when the current is 5 amperes?
    10 gauge.
    12 gauge.
    8 gauge.
    18 gauge.
3. Every electrically operated tool should be grounded.
    True.
    False.
4. When using an electric disk sander, it should be pressed firmly against the surface of the work.
    True.
    False.
5. Orbital sanders are used primarily for what type of work?
    Rough sanding.
    Finish sanding.
    When it is necessary to remove a lot of metal.
6. With what type of sander is it possible to use a dust collector?
    Orbital.
    Disk.
    Belt.
    Flexible shaft, disk sander.
7. Indicate two types of abrasive materials that are used on disks used in auto body repair work.
    Sand.
    Flint quartz.
    Emery.
    Garnet.
    Aluminum oxide.
    Crocus.
    Silicon carbide.
8. What type of abrasive is used for paint removal and cutting down welds.
    Open-grain.
    Closed-grain.
9. Which type of abrasive is the coarser?
    16 grit.
    120 grit.
10. What grit is usually recommended for removing paint?
    16 grit.
    320 grit.
    400 grit.
11. What grit is usually recommended for featheredging?
    16 grit.
    80 grit.
    400 grit.

Chapter 6

SERVICING NEW
SAFETY FEATURES

Because of increased concern for the safety of the occupants of motor vehicles, more engineering design attention has been given to strengthening panels and finding ways to reduce the damaging effects of collisions. As a result, all doors have steel reinforcing beams built in, Fig. 6-1, and bumpers are equipped with energy absorbing units, Fig. 6-2.

Fig. 6-1. Steel reinforcing beams inside doors provide side impact protection on late model cars. Top. Ford. Bottom. Chrysler.

However, these new safety features present the body shop worker with more complex repair problems. More time is needed for replacing parts, and the cost of replacement parts has increased materially. Often, the cost of repairs is more than the vehicle is worth, so it is consigned to the junk yard.

REPAIRING DOOR DAMAGE

In an effort to save certain wrecked vehicles, some body workers will cut out the reinforcing member to permit easier straightening of the panel. The reinforcing member is straightened - or a new one is obtained - and welded in place.

Repairing damaged doors on late model cars is particularly difficult because of the location of the reinforcing member. The added beam creates a problem of poor access to latch, striker and window mechanism.

Another condition that must be considered when working on newer cars is that many of the panels are made of flexible urethane. These panels cannot be straightened, but they are repairable. Since this urethane material is flammable, it presents a fire hazard when using a torch on any nearby metal panel. The proper procedure is to apply a coating of wet flake asbestos to the surface of the urethane panel to protect it from the heat and flame produced by the welding torch.

The repair procedure for urethane panels and bumpers is given in another chapter.

ENERGY ABSORBING BUMPERS

In order to withstand the shock of low-speed front or rear end collisions, many cars are

Fig. 6-2. Oldsmobile's energy absorbing bumpers are typical of General Motors' installations.

equipped with energy absorbing bumpers. The front bumper system on Chevrolets is shown in Fig. 1-8. The installation on an Oldsmobile Starfire, Fig. 6-2, is typical of late model General Motors' cars. Fig. 6-3 pictures the various components of the combination gas and hydraulic energy absorber used by G.M. Chrysler's units are shown in Figs. 6-4 and 6-6.

Basically, these energy absorbing units are similar to conventional shock absorbers. They are placed between the bumper and frame or body, where they provide the mounting for the bumper. The piston tube attaches to the bumper; the cylinder attaches to the frame. These units are designed to absorb the impact energy, then return the bumper to its original position without any serious damage.

The General Motors' unit, Fig. 6-3, has two subassemblies: the piston tube and the cylinder tube.

The piston tube is filled with a pressured gas, and the assembly consists of a bumper bracket, piston tube, orifice, seal, piston seal, piston and stop ring.

The cylinder tube is filled with hydraulic fluid, and this assembly consists of a frame bracket, cylinder tube, mounting stud and metering pin.

During construction, the piston tube assembly is inserted into the cylinder tube assembly, then the cylinder tube is crimped. The crimp mates with the stop ring to hold the unit in place. The recess in the stop ring area is filled with grease to keep out foreign matter.

Fig. 6-3. A cutaway view shows a General Motors' energy absorbing unit in extended position.

Fig. 6-4. *Chrysler's energy absorber is diagrammed in two key positions. Top. Normal. Bottom. Impact.*

Instructions covering the General Motors' unit emphasize that the unit is not to be repaired or welded. Do not apply heat to the unit. Also, do not drive into barriers to test the unit.

If the energy absorbing unit is to be scrapped, or it is bound up, proceed as follows:

1. Relieve pressure by providing a positive restrait, such as a chain or cable, and stand clear of bumper.

2. Relieve gas pressure by drilling a 1/8 in. hole in piston tube near bumper bracket.

3. Remove energy absorbing unit only after pressure has been relived.

4. When removing one unit from vehicle, it may be necessary to support bumper to prevent rotation of other unit.

5. If unit is removed from vehicle intact, vent if before scrapping.

6. Do not immerse energy absorbing units in solvents.

No special precautions are required when servicing energy absorbing bumpers on Chrysler-built vehicles.

To test the operation of a General Motors' energy absorbing system, compress each unit separately and observe whether or not the bumper returns to its normal position. To make the test:

1. Place car approximately 18 in. from a suitable barrier, such as a pillar or wall.

2. Turn off ignition, place transmission in park and apply parking brake.

3. Align a hydraulic jack with energy absorbing unit to be tested, Fig. 6-5.

4. Apply pressure from jack to compress unit 3/8 in. (use a 6 in. scale).

5. Release pressure and note whether or not unit returns.

6. If either unit fails to return to its original position, install a new one.

Fig. 6-5. *Setup is shown for testing the operation of a General Motors' energy absorber.*

Fig. 6-6. *Chrysler's front and rear energy absorber mountings: Top. Front. Bottom. Rear.*

The Ford design impact absorbing bumper system uses flexing rubber blocks to absorb the energy of the collision. The impact absorber consists of a steel ram inside a steel outer case, enclosing flexible rubber blocks. A rectangular block on each side connects the ram to the case. On impact, the ram is driven back, stretching the rubber blocks. After impact, the blocks - and the bumper - return to normal.

LAP AND SHOULDER BELTS

The construction of lap and shoulder belts installed on different makes and types of automobiles varies greatly. However, some general precautions should be observed when servicing these belts. Attaching points and anchor bolt torques also vary. Check manufacturer's specifications.

In most cases, safety belts are serviced in complete sets. In addition, the manufacturers state that no attempt should be made to mix standard and deluxe sets.

When removing or replacing seat belts, keep sharp edges and other damaging articles away from the belt. Care should be taken that buckles and latch plates are not bent or otherwise damaged. The webbing or strap material should be cleaned with mild soap and water. It is not advisable to use commercial solvents. Do not attempt to bleach or dye any part of the belts or webbing.

In the case of defective retractor mechanisms, the complete units should be replaced. The manufacturers state that no attempt should be made to repair such units.

Lap belt to floor pan and shoulder belt to roof panel or quarter panel fasteners are important attaching points, Fig. 6-7, in that they could affect the performance of these safety systems. Manufacturers state that such parts should be replaced with the same part number, or with an equivalent part, should replacement be required. All seat and anchor bolts should be torqued to factory specifications.

When trouble is encountered with recent Fisher bodies installed on General Motors cars, consult the following troubleshooting outline for help in diagnosing the cause.

SEAT BELT REMINDER LIGHT/BUZZER DIAGNOSIS

A. Light and buzzer on continuously, but buckling belt will turn off buzzer.
  1. When diagnosing a warning system failure and the system automatically shuts off because of the 4-8 second timer, a minimum of three minutes must be allowed between the diagnostic steps to allow the timer to reset (key in off position during this period).
  2. Replace timer.
B. Reminder light never on - buzzer normal.
  1. Check connection of lamp ground circuit #1.
  2. Check lamp bulb.
  3. Connect "short" tester to lamp circuit (yellow) at bulb socket.
    a. Test light off: repair yellow wire.
    b. Test light on: repair black wire.
C. Reminder light/buzzer never on.
  1. Check fuse.
  2. Connect short tester to timer feed circuit (pink) at timer connector and to body ground.
    a. Test light off: repair pink wire.
    b. Test light on: connect short tester to timer output circuit (at yellow wire) and to body ground.
    1b. Test light off: replace timer.

Fig. 6-7. Front seat belt attaching locations.

2b. Test light on: check per condition A and condition D.
D. Reminder light normal - buzzer never on.
   1. Check buzzer: replace if defective.
   2. Connect short tester to buzzer feed (pink) at buzzer connector and to body ground.
      a. Test light off: repair pink wire.
      b. Test light on: check continuity of buzzer ground circuit from buzzer connector - including the retractor switch-to body ground.
      c. Repair wire harness or replace retractor switch.

QUIZ - Chapter 6

1. What is the specific purpose of new safety features?
   To protect the car body.
   To protect the passenger.
   To protect both the car and the passenger.
2. When repairing a damaged door, what is the usual practice?
   1. First remove reinforcing beam.
   2. Leave beam in place and use hydraulic press.
3. The General Motors' energy absorbing unit uses gas under pressure.
   True.
   False.
4. Chrysler's energy absorbing unit uses gas under pressure.
   True.
   False.
5. Is welding necessary when repairing a General Motors' energy absorbing unit?
   Yes.
   No.

Chapter 7
USING
PULL RODS

When removing dents and creases from auto body panels, considerable time is often required to remove the interior trim. Also the work is complicated when the damage is located in certain areas such as doors and rear deck lids, because of metal braces and other structural members which make it difficult to use the conventional dolly and hammer method.

On many jobs, the use of pull rods makes it unnecessary to remove upholstery or interior trim, as the work is done from the outside of the damaged panel. The procedure is to drill a series of 9/64-in. holes in the deepest part of the creases. These holes should be about 1/4 in. apart. The crease is then worked up gradually by inserting the hooked ends of the pull rods in the holes and pulling on the handles. Depending on the type of damage, as many as four pull rods, two in each end, may be used. The repair is started in this case, Fig. 7-1, at the front edge of the door. Work to the rear, then start

at the front again. At the rear edge of the door, two pull rods and a hammer with a taped face, Fig. 7-2, are used to prevent chipping the paint. Pull on the rods should

Fig. 7-2. As pull is exerted on the pull rods (hooked in the holes) a hammer is used to force the ridge back into place.

Fig. 7-1. Note the series of 9/64-in. holes drilled along the peak of the ridge.

Fig. 7-3. After surface is smooth, holes are filled with solder. Note shape of point of soldering iron.

be at right angle to the surface of the panel. Be sure to pull and not pry.

In this method of repair, light reflection of the paint helps to locate low spots. To increase reflection of the paint, it is advisable to clean the surface with a wax remover before starting the repair. Place the light at an angle to take full advantage of light reflection on the paint. In a final check use a file to locate low spots.

After the dent or crease has been removed the holes are filled with solder, Fig. 7-3. With special equipment that is available, as many as 30 holes can be filled in one minute. Tip of the soldering iron should not be blunt, but have a long rounded taper so it will enter the hole easily.

OTHER TOOLS AND EQUIPMENT

The same general method also can be used to straighten deeper and more complicated damage by means of a slide hammer or power equipment.

The procedures are as follows:

1. Drill a hole at the deepest part of the crease. Install a pull hook in the hole. Attach a slide hammer to the pull hook. Draw out the damaged area by operating the sliding weight.

2. Drill two holes at the deepest part of the crease. Attach a bar with two pull hooks to the drilled holes. Apply power as required.

QUIZ - Chapter 7

1. Is it necessary to remove interior trim when using pull rods to straighten damaged area?

    Yes.

    No.

2. What size holes are drilled in panel when using pull rods?

    9/64 in.

    9/32 in.

    3/16 in.

3. What is the preferred shape of the tip of the soldering iron used to fill the holes drilled in the panel?

    Blunt.

    Conventional pyramid.

    Long rounded taper.

Details of frame forestructure of late model Chrysler car lines.
(Chrysler Corp.)

Chapter 8

STRAIGHTENING FRAMES AND PANELS WITH POWER TOOLS

CHECKING FOR DAMAGE

In many cases, damage to automobiles, is so extensive that the entire vehicle has become distorted. If the vehicle has separate frame and body construction, the frame will have been bent as well as the body panels. If the vehicle is of unitized construction, the structural members will have been distorted. In other words, the damage is more than simple dents to individual panels of the body.

It then becomes the job of the auto body repairman to restore the body and frame to its original shape and condition. To do so it is necessary to know how far or how much the individual members of the body and/or frame must be straightened. This can only be done by accurate measurements.

In the event of extensive collision damage, major underbody repairs may be required to re-establish proper alignment. Extensive damage may include twist, side-sway, complicated sags, or a combination of these conditions in the underbody area. In most cases, the most practical method is to employ body and frame power straightening equipment to correct the condition. Such equipment offers a variety of controlled pushing and pulling operations as well as accurate frame and levelling gauges which are especially helpful in checking these conditions.

It must be remembered that misalignment of the frame and underbody can affect the fit of doors, hood and trunk lid. Even more important, such misalignment can influence the suspension system and adversely affect drive shaft alignment.

Generally, underbody alignment must be correct within plus or minus 1/16 in. of the car manufacturer's specified dimensions.

A typical separate frame and body design is illustrated in Fig. 8-1; unitized designs are shown in Figs. 8-23 and 8-24. In Fig. 8-1, the dimensions are calculated on a horizontal plane parallel to the plane of the underbody. Measurements are made with a tram gauge which, at all times, must be parallel to the plane of the underbody.

PRINCIPLES OF TRAMMING

As indicated in Fig. 8-1, all diagonal dimensions are of equal distance to the same matching reference points, unless otherwise specified. Remember that all measurements must be made in a horizontal plane. Specifications shown give differences in vertical height of reference points.

In the absence of specialized tramming equipment, an adequate job of alignment can be accomplished with the following procedure:

Place car on a clean level floor. It must be level, because frame measurements are given with a tolerance of 1/16 in. (1.6 mm). Actually, it is much better to make these measurements with car on straightening rack.

Select several points along one frame side rail, Fig. 8-2. Carefully transfer these points to floor by means of a plumb bob. Locate corresponding points along opposite side rail. Transfer these points to floor. Carefully measure distance from floor, vertically, to check points on frame.

Move car away from marks on floor. Measure distance between points, as shown in Fig. 8-2. Corresponding measurements should be the same within 1/16 in.

To isolate certain conditions of frame

Fig. 8-1. Distances on conventional frame and body structure to be measured when checking for misalignment.

Fig. 8-2. Another method of checking frame for misalignment. A plumb line is used to project points of frame to the floor and the distances as indicated are then measured.

misalignment and also on different frame designs, it may be necessary to set up diagonal check points covering other areas than those shown in the illustration. If additional points are selected, be sure they are symetrically opposite.

In addition to checking the frame misalignment, as shown in Fig. 8-2, the body should also be checked by measuring and comparing diagonals as illustrated in Fig. 8-3.

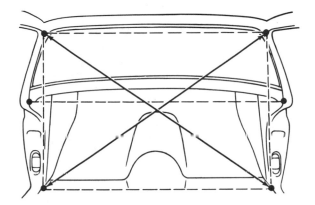

Fig. 8-3. *Typical points within body to be measured when checking for misalignment.*

MISALIGNMENT CORRECTION

Frame misalignment can be corrected by straightening the out-of-line parts and/or by replacing cross members, braces, brackets, etc.

To prevent internal stresses in metal, frame straightening should be limited to parts that are not severely bent. If heat is needed to straighten a frame member, the temperature should be kept below 1200 deg. F. Excessive heat may weaken the metal and cause permanent damage. This is particularly true in the case of heat treated members.

If a frame member is replaced, use the same method of attachment as on the original frame members.

The plumb bob method of checking a frame for misalignment is dependent for accuracy on having a level floor.

TYPES OF FRAME DAMAGE

There are many different ways in which a frame can be bent. The damage can occur as

the result of a collision along the side, from the front or from the rear. Also the car can be rolled.

As the result of a front or rear end collision, the frame may develop a sag in the center, much like a hammock. When struck from the side, the frame will be bent inward and is described as having a "sway." Some types of front or rear end collision will cause the front or rear of the chassis to be bent upward or downward. The frame can assume a diamond shape when struck obliquely. The frame can also become twisted and have any combination of the foregoing.

USING FRAME GAUGES

There are many different types of frame gauges available for determining whether a frame is misaligned. Their use will quickly tell whether the frame is twisted, swayed, sagged or diamond-shaped.

One type of frame gauge is basically a set of sighting points, Fig. 8-4. The points are

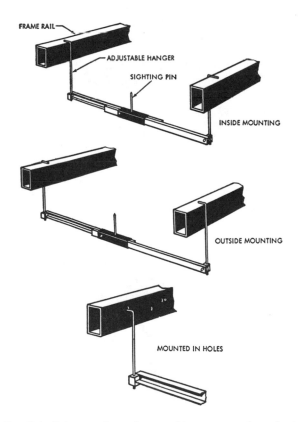

Fig. 8-4. *Points on frame for attaching gauges when checking frame for misalignment.*

Fig. 8-5. Gauges should all be in alignment as shown, if frame is not distorted.

Fig. 8-6. Pins on gauges will not be in alignment if the frame is bent.

hung on the chassis at various points, Fig. 8-5. They can be hung directly on the side rails or in holes in the frame. Such gauges are adjustable to frames of different widths, and the side pieces are adjustable as to length. The center of the gauge is provided with a sighting pin which is always centrally located. A minimum of three gauges should be used. The more gauges used the greater the accuracy and the easier it is to determine the exact location and degree of misalignment.

As an example, when using such gauges to check for misalignment, install one gauge at the point where misalignment is suspected. Install another gauge in front of that area, and a third gauge well behind the suspected area, Fig. 8-5. If one gauge must be lowered to clear an obstruction, the other gauges must be lowered an equal amount.

If one of the sight pins is lower than the others, Fig. 8-6, there is a sag at that point. In the case of a twisted frame, none of the sight pins would be in alignment and one or more of the horizontal bars of the gauges would be tilted.

For a diamond-shaped frame, the diagonal dimensions of the frame are measured with a tram gauge. To determine whether the rear wheels are tracking the front, place the front wheels in the straight ahead position and compare the wheelbase on both sides of the vehicle.

MODERN FRAME AND BODY DESIGN

Originally, automobiles were built with a heavy frame to which the body was bolted. These frames were of various types. Among the most popular designs were the ladder frame, X-frame and hour glass frame.

More recently, the unitized body was introduced. In this design, the body and frame are manufactured as a single unit (frame built into body). However, various problems were encountered, particularly in larger vehicles. Now, many cars use a "perimeter" frame, Fig. 8-7, with the body coming down over the frame to form an integrated structure. Others use a unitized body with a partial frame that supports front end sheet

Fig. 8-7. Type of perimeter frame. Letters denote frame alignment reference points.
(Pontiac Motor Div., General Motors Corp.)

Fig. 8-8. *Chrysler frame with bolt-on frame section (stub frame).*

Jack stand made of strong alloy steel. Locks automatically in any location on application of power. Set-up shown for straightening diamond frame.

Front end designed to accommodate Bear Axle Press.

Diamond beams for pulling diamond frames.

Runways are adjustable to all wheel treads.

Adjustable standards made of strong alloy steel adjustable to various heights and locations on jack rail.

Upright bar adjustable to any height. Held in position by locking screws.

Detachable heads for upright bars.

Movable wheel stops.

Removable ramps

Turning plate recess in runways.

Hydraulic power. All power self-contained in powerful hydraulic jacks of special construction.

Jack holder distributes power from jack to entire surface of runway beam.

Combination jack stop and jack rail lock made of strong alloy steel. Locks automatically on application of power.

Jack stand for vertical jacking

Heavy steel beams under runways provide adequate rigidity for all straightening jobs.

Movable jack rails adjustable to any angle or location on runway beams.

Fig. 8-9. *Typical stationary rack type frame straightening equipment.*

metal, front suspension, engine, etc. Some of these designs use "MacPherson Strut" or Hybrid MacPherson Strut suspension. (See end of chapter for details.)

Most Chrysler-built cars have unitized construction with a bolt-on (stub) frame section, Fig. 8-8. Overall strength and rigidity is obtained by combining the frame and body.

CAREFUL INSPECTION NEEDED

Before attempting any repairs on a damaged vehicle, first make a careful inspection to determine the full extent of the damage, how it occurred, and in what direction, or directions, the pull will have to be applied to correct the condition. Then, with the aid of gauges previously described, measure the extent of the damage.

REPAIRING FRAME DAMAGE

There are three basic types of equipment used for auto body and frame repair:

1. Stationary rack type. Vehicle is chained and clamped to a heavy-duty rack, Fig. 8-9. Hydraulic jacks are used to apply pressure where needed to straighten frame.

2. Portable (dozer) type. Vehicle is placed on safety stands, and equipment is moved to desired position. See Fig. 8-13.

3. Rail or floor type. In rail applications, rails are placed in the floor and equipment is attached to rails at any convenient point, Figs. 8-17 and 8-18. In floor applications, pot holes are installed in floor to form anchor points for straightening equipment, Fig. 8-19.

USING STATIONARY EQUIPMENT

Rack type body and frame repair equipment is drive-on type, Fig. 8-9. Generally, the rack is about 18 in. above floor level. This equipment provides an accurate base from which measurements can be made to determine the extent of the damage.

Rack type equipment usually consists of heavy steel members to which the vehicle is fastened with chains and clamps. The steel

Fig. 8-10. Method of anchoring car to rack. (Bee Line Co.)

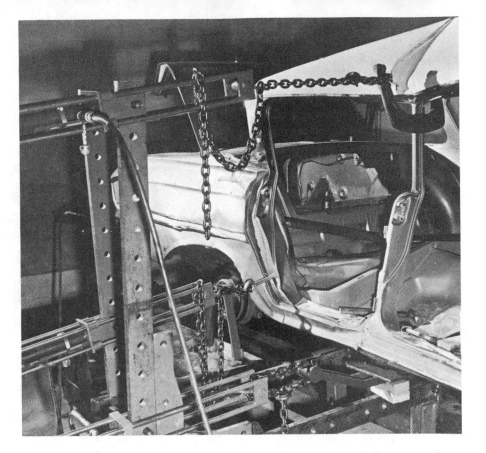

Fig. 8-11. Preparing to straighten body on rack type equipment. (Bee Line Co.)

racks are used to hold the vehicle fast. They also serve as a base for hydraulic jacks, which are used to force the damaged members back into alignment.

Examples of work being done on a rack type of equipment are shown in Figs. 8-10, 8-11 and 8-12. Fig. 8-10 illustrates one method of anchoring a body to the frame. Note the round bar placed across the rack and the heavy chain securing the body to the rack.

The vehicle shown in Fig. 8-11 was struck on the side, damaging the top, door pillars, floor pan rocker panel and side bar. Note the rig for pulling the roof and door frame into alignment.

Fig. 8-12 shows correction being made to a damaged rear fender panel. The method of anchoring the body to the rack is illustrated. Also shown are the points where pulling power is applied to straighten the panel.

PORTABLE EQUIPMENT

Portable units for body and frame repair frequently are called "dozer" units. A dozer unit has one big advantage in that it can be moved to the job. Stationary equipment requires that the car be driven or towed to the equipment. If the equipment is the drive-on type, there may be quite a problem in getting the car on the rack.

When correcting damage with portable equipment, attach the equipment to the wrecked car so that the car frame or chassis members will serve as a base against which the force of the hydraulic jack is exerted. Fig. 8-13 shows a car with front end damage. The car is resting on jacks and the beam of the dozer is chained to a cross bar under the car. The pull with the chain is forward with a slight lift.

Fig. 8-14 shows the method of correcting sag in a car frame. Note that the main beam of the equipment is placed under the car, and the beam is chained to the frame. Hydraulic jack A is placed between the beam and the frame at the center of the sag area. As jack A is raised, jack B is also operated, pulling the front of the frame forward.

One method of correcting sway damage is

Fig. 8-12. Pulling rear panel to original contour. (Bee Line Co.)

Fig. 8-13. Using portable equipment to repair front end damage. Note safety stands.
(Blackhawk Collision Repair Div., Applied Power, Inc.)

shown in Fig. 8-15. Sway damage results when a car is struck on the side. Note the method of side anchoring from the anchor post of the equipment. This setup is required when correcting center sway damage.

In both examples, Figs. 8-14 and 8-15, the car frame itself is used as an anchor to push and to pull against. Similar arrangements can be made with this type of equipment for correcting other types of frame damage.

Fig. 8-14. Setup for correcting sag condition in car frame. (Blackhawk Collision Repair Div., Applied Power, Inc.)

Fig. 8-15. Equipment setup for correcting sway damage.

HAND PORTABLE EQUIPMENT

Another type of portable equipment that can be carried by hand is used primarily for straightening sheet metal rather than heavy frame members. This equipment can be used for either pushing or pulling. When used with special hooks, clamps and accessories, this equipment can straighten any type of sheet metal damage.

Fig. 8-16 shows this equipment being used to remove a crease from the roof of a car. Pull is being exerted on a strap that was soldered or welded to the roof panel. Note that, as pull is exerted to remove the crease, pressure is also applied on the underside of the crease.

Special attachments are provided that can be placed within a door panel to spread out and remove dents.

KOREK STRAIGHTENING SYSTEM

A recently developed system for straightening autobodies and frames uses a flat reference plane consisting of specially designed steel members set into the floor of the shop, Fig. 8-17. These members provide firm anchorage for necessary pushing and pulling required to straighten damaged areas of the

Fig. 8-16. Using hand portable equipment to correct damage to a roof.

body or frame.

With this system, it is possible to push, pull and anchor from any point around the vehicle. Force can be exerted upward, to the side or downward as desired. In addition, the straightening forces can be applied in several directions at the same time.

When using the Korek system to correct damage on a vehicle, place the car on safety stands so the extent of the damage can be accurately gauged. The stands also place the vehicle at a convenient working height.

Proper anchoring of the vehicle to the base is very important, since any pulling or pushing force will have an opposite reaction on the anchoring system. Anchoring at or near the safety stands is recommended when ever possible. With anchors close to the supporting stands, downward bending of undamaged portions of the vehicle is avoided.

With the Korek system, pull forces are applied by 10 ton hydraulic rams which can be placed at any point around the vehicle as well as underneath it.

Fig. 8-17 shows four different pulls being placed on a car that was struck in the left rear. Note that three of the pulls are hori-zontal. The one attached to the corner of the trunk opening is pulling upward at an angle. The forces can be applied simultaneously or independently, as desired.

Fig. 8-18 shows a car with heavy damage at the right front. The alignment gauges are attached to the underside of the car. The car is anchored with the help of a round bar going from one side of the car to the other. To straighten the damage, two pulls are being made, one is a direct forward pull; the side pull is slightly downward.

MITEK SYSTEM OF DAMAGE REPAIR

A variation of the Korek system is found in the Mitek system. Mitek provides portable power units that can be moved around the vehicle as needed. Anchorage for the power units is provided by "pot" holes in the floor. The power units are mounted on rollers for easy positioning. Fig. 8-19 shows a power unit attached to the damaged area of a door. Additional pot holes are shown in the illustration.

Basic pulling setups for straightening damaged cars are shown in Fig. 8-21.

*Fig. 8-17. Korek setup of four different pulls to straighten rear end damage.
(Blackhawk Collision Repair Div., Applied Power, Inc.)*

Fig. 8-18. Korek setup for correcting front fender damage, using two hydraulic rams for straightening.

Straight pulls, vertical pulls and angle pulls with variations are easily applied with proper equipment.

The power units are of the hydraulic ram type. They provide up to 10 tons of pulling power. The direction of the pull can be changed by altering the direction of the ram and by adjusting the length of the tubing used with the ram. Naturally, the longer the pull, the longer the length of the tubing needed. For a down pull, the ram is placed at a low angle to the floor.

Accessory equipment, Fig. 8-20, is available for correcting damaged MacPherson type front suspension systems.

BASIC SETUPS

Damage can occur to any area of a vehicle: front, rear, sides, top or bottom. Therefore, auto body shops must be prepared and equipped to make corrections of all types.

Various methods of correcting damage are shown in Fig. 8-21.

One diagram shows a high-pull setup. In this pulling arrangement, the ram strut is placed close to the vehicle with the chain attached to a plate welded to the roof at the point of damage.

In the setup for a straight forward pull, additional tubing is installed on the ram to bring it to the desired height. Also note in Fig. 8-21 that a downward pull at the front of the frame is made with a chain bridge.

SAFETY PRECAUTIONS

When using chains to anchor a chassis, several safety precautions must be remembered:

1. Do not pull chains around sharp corners. Otherwise, the chain links will be nicked,

Fig. 8-19. Using Mitek equipment to pull out a damaged door panel. Note "pot" holes in floor for anchoring equipment. (Blackhawk Collision Repair Div., Applied Power, Inc.)

Fig. 8-20. Details of special equipment designed to correct damaged MacPherson front suspension systems.

develop a crack and, eventually, break.

2. Never heat chains with a torch. High temperatures will destroy the heat treatment and seriously weaken the chain.

3. Do not bolt chains together. The bolt may not be strong enough to withstand the forces being exerted.

4. When a chain breaks, the ends fly about with a whip-like action that could cause severe injury. To be on the safe side, cover the chain with a tarpaulin or other heavy material. In that way, any whip back of the chain will be smothered by the covering.

5. In working with the Korek system, make sure that all chain anchors are secure. Any pulling force exerted on vehicle

Placing the ram at about a 45° angle and at this height produces a straight-out pull.

This set-up produces a down and out pull pattern. Ram is placed low near the floor.

The cowl is lifted upward. The front end is tied down with chains to maintain its position.

For a horizontal pull on the cowl, add tubing to the ram and place the ram at an angle.

Using a chain "bridge," force is applied to the chain, and the frame is pulled downward.

Pull upward and outward using ram with extension tubing. The ram is placed in a vertical position.

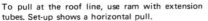

To pull at the roof line, use ram with extension tubes. Set-up shows a horizontal pull.

For pulling roof damage up and out, the ram strut is positioned higher than the roof area.

Fig. 8-21. Basic pulling hookups for power straightening various types of damage.
(Blackhawk Collision Repair Div., Applied Power, Inc.)

attachment point will create an equal reaction force on anchors.

6. When hooking the chain into an anchor, remember that the anchor, ram foot and attachment point on vehicle must be in a straight line in direction of pull.

7. Use a double-grab hook to add a hook to a hookless chain, or use it to take up slack in a chain being used for pulling or anchoring.

8. When attaching a pulling chain to frame of car, use short pieces of angle iron to pad corners where the chain wraps around frame section.

9. When using a portable body and frame straightener, both the holding chain and the pulling chain should be attached to the pivot arm at the same location to avoid tipping the straightener while the pull is being made.

STRAIGHTENING UNITIZED BODIES

With more cars such as Omni, Ford Fairmont, Fig. 8-22, Zephyr, Mustang, GM X style, Fig. 8-23, and many imported cars, there will be increased problems for auto body shops.

The construction of these cars closely follows the design used on many European and Japanese cars. In the past, standard design of domestic cars has been separate frame and body as well as American style unitized bodies. The new designs feature front engine, front wheel drive, strut suspension type. The load carrying body parts are made of thinner, but higher strength steel. All of these components form part of this new construction.

CONSTRUCTION DETAILS

Some body shop mechanics call this new construction a "hybrid" MacPherson strut. The spring is not wrapped around the shock absorber as it is in the true MacPherson strut design. Instead, the spring is placed between the lower control arm and a picket in the front cross member.

The upper part of the strut is bolted

Fig. 8-22. Ford Mustang on bench type straightening system.

Fig. 8-23. Using hand operated power equipment to straighten unitized body structure. (Kansas Jack)

Fig. 8-24. Underbody dimensions of Ford Fairmont and Zephyr X models.

directly to the body sheet metal at the inner fender panel. In that way, the upper control arm is eliminated. The lower part of the strut is bolted to the spindle, which is mounted on the lower control arm. Extreme precision and great accuracy are required in the assembly of this design.

During Ford's manufacturing process, the underbody starts as three separate pieces. The first piece is the rear floor pan, which is formed from several pieces by welding in a fixture. Next is the front floor pan, which also is welded in a fixture. The third piece is the front structure, which includes the toe pan, fender inner panels and radiator core support.

These three subassemblies are placed in a fixture and welded together to form the underbody assembly. Next, the remaining body structure is added and the "hang-on" sheet metal parts are attached. Attachment of the front cross member completes the assembly which, at this point, is ready to go to the paint shop.

The next step is the installation of the front shock absorbers. Then, the top plates are added and riveted in place. The top plate provides camber adjustment of about 1/2 deg. in either direction. However, in the Ford design, camber and caster adjustments are made after assembly. You will find that many cars using strut suspension systems have no caster or camber adjustment.

ACCURACY REQUIRED

From the foregoing, it can be seen that the assembly is made with extreme accuracy. Note in the underbody dimensions in Fig. 8-24 that a measurement of 14.03 in. is specified for the Ford Fairmont and Zephyr. That is: in a measurement of 14 in., the accuracy is kept within 1/32 in.

A dimensional diagram of the GM X style body is shown in Fig. 8-25. With conventional separate body and frame construction, some adjustment of caster and camber is provided. With this new "hybrid MacPherson Strut" design, there is little or no adjustment. As a result, the body shop mechanic has to restore the complete structure to its original form and condition. It is not enough to get the underbody straight. It is equally important

Fig. 8-25. Checking dimensions for General Motors X style cars. Horizontal: A-31 3/4 in. (806.5 mm). B-33 1/16 in. (839.8 mm). C-50 1/16 in. (1 271.6 mm). D-44 9/16 in. (1 131.9 mm). E-33 3/4 in. (857.3 mm). F-79 1/16 in. (2 008.2 mm). G-69 in. (1 752.6 mm). H-33 11/32 in. (846.9 mm). I-54 7/8 in. (1 393.8 mm). J-66 9/16 in. (1 690.7 mm). K-42 3/4 in. (1 085.9 mm). L-40 1/4 in. (1 022.4 mm). M-45 in. (1 143.0 mm). N-61 7/16 in. (1 560.5 mm). O-72 3/8 in. (1 838.3 mm). Vertical: a-5 5/32 in. (131 mm). b-10 15/16 in. (261.9 mm). c-11 13/16 in. (300 mm). d-3 21/32 in. (92.9 mm). e-1 7/8 in. (47.6 mm). f-13 7/16 in. (341.3 mm). g-9 21/32 in. (245.3 mm). h-9 3/32 in. (231 mm).

to get the body itself straight and in alignment.

When straightening one of these models, you cannot start pulling in one place. According to equipment manufacturers' engineers, no single area of the structure is built strong enough for such corrective measures. Instead of pulling at one place, it is necessary to start corrective pulls at several points at the same time. Also the applied forces must be relatively light and all should be exerted at the same time.

STRAIGHTENING SYSTEMS

Currently, there are two basic systems for making such corrective measures, according to equipment engineers. One is known as "bench type." The other is known as the "universal type."

Bench type equipment is used to correct the collision damage in a few basic models - usually those produced by a single car manufacturer. The universal system, on the other hand, is used to correct damage in virtually all makes of cars, regardless of the manufacturer and variations in design. Obviously, such equipment is well suited for use in the independent body repair shop that caters to owners of all makes and models of cars. Bench type straightening system has greater appeal to equipment operators in the body shop of a new car dealership that does corrective work on only one make of car.

BENCH TYPE SYSTEM

Briefly, the bench type system shown in Fig. 8-26, has a fixture with holes or pins built into each transverse beam or anchoring device. These are fastened to key points on the car body. Each set of fixtures is made as exact duplicates of the car manufacturer's specifications. As pressure is applied, the car body aligns with the holes or pins in the fixture and full correction to the damaged body is made.

The bench system can be used with virtually any floor-mounted or portable straightening system. Also, when it is necessary to replace a severely damaged area, the fixtures can be used as welding jigs.

Fig. 8-26. This heavy-duty bench type straightening system provides a range of fixed measuring and anchoring devices with two combined hole patterns. (Blackhawk Collision Repair Div., Applied Power, Inc.)

UNIVERSAL SYSTEMS

The universal straightening system shown in Fig. 8-27 differs from the conventional system since it measures the distance in length, width and height between special points in the body. This system is made of an aluminum frame support that supports eight sets of measuring slides. Attached to each slide is a second slide (also on rollers) for measuring the width. Special telescoping tubes are attached to the slides for measuring the height.

With this equipment, the manufacturer states that it is possible to measure each strategic point in three directions at the same time. In that way, it can be used for all cars. A set of adapters is provided with different size holes, bolt heads and thread sizes.

FORD UNITIZED BODIES

Ford states that the unitized body should present no unusual difficulties or necessitate the use of additional equipment. The application of heat and the use of heavy-duty jacks must be carefully controlled. Care is required because of the difference in the gauge of the metal in the sub-frame of a unitized body and the stress points developed in a single welded unit construction. It is possible to pull damaged areas back into alignment by the use of lightweight jacks and hydraulic equipment without heating the metal.

In the case of severe or sharp bends, it may be necessary to use heat. Any attempt to cold-straighten a severely bent bracket may cause ruptures of the welds and/or cracks in the bent part. Never heat the area more than a dull red.

QUIZ - Chapter 8

1. How do you determine the extent of damage to the structural members of the vehicle?
   By observation.
   Accurate measurements.
2. What is the usual tolerance for underbody alignment?
   1/4 in.
   1/16 in.
   .005 in.
3. When checking a frame for misalign-

Fig. 8-27. *The universal measuring and correction system measures in three directions at the same time. The system is fully mobile even when pulling.*
(Blackhawk Collision Repair Div., Applied Power, Inc.)

ment, how are the measurements made?

Horizontally.

Vertically.

Diagonally.

4. If specialized tramming equipment is not available, how are points on the frame transferred to the floor?

With a tape measure.

With a plumb bob.

With a carpenter's square.

5. What is the limit of temperature that can be applied to a frame member to aid in straightening?

2000 deg.

1200 deg.

1750 deg.

6. When using sighting points (gauges) to locate misalignment of frames, what is the minimum number that should be used?

Two.

Three.

Four.

Five.

7. If one of the sight pins of a tram gauge is lower than the others, what is indicated?

Damage exists at that point.

There is no misalignment.

8. What type of equipment is used for straightening frames?

Hydraulic jacks.

Steam hammer.

Screw jacks.

9. When using chains to anchor a chassis, should the chains be passed around sharp corners?

Yes.　　　　　No.

10. Name three types of body and frame straighteners.

11. Any pulling force on the attachment point on the vehicle will create an equal reaction force on the anchors.

True.

False.

12. When hooking the chain into the anchor, the anchor, ram foot and attachment point must be at right angles to the direction of pull.

True.

False.

13. What type of accessory is used to take up slack in a chain?

Twin pull hooks.

Double-grab hook.

Chain lock head.

14. When attaching a pulling chain, what should be used to pad the corners where the chain wraps around the frame section?

Shop towels.

Molded rubber pads.

Short pieces of angle iron.

EXTRUDED HOLE

DIMENSIONS FOR X, Y, AND Z ARE NOT GIVEN AS THEY ILLUSTRATE POINTS FOR TAKING DIAGONAL MEASUREMENTS FOR CHECKING THE SQUARENESS OF THE FRAME EASILY IDENTIFIABLE FEATURES OF THE FRAME ARE LOCATED AT THE APPROXIMATE TERMINAL POINTS OF THE ARROWS AND SHOULD BE USED IN MAKING THESE MEASUREMENTS.

A	B	C	D	E	F	G	H	J	K	L	M	N	P	R	S	T	U
1158.0	1104.0	928.0	1266.0	1375.0	1186.0	1376.0	1444.0	742.7	603.0	1607.0	1552.0	165.5	214.5	117.5	28.5	168.5	142.5

Frame dimensions on late model Buick "E" series cars. (Buick Motor Div., GMC)

Chapter 9

WELDING WITH OXYACETYLENE, ELECTRIC ARC

Welding is a metalworking process in which metals are joined by heating them to the melting point, and allowing the molten portions to fuse or flow together.

There are two basic methods used for welding in the auto body shop:

1. Oxygen acetylene.
2. Electric arc.

In the auto body shop, oxyacetylene welding equipment is used not only for welding, but also as a source of heat for soldering, shrinking metal and for softening the metal so that it can be more easily straightened. Oxygen acetylene is also used for cutting metal.

In oxyacetylene welding, the mixture of the two gases produces an intensely hot flame that will melt and fuse metals. When cutting metals with a special torch, a jet of oxygen striking a piece of iron or steel heated to its kindling temperature will cause the metal to burn away quickly. Chemically, oxygen cutting is similar to the eating away of iron and steel by ordinary rusting only much faster. In rusting, the oxygen in the air or water affects the metal slowly. Directing a jet of oxygen at metal heated almost to its melting point, actually speeds up rusting and burns away the metal. The iron oxide melts and runs off as molten slag and exposes more iron to the action of the oxygen. When welding, two pieces of metal are placed together. The edges are melted with the flame and the molten metals flow together. In most cases, welding rod or electrode is added to strengthen the joint.

ELECTRIC ARC WELDING

Electric arc welding is a process whereby the heat necessary to bring the metal to a molten state is obtained by a continuous electric arc formed between a welding rod and the work. In electric arc welding, where a generator supplies the current in the shop, one terminal of the generator is grounded on the work and the other is connected to the welding rod or electrode. As the electrode is brought into contact with the work an electric arc is formed. This has sufficient heat to fuse the work.

The coating on welding electrodes is composed of a number of chemicals blended together and bonded to the wire or electrode. The object of the coating is to provide protection for the weld metal from oxygen and nitrogen in the air. As the coating burns it produces a gaseous shield which protects the metal as it flows from the electrode to the work. The coating contains alloys which combine with the weld deposit to form a slag or covering over the bead to protect it from the atmosphere and too rapid cooling. See Fig. 9-1. In auto body work, this method, arc welding, is frequently used when rewelding seams which have been spot welded originally, but cannot be spot welded again.

Fig. 9-1. Close-up showing electric arc welding procedure.

When using arc welding it is important that the two sections be brought into close alignment. Relatively large space between sections cannot be repaired satisfactorily by arc welding. In such cases gas welding becomes necessary.

OXYACETYLENE EQUIPMENT

When welding with oxyacetylene the following equipment is needed:
1. Oxygen cylinder.
2. Acetylene cylinder.
3. Oxygen regulator.
4. Acetylene regulator.
5. Welding torch.
6. Connecting hoses.
7. Protective goggles.
8. Lighter.

In most cases the oxygen and acetylene are in tanks. However, equipment for generating acetylene is also available. Oxygen and acetylene cylinders must be kept away from heat. Never allow the flame of a torch to play on a cylinder as it might melt the safety fuse plugs. In storing and using cylinders always keep the valve ends up. During shipment the heavy cylinder cap is screwed over the valve to protect it from injury. If a cylinder valve should be broken off, the terrific pressure of the gas escaping from the cylinder would burn any material touched, and would give the cylinder jet velocity. It is essential that all cylinders be handled carefully, and be clamped or chained to a post or placed in a special cylinder truck, see Fig. 9-2, so there is no danger of being tipped over or dropped.

SETTING UP ACETYLENE EQUIPMENT

With the cylinders correctly placed, remove the oxygen cylinder cap, then stand to one side of the valve outlet and open the valve slightly. When it hisses, close the valve. That procedure gets rid of any dust around the valve seat.

Attach the oxygen regulator, Fig. 9-3, to the oxygen cylinder, using an open-end wrench. The threads on the oxygen regulator are conventional right-hand threads. Be sure to keep oil and grease away from oxygen equipment. Do not lubricate the threads. In

Fig. 9-2. Oxygen and acetylene cylinders should be mounted vertically in a truck or chained to a post.

addition to having right-hand threads, the oxygen regulator can be recognized by noting the pressure range on the gauges. One of the gauges will indicate up to 4,000 psi. Also, oxygen regulators are usually painted green.

With the regulator attached to the oxygen cylinder, loosen the regulator handwheel. Stand away from the other regulator and open the cylinder valve. The lower gauge will indicate the cylinder pressure.

INSTALLING ACETYLENE REGULATOR

Blow the dust out of the acetylene cylinder valve by opening the valve one-quarter turn. Then close it quickly. No flame or lighted cigarette should be nearby as acetylene is highly flammable. Attach the acetylene regulator (usually painted red), also shown in Fig. 9-3, to the cylinder. The connections have left-hand threads so it is not possible to install an acetylene regulator on an oxygen tank.

Loosen the regulator handwheel. Open the cylinder valve slightly, then one and one-half turns. Leave wrench in position on acetylene tank valve.

CONNECTING HOSES

The oxygen hose is connected to the oxygen regulator, and the acetylene hose to the

Fig. 9-3. Basic accessories for welding with oxyacetylene.

acetylene regulator. In the case of new hose, it is necessary to first blow out loose talc powder. This is done by attaching one end of the hose to the oxygen regulator outlet and opening the valve to 5 lb. pressure. Do the same with the acetylene hose.

SIZE TIP TO USE

The size tip to use on the welding torch depends on the thickness of the metal to be welded. Most auto body sheet metal is approximately 20 gauge, or .032 in. Body men generally use a number two or number three tip. The tips recommended by Linde Air Products are as follows:

METAL THICK- NESS		WELDING HEAD SIZE ON TORCH			PRESSURE FOR OXYGEN AND ACETYLENE
IN.	GAUGE	W109	W110	W111	
..	32	1	1	1	5-7
..	28	1	1	1	5-7
..	25	2	2	2	5-7
1/32	22	2	3	3	5-7
1/16	16	3, 4	4	4	5-7
1/8	11	4	5	5	5-7
3/16	..	4, 5	7	7	5-7
1/4	..	6	8	8	6-9

LIGHTING TORCH

Different pressures are needed for welding different thicknesses of metal as noted in the preceding table. First open the torch oxygen valve one full turn, turn in the oxygen regulator handwheel until correct pressure for the job shows on the gauge. For auto body sheet metal this is usually 5 to 7 lbs.

Then close the oxygen valve. Next open the torch acetylene valve one full turn and turn on the acetylene regulator hand valve until the correct pressure shows on the gauge. Close the torch acetylene valve promptly.

After putting on protective goggles, Fig. 9-3, point the torch down and away from you. Open the torch oxygen valve about one-quarter turn, then the torch acetylene valve one full turn. Light the gas at the tip with a friction-type lighter, Fig. 9-3. Open both valves wide and adjust torch acetylene valve slowly until a neutral flame is obtained, Fig. 9-4.

ADJUSTING THE FLAME

With the gas burning as outlined in the preceding paragraphs, open the oxygen valve slowly. The flame should gradually change

Fig. 9-4. Illustrating method for indicating amount of excess acetylene used. After the flame has been adjusted to neutral, the torch acetylene valve should be opened, or the oxygen valve closed until the desired acetylene feather is obtained.

from a yellow acetylene flame, to a blue carburizing, or reducing flame, Fig. 9-4. Starting with an excess acetylene flame, a neutral flame is obtained by slowly closing the pipe acetylene valve until the acetylene feather disappears.

To obtain an oxidizing flame, either increase the oxygen or reduce the acetylene.

WHAT TO DO ABOUT BACKFIRE

Improper handling of the torch causes the flame to backfire; that is, go out with a loud snap. It may happen if you touch the work with the tip or nozzle, overheat the tip or nozzle, operate at incorrect pressures, if the head or nozzle is loose, or if there is dirt on the head or nozzle seat. The torch may be relighted as soon as the trouble is corrected.

WHAT TO DO ABOUT FLASHBACKS

A flashback occurs when the flame disappears and gas burns inside the equipment.

This is usually accompanied by a squealing or hissing noise from inside the torch, sparks coming out the nozzle, heavy black smoke coming from the torch, blowpipe handle getting hot. In some cases the flame may go back far enough so that it will burst through the hose. When this happens, close the oxygen needle valve immediately. Then close the acetylene valve. After allowing time for the equipment to cool, relight the torch in the usual manner.

Flashbacks can usually be eliminated by using the correct pressures for each welding head or cutting nozzle. If flashbacks occur frequently there is a strong possibility that the torch and/or tip are defective.

AT THE END OF THE JOB

Turn off the torch. First close the torch acetylene valve, then the torch oxygen valve.

If you are stopping work for only a few minutes:

1. Turn out oxygen regulator valve until loose.
2. Open torch oxygen valve.
3. Close torch oxygen valve.
4. Turn out acetylene regulator hand valve until loose.
5. Open torch acetylene valve.
6. Close torch acetylene valve.

If you stop work for more than ten minutes:

1. Close oxygen cylinder valve.
2. Open torch oxygen valve until all pressure goes down to zero.
3. Turn out oxygen regulator handwheel until loose.
4. Close torch oxygen valve.
5. Close acetylene cylinder valve.
6. Open torch acetylene valve until all pressure goes down to zero.
7. Turn out acetylene regulator handwheel until loose.
8. Close torch acetylene valve.

WELDING PRACTICE

To weld sheet metal, a neutral flame (flame obtained by burning approximately one-to-one mixture of acetylene and oxygen) should be used. Skill can be attained by practicing on strips of sheet metal. At first, do not attempt to weld two pieces of sheet metal together, but move the flame across the surface of the sheet metal, carrying the "puddle" along the surface, Fig. 9-5. Do not

Fig. 9-5. A practice piece with good results shown at A and D. Excess heat caused holes to be burned as shown at B, while too little heat was used at C. No welding rod was used when making this practice piece.

use any welding rod. The purpose of this exercise is to obtain skill in carrying a puddle across the surface of the sheet. The torch should be held so that the flame points in the same direction that the weld will be made and at an angle of about 45 deg., Fig. 9-6. The

Fig. 9-6. Note angle of welding rod and torch.

inner cone of the flame should be about 1 in. away from the surface of the sheet. Hold the torch in this position until a pool of molten metal about 3/16-in. to 1/4-in. in diameter is formed. Then move the torch slowly so as to move the puddle in the desired direction to obtain an even ripple effect. To do this, the torch should be swung from side to side in a small arc. If the torch is moved too slowly, holes may be burned through the sheet metal. If the torch is moved too quickly, the desired degree of melting and overlapping of the puddles will not be obtained.

After some skill is obtained without using a welding rod, repeat the preceding exercise, using a welding rod, Fig. 9-7. In this case, the addition of the welding rod will produce a slight ridge of metal above the surface of the sheet. The position of the welding rod should be similar to the welding torch, except that it is held in the left-hand and at an angle of slightly more than 45 deg. The spot on the sheet, and the tip of the welding rod should be brought to the melting temperature

Fig. 9-7. Examples of good and poor welds. Those at A and D are satisfactory, while the weld at B shows the effects of too much heat. Insufficient heat, little fusion and improper melting of the welding rod produced the weld shown at C.

at the same time. It will be found that the best position for the end of the welding rod is just inside the outer end of the flame while the flame is being concentrated on the spot at the start of the weld.

After practicing the use of the welding rod, place the edges of two pieces of sheet metal 1/16 in. apart and weld them together. In this case it is important that the welding action penetrate completely through to the inner side of the sheet.

STEP 1 — WELD

STEP 2 — WELD HAMMERED BELOW METAL SURFACE

STEP 3 — METAL FINISH TO LEVEL BOTH SURFACES

STEP 4 — TINNING OVER WELD

STEP 5 — SOLDER OVER WELD

STEP 6 — METAL FINISH

Fig. 9-8. Typical welding operations used when replacing a body panel.

During the welding action, the welding puddle must be controlled so that it will not fall through the gap. However, the metal added from the rod must be thoroughly fused with the base metal on both sides of the joint for the entire thickness of the sheet.

After sufficient skill has been attained on welding small sheets of metal together, work on an actual fender or body panel can be attempted.

WELDING A PANEL

After welding two pieces of sheet metal together, there will be a slight ridge along the welded seam, Step 1, Fig. 9-8. This must be hammered below the contours of the surface approximately 1/16 in., Step 2. Using a disk sander, make the surface clean and smooth, Step 3. The groove and weld is then tinned, Step 4, and filled with solder, Step 5. The final step in preparation for painting is to sand the surface, Step 6.

ELECTRIC WELDING

When two electrical conductors are brought together to form a contact, current will flow. Then when the conductors are separated a short distance an arc will be formed, and the current will continue to flow through the arc. This will produce such high temperatures that metal is melted. Under extreme conditions temperatures as high as 6300 deg. F. are obtained.

To maintain such an arc as used for welding, special equipment is needed. Such equipment will generate current of the correct specification, or transform it from a power supply line. A flux-coated filler rod or electrode is used to maintain the arc and to supply metal needed to fill the gap separating the metals being welded. Such welding is used extensively when rewelding seams which were originally spot welded.

A difficulty in the use of arc welding on sheet metal is that it cannot be used to fill wide openings or gaps. The intense heat of the arc tends to melt away exposed edges faster than the filler metal can be deposited.

It is not necessary to leave a gap between the edges being welded. Care must be exercised to avoid burning through the thin metal of which the auto bodies are made. When the electric arc is used on a lapped sheet metal joint, the surfaces must fit tightly together, otherwise holes will be burned in the work.

A big advantage of using electric arc welding on body sheet metal is that it causes less heat distortion than oxyacetylene. This is true because it progresses more rapidly, and without the blast of the heated gases. There is also reduced fire hazard when used close to flammable materials, such as upholstery and other interior trim. There is, however, still some hazard caused by sparks which are thrown off.

When welding the heavier section materials used in the frame of the automobile, electric arc has a big advantage of speed with reduced distortion.

ARC WELDING EQUIPMENT

In arc welding, the metal being welded forms part of the electrical circuit. One terminal from the power source is connected to the work, and the other terminal is connected to the electrode holder. When the electrode is touched to the work, the circuit is completed, the arc is formed and a very heavy current flows. It is this heavy current which melts the electrode and causes it to stick to the work. Special procedure must therefore be followed when forming the arc.

FORMING ARC

A difficulty experienced in forming or striking the arc, especially by beginners, is that the electrode fuses to the work. While there are several methods of striking the arc, the following is the method most frequently used.

First move the electrode toward the work, moving it downward and vertically, as shown in Fig. 9-9. Just as soon as the electrode touches the surface of the work, withdraw it to the correct arc length.

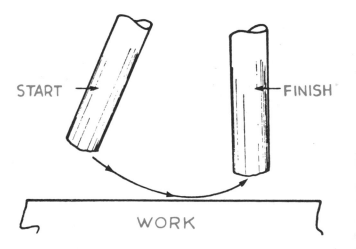

Fig. 9-9. One method of striking an arc is to move the electrode downward and vertically. As soon as electrode touches surface of work withdraw it to correct length of arc.

Another method, which is a variation of that just described, is to move the electrode at an angle to the work in a sort of scratching surface method. The electrode will scratch across the work to form the arc, Fig. 9-10.

When the arc is formed withdraw the electrode to form an arc of the proper length.

The second method may be easier for beginners, particularly when using an AC machine.

If the electrode fuses to the work, give the holder a quick twist. If this does not free the electrode, it will be necessary to open the

Fig. 9-10. In this method of striking an arc, the electrode is moved across surface of work in scratching motion.

circuit by letting go of the electrode with the holder. Never, try to free a fused electrode without the protective helmet on. Do all loosening of the electrode with the shield in front of your eyes. The student should practice the motion of striking the arc, with the current turned off. Then after having become familiar with the proper motion, the current may be turned on and the actual arc formed. The correct length of the arc work on sheet metal is approximately 1/8 in. to 3/16 in.

Fig. 9-11. Electric welding equipment that uses alternating current. Note safety helmet.

Fig. 9-12. Mechanic brazing a car roof to front header. Note original spot welds and self-locking pliers holding panels in alignment.

AC AND DC WELDERS

Both AC or DC welders may be used for auto body work. The DC welder can be used to do all types of welding, and in any position. However, the cost of the equipment is usually greater than an AC welder, see Fig. 9-11.

The direct current welder consists basically of a direct current generator with the necessary controls. The alternating current arc welder consists of a transformer which is connected to the commercial power lines.

SPOT WELDING

Instead of having a continuous weld to join two pieces of sheet metal together, welding in spots less than an inch apart is often done. Such welding is used largely in production work. It is often used to weld the roof to the side panels, Fig. 9-12. Similar welding in spots can be done in the repair field by using an arc spot welding gun, as shown in Fig. 9-13. Such equipment produces a weld spot to join two pieces of overlapped sheet metal. It is designed for use in any position and on any seam which was originally welded by resistance type spot welding by the manufacturer. When using an arc spot welding gun, welding rod is also used so a slight hump is made at each weld.

As little heat is produced with arc spot welding, little distortion results. This method is therefore used frequently when the welds are made in close proximity to upholstery and other flammable materials.

RESISTANCE SPOT WELDING

Many auto body panels are joined together at the time of manufacture by resistance spot welding. Panels are joined by a series of spot welds. The welds are placed about 1 in. apart instead of using a long continuous weld.

Fig. 9-13. Spot welder being used on rocker panel.

In this production type welding, the weld area is gripped between the electrodes of the spot welding machine and a high amperage low voltage current is passed through it. The electrical resistance of the overlapping layers of the joint is much higher than that of the electrodes, and consequently as the current passes through it, a high degree of heat is generated. This heat is sufficient to melt the metal at points of contact and welds are formed.

An example of this type of spot welding is shown in Fig. 9-12.

Fig. 9-15 shows the schematic drawing of an electric or resistant spot welding operation. The usual method of breaking these welds apart is to insert a cold chisel between the two sheets of metal and force it through with a hammer.

The use of resistance spot welding is difficult in the repair shop because of the problem of obtaining access to both sides of the panels being welded, as required in this type of welding.

ARC WELDING SAFETY

When arc welding, wear a special helmet to protect your eyes from the brilliant light given off by the arc. See Fig. 9-14. Think about what you are doing and know what others are

Fig. 9-14. One type of arc welding helmet.

doing around you. Before starting to weld, warn those nearby to "cover."

Also wear protective clothing and gloves to prevent injury from flying sparks (arc showers). Molten metal can cause serious burns.

Special screens should also be provided to protect other workers in the shop. Welding

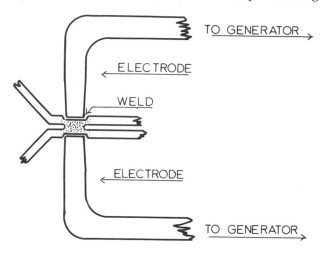

Fig. 9-15. Schematic drawing of resistance spot welding operation.

should not be performed in any area where there is any possibility of sparks falling on flammable material.

All electric cables should be examined periodically to make sure that the insulation is in good condition, so there will be no danger of electric short circuits.

BRAZING

Brazing is another method of joining two pieces of metal by means of heat. In brazing a nonferrous (nonferrous means without iron) filler rod, which melts at 800 deg. F., is used. The 800 deg. temperature for brazing compares to 400 deg. F. for soldering, and 2800 deg. F. for welding steel.

In auto body repair work, brazing is sometimes used for repairing seams which were originally electric spot welded. In order to make a strong joint, it is essential that the two surfaces be close together. The usual recommendation is .003 in. to .005 in.

When brazing, the nonferrous filler rod actually diffuses and penetrates into the metals being joined to form an alloy. Brazing is done only on metals that have a higher melting point than the brazing material or filler rods. Metals being brazed should not be heated to the melting point.

In brazing the alloy formed on each of the two metals will join and intermix so that a joint of maximum strength is formed.

As in the case of soldering, a flux is needed when brazing. This flux is available in plastic, liquid and powder forms, and also as a solid coating on the nonferrous filler rod.

Many body men use a paste or powder form of flux, and apply it in the following manner. The filler rod is heated, and then is dipped into the container holding the flux. The end of the rod is coated with flux when it is withdrawn. Then as the filler rod is melted, the flux is also melted and runs ahead to clean the surface and prevent oxidation.

Filler rods that are coated with flux eliminate the necessity of dipping the rod into the can of flux, and in that way time is saved.

When brazing, molten brazing material flows back through the joint as the result of capillary action. This is caused by the attraction of the surface for any liquid that will wet it. Other examples of capillary action are oil running up a wick, and ink being drawn up by blotting paper.

An advantage of brazing is that it requires less heat than fusion welding and therefore there will be less distortion, particularly when the brazing is done on low crown sections of panels.

QUIZ - Chapter 9

1. Is oxyacetylene welding equipment used only for welding?
   Yes.
   No.
2. How should oxygen and acetylene cylinders be stored?
   Valve ends up.
   Lying on side.
   Kept in cartons.
3. When setting up oxyacetylene welding equipment, how should you get rid of dust around the valve seat?
   Wipe away with clean cloth.
   Use camel's hair brush.
   Open valve slightly.
4. The threads on the oxygen regulator are right-hand threads?
   True.
   False.
5. What is the usual color for the connections on the oxygen regulator?
   Red.
   Green.
6. What color are the connections of the acetylene regulator?
   Red.
   Green.
7. Should threads of oxygen equipment be lubricated?
   Yes.
   No.
8. What size tip is usually used when welding auto body sheet metal?
   2 or 3.
   4 or 5.
   0 or 1.
9. When lighting the welding torch, what method should be used.
   Friction lighter.
   Match.
10. If there is an excess of acetylene, what color is the flame?
    Blue.
    Yellow.
    Red.
11. What color is a carburizing flame?
    Blue.
    Yellow.
    Red.
12. When welding sheet metal, what type flame should be used?
    Carburizing flame.
    Neutral flame.
    Oxydizing flame.
13. How far should the inner cone of the flame be from the surface of the work?
    2 in.
    1 in.
    3 in.
14. When arc welding sheet metal, is it possible to fill wide gaps?
    Yes.
    No.
15. Does electric arc welding cause much or little heat distortion?
    Much.
    Little.

16. Alternating current is never used when welding sheet metal.

    True.

    False.

17. What kind of rod is used when brazing?

    Nonferrous rod.

    Swedish iron rod.

    Nickel-steel alloy.

18. What two basic methods of welding are used in auto body shops?

19. What is the object, or function, of the coating applied to arc welding electrodes?

20. How can flashbacks in oxyacetylene welding be eliminated?

21. Give one advantage of brazing.

22. At what temperature is brazing done with a nonferrous filler rod?

    400 deg. F.

800 deg. F.

2800 deg. F.

23. Metals being brazed should not be heated to the melting point.

    True.

    False.

24. Spot welding joins two pieces of over-lapped sheet metal. When joining panels by a series of resistance spot welds, how far apart should the welds be placed?

    1 in.

    3 in.

    5 in.

25. Arc spot welds may be made close to upholstery or other flammable materials.

    Yes.   No.

26. What is the usual method of breaking spot welds apart?

Pontiac Fiero "space frames" utilize 39 mounting pads to locate and support the exterior body panels. These pads (blocks of sheet metal 3/4 in. square and 1/2 in. high) are filled with epoxy compound and spot welded to the frame at points where the plastic body panels are to be attached.

OXYGEN
CYLINDER
VALVE

OXYGEN
REGULATOR

OXYGEN
SAFETY
VALVE

OXYGEN
CYLINDER

ACETYLENE
CYLINDER VALVE
WRENCH

ACETYLENE
REGULATOR

OXYGEN
HOSE

TORCH
OXYGEN
VALVE

TORCH

ACETYLENE
HOSE

CYLINDER
SUPPORT

TORCH
ACETYLENE
VALVE

ACETYLENE
CYLINDER

FUSIBLE
PLUGS

A complete oxyacetylene welding station basically includes gas cylinders, pressure regulators and gauges, hose and welding torch. Tanks must be chained or strapped in place so there is no chance of upsetting them.

DIRECTION OF TRAVEL

ELECTRODE HELD AT AN
ANGLE OF APPROXIMATELY
5 DEG. TO THE PLATE

5 DEG.

GROOVE

AIR
BEHIND
ELECTRODE

An increasingly popular auto body metal cutting method uses an air carbon arc electrode holder and carbon electrode. The holder has air passages, an on-off valve and an air orifice. When the electrode is held at the angle shown, the jet of air is directed at the arc crater immediately behind the arc to speed the cutting operation.

Chapter 10
CUTTING
SHEET METAL

There are six principal ways of cutting sheet metal as used in the auto body shop.

A. Oxygen-Acetylene Torch.
B. Electric Arc.
C. Abrasive Wheel.
D. Power Saw.
E. Shears.
F. Impact Hammer and Cutter

CUTTING WITH OXYGEN-ACETYLENE

Cutting with the oxyacetylene is one of the fastest methods of cutting sheet metal. An objection to its use is that a relatively wide cut is made and consequently more metal is wasted than when an abrasive wheel or power saw is used. When cutting with oxyacetylene, a small area is heated with the flame until it is bright red and starts to melt. Then a jet of oxygen is directed against the preheated area and a narrow slit is quickly burnt through the metal, Fig. 10-1.

Oxygen is what does the cutting. It makes a liquid iron oxide as it joins with the hot steel. This flows out or is blown away, exposing more metal to the jet of oxygen. By moving the blowpipe or torch, Fig. 10-2, the jet of

Fig. 10-1. Cutting door inside panel with oxyacetylene torch.

oxygen is guided to cut a straight line, curved or irregular line as desired.

The nozzles for cutting have one center hole surrounded by four smaller holes, Fig. 10-3. The outer holes provide the small oxyacetylene flame to preheat the metal to start cutting, and to keep the cut going after it has started. The jet of oxygen is regulated by the cutting oxygen lever and comes from the center hole.

Fig. 10-2. Details of oxyacetylene torch construction.

For cutting sheet metal a #0 nozzle is normally preferred, with about 15 lb. oxygen and 4 to 5 lb. acetylene pressure.

When cutting with oxygen, the first step is to clean the area being cut, using a wire bristle brush, power sander or other suitable means. Then, mark the line to be cut. A soapstone pencil is usually recommended for drawing the line, although chalk is also used extensively. This line is then center punched every one-half inch so it can be seen while working.

Light the torch. Hold the nozzle so that the cutting oxygen hole is over the edge of the panel being cut and at the marked line. The preheat flame will heat both the top of the panel and the side edge. Keep the edges of the pale blue core for preheating flame about 1/16 in. away from the metal for best results. Also keep the nozzle of the blowpipe at right angles to the surface of the panel until a spot under the preheating flame starts to melt. Then tilt the nozzle so that the flame points toward the edge of the panel. Slowly open the cutting oxygen valve by pressing down on the lever. As soon as cutting starts, as indicated by a shower of sparks, slowly straighten the nozzle again and press the oxygen lever all the way down. When the cut has gone all the way through the panel, tilt the nozzle forward a little in the direction of cutting. If the blowpipe is moved too fast the cutting will stop. Should this occur, release the oxygen lever and start the cut over again with the preheat flame.

When using a cutting blowpipe, both hands are needed. The right hand is used to control the oxygen lever and guide the blowpipe, while the left hand is placed slightly forward of the right and is used to balance the weight of the blowpipe and support its weight. When cutting an arc, the left hand is used as a pivot or axis and the gun is swung about that point. To cut a straight line, simply roll the hand that supports the blowpipe.

When cutting thick sections of metal a somewhat similar technique is followed. However, larger size nozzles are needed and the rate of cutting is much slower.

When making a square cut, that is a cut that goes straight through the metal, set the nozzle so that the two preheating jets fall directly in line to be cut - one in front and the other behind the cutting oxygen, Fig. 10-3. When making a bevel cut, as is sometimes neces-

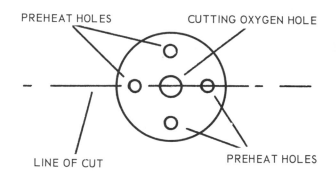

Fig. 10-3. *Cutting torch should be held as indicated when cutting straight through the metal.*

sary when cutting thick pieces of metal, such as the vehicle frame, set the nozzle so that the preheat holes are in the position shown in Fig. 10-4. This provides the additional preheating required when making a double cut.

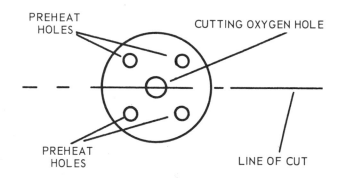

Fig. 10-4. *When making a bevel cut through thick metal, make sure preheat holes of torch are held as shown.*

CUTTING WITH ELECTRIC ARC

When cutting sheet metal with an electric arc, usually a direct current machine, carbons are generally used. Electric negative should be used in all cases, and a current of 50 to 100 amps. is all that is needed for cutting the sheet metal used in auto bodies, Fig. 10-5.

The arc should be started at some point from which the molten metal will easily flow. By starting at the bottom and working up, the molten metal will flow out of the cut. Also the cut should start at the edge of the panel.

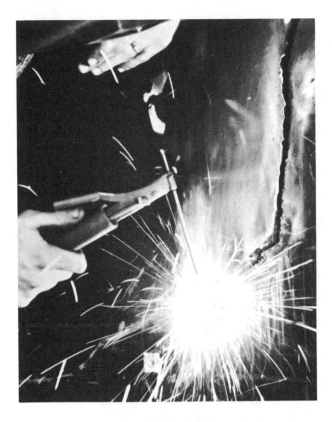

Fig. 10-5. *Cutting a body panel with an electric torch.*

CUTTING WITH ABRASIVE WHEELS

A fast way to cut sheet metal is to use special abrasive wheels and saws designed especially for the purpose, Fig. 10-6. Very little metal is wasted by this method. With disks or circular saws of large diameter, it becomes difficult to cut curves of small radii, but in straight line cutting operations disks and circular saws are preferred by many mechanics. In addition there is no fire hazard when using grinding wheels or saws. The same equipment can be used for slotting

Fig. 10-6. *Using a circular saw to cut a body panel.*

Fig. 10-7. *A jigsaw being used to cut a body panel.*

sheet metal, cutting old bolts, removing welds, and for miscellaneous grinding.

Fig. 10-6, shows a truck trailer panel being cut by this method. When using an abrasive wheel or circular saw for cutting, care must be exercised that the saw is moved in a straight line. If curves are attempted, the saw will bind and quickly become dull.

POWER JIGSAWS FOR CUTTING

There are several different types of equipment that are broadly classed as saws. One saw that is used for cutting sheet metal in the body shop is the jigsaw as shown in Figs. 10-7 and 10-8. This electric driven tool will cut arcs of small radii, and is also used for straight line cutting.

When using this method, the cut should not be forced but the saw should be moved along smoothly without attempting to cut too fast.

Fig. 10-8. *Another type of saw designed to cut body panels.*

CUTTING WITH SHEARS

While power driven equipment is used for all major cutting of sheet metal in auto body shops, hand shears are still used extensively for small work and close fitting of panels.

CUTTING WITH IMPACT HAMMER

An impact hammer, fitted with a cutting chisel is also used for cutting sheet metal. However, this frequently results in a rough ragged cut and as a result other methods are usually preferred.

QUIZ - Chapter 10

1. Name four ways to cut sheet metal.
2. Cutting sheet metal with oxyacetylene is one of the quickest methods of cutting sheet metal.
   True.
   False.
3. It is not necessary to first clean the surface of the metal before cutting with oxyacetylene.
   True.
   False.
4. The edges of the pale blue cone for preheating flame should be kept how far away from the work when cutting with oxyacetylene?
   7/8 in.
   1/16 in.
   1/4 in.
5. When cutting with abrasive wheels, it is easy to cut an arc of small radius.
   True.
   False.

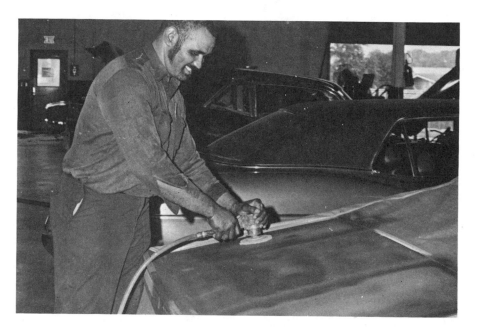

Using machine with polishing compound to give a higher than normal lustre to finished surfaces.

Chapter 11
HOW TO
SHRINK SHEET METAL

In many cases, as a result of a collision, the sheet metal will become stretched. In addition, as a result of using a dolly block and dinging hammer, the metal will be reduced in thickness and will therefore tend to occupy a greater area than originally. When this occurs the metal will tend to bulge, as shown in Fig. 11-1.

Fig. 11-1. As the result of either hot or cold working, sheet metal will become stretched, and will bulge as shown.

When metal becomes stretched or bulges, it is necessary to shrink it so it will occupy the same space as originally.

There are three major methods of shrinking sheet metal:

A. Using a special shrinking hammer.
B. Cutting slits in the bulged area.
C. Use of heat.

The hammer used for shrinking sheet metal is the same as a conventional dinging hammer, except that the face of the hammer is cross-grooved, Fig. 11-2. These grooves are quite deep and when used will mark the metal with a series of square dots. The hammer is used with a dolly in the usual manner, but instead of making the metal thinner, it will tend to shrink it as a result of the many tiny dents formed by the grooved face of the hammer. When using a shrinking hammer, care must be taken that the full face of the hammer strikes the surface of the panel.

A bulge or stretch can also be removed from the panel by cutting slits in the metal and allowing the edges of the slits to overlap. The overlapping surfaces are then welded together, after which the weld is countersunk and the surface smoothed with a disk grinder or a file. This method, however, is not considered good practice and is seldom used by skilled body men.

The best and most frequently used method of shrinking metal is by means of heat. The complete shrinking process is to heat a spot at the center of the bulge, as in Fig. 11-3.

Fig. 11-2. Face of hammer used for shrinking metal. Note that face is cross-grooved.

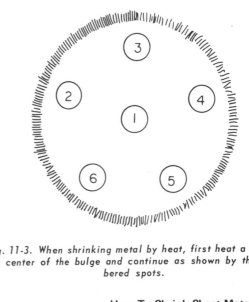

Fig. 11-3. When shrinking metal by heat, first heat a spot at the center of the bulge and continue as shown by the numbered spots.

Using a dolly block and hammer, this is then hammered down, Fig. 11-4. In successive rim heats, Fig. 11-3, additional spots are heated and hammered down. This is a basic procedure, and an area being shrunk by this method is shown in Fig. 11-4.

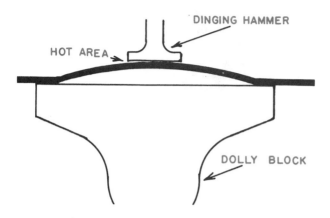

Fig. 11-4. *After heating the area, the surface is worked with hammer and dolly.*

Naturally, no attempt should be made to shrink a panel until the surface has been worked over and has been made relatively smooth. In addition, the lacquer or enamel should also be removed before starting the shrinking process.

Three different sizes of heat spots will be found sufficient to cover practically any type of shrinking. On compound curved surfaces a spot not more than 1/8-in. in diameter should be heated at one time. On plane flat surfaces, 1/4 to 5/8-in. heat spots can be used. Larger heat spots are used in cases of excessive bulge, but at no time should a heat spot larger than 5/8 in. be used.

It is well to remember that auto body sheet metal loses its temper or springing effect when heated to a cherry red. By heating small spots, the natural spring and resiliency of sheet metal is retained in the metal between the spots.

Most body panels have at least a slight curve. Therefore, if the metal is shrunk too much it will cause a flat area at that point and sometimes causes buckles to appear elsewhere in the panel. The flat area would then have to be stretched to the proper degree with a hammer and dolly.

The first heat should be applied in the approximate center of the bulge, heating a spot to a cherry red about 1/8-in. to 1/4-in. in diameter, depending on the size and height of the bulge. This spot is then hammered down while red hot, directing the blows against the red spots with the flat face of a dolly underneath. After this initial heating and hammering operation, the bulge assumes a crater like shape, Fig. 11-5. The next step is to

Fig. 11-5. *Shrinking an area with a torch.*

shrink the rim of this crater in successive stages, Fig. 11-3. Selecting the highest point of this rim, the heating operation is then repeated, and hammer and dolly used as on the first spot.

On the next high spot, which is No. 3, Fig. 11-3, the preceding operations are again repeated. It will be observed the bulged surface is being brought down and begins to assume its former shape and contours. The procedure is continued, taking five successive steps, until the entire bulged area is brought down to the level of the first spots.

Due to the expansion of the metal while hot, the surface will be slightly bulged after the last spot is hammered down, but will continue to shrink until the metal is thoroughly cool. It is very important to allow the metal to become thoroughly cool before any final dinging is done, after which it can be determined whether the surface is at its proper level. Should there be one or more high spots remaining, these should be shrunk again, using very small heat spots.

The panel surface is then ready for final sanding and preparation for priming. It is always good practice to clean and paint the underside of the area that has been shrunk too, otherwise rust will quickly form.

In the case of a long narrow stretch, the shrinking is started at either end instead of the center.

Aluminum shrinking follows the same general procedure as steel, except that care must be used to avoid burning through the metal at point of contact with the flame because aluminum absorbs heat much more rapidly than steel, and does not change color under heat. It also cools more quickly. Just as soon as the metal starts to blister where the flame contacts the metal, the flame must bo removed and hammering done quickly with a wood or fiber mallet.

1. How does a shrinking hammer differ from an ordinary dinging hammer?
   Has a heavier head.
   Has a longer handle.
   The face is cross-grooved.
2. When shrinking metal with a torch, where should the heat be first applied?
   At the center of the area.
   At the edge of the area.
3. When shrinking an area on a plane flat surface, how large should the heat spots be made?
   1/8 in.
   1/4 to 5/8 in.
   1 in.
4. When shrinking sheet metal, what should be the color of the heated spot?
   Red hot.
   White hot.
   Straw color.

Chapter 12

REPLACING
PANELS AND FENDERS

In many cases the damage to fenders and other panels can be repaired by dolly block and hammer, or other straightening methods. However, in other cases, considerable time can be saved by removing the damaged panel and installing a new one, or by cutting out the damaged area and inserting a new section.

Fig. 12-1. Typical replacement panels.

Whether to repair the original panel or install a new one depends on the extent of the damage, and which repair method would cost the least. This can be determined only as the result of experience and accurate estimates of the time involved in making repairs and replacements, together with the cost of parts.

Some of the frequently replaced panels are shown in Fig. 12-1. Some others are illustrated in Chapter 1, on Auto Body Construction.

At this point it should be emphasized that great accuracy is required in straightening work in order that doors and windows will operate correctly, and in the case of front end work the front suspension cross member is made to unusually close limits. This is necessary to insure proper front wheel alignment. Therefore, in many cases it is better practice to replace a member than to attempt to straighten it.

REMOVING A FENDER PANEL

When it is desirable to replace a complete panel, it is necessary to remove the bolts securing it to the rest of the structure, or cut through the spot welds as the case may be.

In most cases the front fender panel is bolted to the rest of the structure, Fig. 12-2. Other panels may be spot welded, Fig. 9-13, or fusion welded, Fig. 12-3. In the case of spot welds, Fig. 12-4, most mechanics usually drill through the spot welds and then use a power chisel to completely separate the panel from the rest of the body structure.

Installation of a new panel is not difficult provided the rest of the body has not been damaged. The alignment of a new front fender, Fig. 12-2, is simplified, for in most cases the bolt holes are elongated so that the position of the panel can be shifted and correctly aligned. In general, only front fender panels

ATTACHING POINTS FOR STONE DEFLECTOR

Fig. 12-2. Attaching points of fender and stone deflector. (Typical)

are bolted in position, while rear fender panels, or rear quarter panels, as these are known, are generally welded in position, Fig. 12-3.

SIDE OUTER
PANEL

WHEELHOUSE

OUTER EXTENSION PANEL

Fig. 12-3. Illustrating outer extension panel, wheelhouse and side outer panel.

REPLACING A COMPLETE PANEL

Typical service panels are shown in Fig. 12-1. If the complete panel is to be replaced, the old panel should be removed by cutting

along the weld, if fusion welded in place, or by drilling out the spot welds, if it is spot welded in place. Car and body manufacturers have the panels welded at different places, and it is necessary to examine the body to determine where the welds are located in each case. In addition, collision manuals will give diagrams of the panels for the different makes and models of cars which indicate where these welds are located.

Before cutting out the old panel, it is important that the damage to the area be restored to its original shape and alignment. This can be checked by comparison with the other side of the vehicle.

After removing the old damaged panel, the inner panel, such as the wheelhouse, rocker and other inner panels are carefully checked and straightened or replaced, as the case may require. The new outer panel is placed in position by means of vice-grip pliers, or by

Fig. 12-4. Drilling out spot welds at front edge of roof.

C clamps. The welder then starts at the center, and proceeds first in one direction, then the other. In order to reduce distortion due to heat, it is advisable to weld a space of only 2 or 3 in. at a time. Leave a gap and weld another short length. In that way temperatures are kept down, and distortion kept to a minimum. When the weld is complete, it is hammered down, filled and finished as described in the chapter on Welding.

REPLACING PARTIAL PANELS

In many cases it is desirable to replace only the damaged area of a fender or panel. In general, the decision on whether to replace a panel or repair the existing panel depends on the length of time required to straighten the damaged area. Such a decision is dependent on the availability of a replacement panel, its cost, and also the cost of labor.

When only a portion of a panel is to be replaced, the first step is to straighten the area so that it is in alignment with the body. Then outline the damaged area with chalk making sure the undamaged area is not sprung out of proper contour. Take measurements carefully from the edge of the panel, the molding, or beading, and transfer these measurements to the replacement panel, scribing lines where the panel is to be cut.

Cut along these lines to obtain the desired area of the replacement panel. There are several different methods of cutting a panel, and these were described in the chapter on Cutting Sheet Metal.

After straightening the cut edges of the replacement panel, position it over the damaged

Fig. 12-5. Damaged area is carefully marked off before it is cut out.

area. Scribe a line on the damaged panel, outlining the new replacement panels, Fig. 12-5. Then cut out the damaged area.

Straighten the cut edge of the damaged area, and fit the service panel portion into the cut out area in the body panel. Be sure that two parts do not overlap at any point. The new section can be held in position by C clamps, or by vise-grip pliers, Fig. 12-6.

Fig. 12-6. Section of service panel is then held in position with clamps while it is welded in place.

Tack weld at intervals, starting at the center and working toward each end. Then make a continuous weld around the two pieces. By welding at intervals, and only about 4 in. at a time, the possibility of distortion due to heat is minimized.

Details on welding and hammering the weld below the surface are given in the chapter on Welding.

DOOR PANEL REPLACEMENT

If a door outer panel is severely damaged and the door inner panel is undamaged, or is in a repairable condition, a door outer panel is available for service as well as a complete door.

If the outer panel is to be replaced, first remove the door assembly and the exterior moldings and hardware. It is not necessary to remove the window regulator, and remote control mechanisms, lock and runs.

Place the door on a flat surface with its edges extending over the edges of the surface, Fig. 12-7. Remove the hem flange by grinding, and repair any damage to the inner panel. Position the new outer repair panel, and bend the end flange over the inner flange. Spot braze the hem flange to the inner panel. Metal finish the exterior surface, paint it and assemble the interior trim and hardware.

INNER PANEL

OUTER PANEL

HEM FLANGE STRIP

Grinder

SPOT BRAZE OUTER PANEL REINFORCEMENT

OUTER PANEL

OUTER PANEL REINFORCEMENT

INNER PANEL

Fig. 12-7. Removing hem flange of door, prior to replacing the outer panel.

It will be necessary to break the weld on the door with an outer panel reinforcement. Spot braze the reinforcement when assembling the new panel.

TOP PANEL REPLACEMENT

Before replacing a top it is important to have the basic body dimensions correct. These can be determined by triangular measurements as shown in Fig. 8-3. Also try the new top panel in position and use it as a template to check for any distortion of the body. After making sure the body is in alignment and not distorted, the new top panel is carefully positioned on the car, and a line is scribed around the edge of the panel.

The old roof is then cut out with one of the methods described in a previous chapter. The new panel is again positioned on the body and is tacked in place with an occasional weld. After again checking for accurate alignment of the new panel with the body, the welding is completed. As in the case of welding other panels in position, only a few inches should be welded at a time.

QUIZ - Chapter 12

1. How is the front fender usually attached to the rest of the vehicle?
   By means of bolts.
   Spots welds.
   Sheet metal screws.

2. Is the position of the front fender panel adjustable?
   Yes.
   No.

3. Before replacing a damaged panel, what should be done?
   Clean the damaged area.
   Straighten the area so it is in alignment with the body.
   Obtain a replacement panel.

4. When welding a replacement panel in place, where should the welding start?
   At the right edge.
   At the left edge.
   At the center.

5. When welding a replacement panel in place, it should first be tack welded in place.
   True.
   False.

6. Door outer panels are available for replacement.
   True.
   False.

7. The basic body dimensions should be checked by triangulation, before installing a new top.
   True.
   False.

Chapter 13

FILLING DENTS WITH
SOLDER, PLASTIC OR FIBER GLASS

On certain areas of an auto body, it is difficult to remove dents. This is particularly true in the case of doors, deck lids and hoods. These panels are built-up sections and it is difficult to back up the dinging hammer, dolly block or spoon. Even when using the pull rod system some fill-in is required. Therefore, after making the area as smooth as possible, the remaining dents are brought up to the level of the undamaged panel by filling in with solder, plastic or fiber glass. Plastic is now the most popular material used for "filler," having superceded solder which requires more skill to apply.

mer and dolly or other means. The metals are joined without melting the base metal.

When filling dents on auto body work, the air-acetylene torch is used. Oxygen is not necessary. The melting point of the solder used to fill dents is 361 to 437 deg. F. Solder flows at 469 to 543 deg. F. The composition of auto body solder varies with different manufacturers. The tin content may range from 15 to 35 percent and the lead content from 65 to 85 percent. The higher the percentage of tin, the lower the melting point.

In order to get the solder to adhere to the sheet metal of the body, it is first necessary

Fig. 13-1. Using acid core solder and torch to tin an area to be filled with solder.

Fig. 13-2. Either a clean cloth or steel wool can be used to spread the solder over the surface being tinned.

SOLDERING

In auto body work, tin-lead mixture, known as solder, is melted and is used to fill indentations that cannot be removed by ham-

to clean and tin the surface. The paint can be burned off with the torch and the surface is then further cleaned by sanding. The next step is the application of the flux. This can be either a liquid or a paste type. Its purpose is to still further clean the surface by removing any oil or oxides that may be present. Commercial fluxes in both paste and liquid form are available for soldering all types of metals. After the application of the flux, following the manufacturer's instructions, the surface is tinned. That is, the surface is heated and then solder is melted onto the area by means of the acetylene torch. Instead

Fig. 13-3. Melting solder on tinned surface.

of using a paste or liquid flux, some mechanics will use an acid core solder for tinning, Fig. 13-1. The melted solder is then spread over the area by means of some steel wool, or a cloth, Fig. 13-2. When the tinning is completed the surface will have a bright shiny appearance and there will be a strong bond between the tin and the sheet metal of the body. Also when additional solder is added to fill the dent, there will be a strong bond between this filler solder and the tinned surface.

After the tinning operation, the body solder (usually in bar form) is melted onto the area, Fig. 13-3. Care must be exercised so that just enough heat is applied to keep the solder plastic, but not molten. Keeping the solder in this plastic condition, it is then smoothed with a maple wood paddle, Fig. 13-4. Suffi-

cient solder must be applied so that it is slightly higher than the surrounding panel. When cool, the surface of the solder is sanded with an open-coat No. 24 grit abrasive, or with a body file.

SOLDERING ALUMINUM

Some automobiles and some truck bodies are made of sheet aluminum. Such bodies can be soldered, although welding is usually used to join aluminum parts. For filling dents special plastics are often used. Aluminum solders are generally self-fluxing, and when using such solders instructions provided by the manufacturer should be followed.

Fig. 13-4. Spreading soft solder over the surface with a wooden paddle.

The reason why aluminum and aluminum alloys are hard to solder is that they conduct heat away rapidly, and they oxidize faster than most metals. The most difficult part of the operation is tinning the surface. Once that has been accomplished, the remainder of the job is easy. In many cases, the special aluminum solders can be used for tinning and conventional solders for the remainder of the job.

HOW TO FILL DENTS WITH PLASTIC

Instead of solder, most shops are now using plastic materials to fill depressions in bodies. There are many different makes of such plastics available. The method of applying the plastic varies somewhat with different manufacturers.

Before attempting to apply any plastic to a

rusted or dented area, it should be carefully sanded, with a disk sander to remove paint and rust, Fig. 13-5. A coarse grit such as

Fig. 13-5. Before applying plastic filler to a car body, it should be carefully sanded.

No. 24 open grit should be used to make the surface slightly rough and provide "bite" for the plastic. In addition the area surrounding the damaged area should be cleaned with a grease and wax remover. Also featheredge

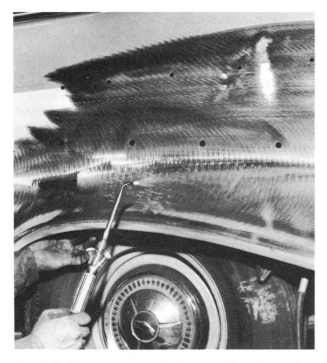

Fig. 13-6. If necessary, shrink the area with torch and then use hammer and dolly.

the area with a No. 80 feathering disk to taper back the paint around the area.

If the metal has been stretched and a bulge is present, heat the area until it is red hot, Fig. 13-6, and shrink it with a dolly and shrink hammer.

Then mix the plastic in accordance with instructions on the container. In most cases, two materials are provided, a resin and a catalyst. Both materials are mixed with a putty knife, Fig. 13-7. Instead of using a box lid, some mechanics prefer to mix the ingredients on a sheet of glass.

Fig. 13-7. Mixing plastic resin and catalyst.

The plastic is then applied to the surface with a rubber squeegee, Fig. 13-8. If the dents are deep and a thick application is necessary, it is advisable to apply several thin layers and allow each layer to dry before applying the next coat.

Fig. 13-8. Applying plastic with rubber squeegee.

Fig. 13-9. Heat lamp being used to speed drying of plastic.

To hasten the drying, heat lamps may be used, Fig. 13-9. Or if heat lamps are not available, the flame of a welding torch can be played over the surface. However, care must be taken not to apply too much heat at one time by this method.

Plastic patches can be cured in about 30 minutes if a battery of infrared lamps is used.

After the plastic filler is dry, it is sanded in the usual manner and then primed and painted.

FILLING RUSTED AREAS

A somewhat different procedure and materials are used to repair rusted areas. In general, the materials include fiber glass cloth, epoxy resin, and hardener.

The procedure is to first sand the surface in the usual manner to remove rust, dirt and paint. Then wipe the surface with an oil-free, wax-free cleaning solvent.

Drill a series of small holes through the metal all around the damaged area. This will insure quicker adhesion of resin to the metal.

Cut the fiber glass cloth. The cloth should be large enough to lap two or three inches over the damaged area, Fig. 13-10. If the rusted area is depressed below the surrounding surface, several layers of fiber glass cloth should be applied. These should be cut

in progressively larger sizes so each succeeding patch will overlap the preceding patch. Wadded newspaper can be used to support the fiber glass when covering large

Fig. 13-10. Cutting fiber glass cloth prior to application on rusted area.

Fig. 13-11. Area is first sanded and then heated with heat lamps, prior to application of fiber glass cloth.

holes and bridging deep dents. At this point, direct the rays from a heat lamp on the surface, Fig. 13-11. This will provide better adherence and reduce curing time.

Fig. 13-12. Before applying the fiber glass patches, they are impregnated with epoxy resin and hardener.

Wearing rubber gloves to protect the hands, mix enough epoxy resin and hardener to impregnate all patches. Care must be taken to use correct proportions of materials for if the mixture is too liquid, it will run when used on a vertical surface. The resin should be mixed in a glass tray.

Dip each of the fiber glass patches in the mixture, Fig. 13-12. When the patch is saturated apply it to the rusted area, Fig. 13-13.

Fig. 13-13. Applying the fiber glass cloth patches to the rusted area.

Fig. 13-14. The patch is first dried and then sanded. Paint is sprayed in the usual manner.

Use heat lamps, Fig. 13-14, to hasten drying time. Then, sand and refinish the surface in the usual manner.

SPRAYABLE BODY PUTTY

A sprayable polyester body putty is available. It is sprayed in the same manner as paint and is said to eliminate the usual glazing putty operation. It is designed to seal and fill hairline cracks, pin holes and other minor imperfections in both metal and fiber glass. In addition, it eliminates the first application of lacquer primer and provides a base for all types of paints, including acrylic.

This polyester body putty comes with a tube of hardener, which is mixed with the material just prior to application. It is applied in several coats and is ready for block sanding and painting after 45 minutes.

QUIZ - Chapter 13

1. Which method of filling dents is faster, lead or plastic?
    Lead.
    Plastic.
2. Solder is a mixture of what two metals.
    Zinc and tin.
    Lead and zinc.
    Lead and tin.
    Copper and zinc.
3. What is the melting point of solder used to fill dents on auto bodies?
    361 to 437 deg.
    500 to 570 deg.
    560 to 670 deg.
4. What is purpose of soldering flux?
    Help clean the surface.
    Roughen the surface.
5. When applying solder to the tinned surface, in what condition should it be?
    Molten.
    Plastic.
6. When using a disk sander to smooth the surface of solder, what grit should be used?
    No. 24 grit.
    No. 240 grit.
    No. 180 grit.
7. When using plastic to fill a dent it is not necessary to featheredge the area.
    True.
    False.
8. Plastic is usually applied to the surface with what type of tool?
    Wooden paddle.
    Rubber squeegee.
9. When covering a rusted area with fiber glass cloth, what is the purpose of drilling holes through the metal?
    Provide better adhesion.
    Necessary for the pull rods.
    Used to attach the fiber glass.

Chapter 14

REPAIRING
FIBER GLASS BODIES

Fiber glass car bodies are formed from chopped fiber glass preforms and fiber glass mats fused together with a polyester resin. Fiber glass is a fiber made by drawing out molten glass into long thread-like fibers. When resin cures or hardens, it binds fiber glass filaments together to form a solid reenforced panel having unusual strength. A reenforced fiber glass body has a high resistance to impact, which means it will not dent. In most minor accidents the body would be undamaged. If damage does occur, it would tend to be localized, not transmitted through the body and cause damage at a point away from the impact (as in the case of metal bodies). Various replacement panels are available for service. Complete panels may be used, or sections may be cut from the panels to accomodate the repair necessary.

The following steps should be used in repair of reenforced fiber glass parts:

1. Study the repair to be made.
2. Remove the damaged material.
3. Fill the damaged area with the proper mixture of resin and fiber glass.
4. Allow the activated resin to cure and harden.
5. Finish and paint the repaired area.

In general the following materials are needed for repairing fiber glass bodies:

Polyester resin.
Polyester filler.
Catalyst.
Fiber glass cloth.
Fiber glass powder or chopped fibers.
Fiber glass bonding strip.

These items are readily available in kit form. In cases where the kit is to be used for repairing both fiber glass and metal bodies, epoxy resin rather than polyester resin should be obtained, as polyester resin does not stick to metal satisfactorily.

The resin is activated by the addition of a catalyst in proper proportions, as specified by the manufacturer.

SAFETY PRECAUTIONS

When making repairs:

1. If resin causes skin irritation, apply protective cream to hands or, preferably, use rubber gloves when working with resin or filler and hardener.
2. Use lacquer thinner to remove any resin accumulated on hands, tools or clothing (before resin starts to jell or harden).
3. Use caution when handling filler. It is highly flammable.
4. Be sure work area is well ventilated. Working with resin creates toxic fumes.
5. Do not let mixed resin and catalyzed material stand in the shop for extended lengths of time, or undisposed of when the shop is closed. Chemical action results in rapid heat buildup, which is a fire hazard.
6. Keep a water container available that is large enough to provide for ready disposal of left over or unused mixed material.
7. When grinding or polishing resin repair areas, use a belt sander with a vacuum attachment for dust control, Fig. 5-7. If a vacuum attachment is not available, wear a respirator mask to avoid inhaling resin dust.
8. Wear a disposable shop coat to keep dust and fiber slivers from becoming embedded in clothing.

RESIN PREPARATION

Typical instructions are as follows: Place one ounce of resin in a wax-free container, and add 10 drops of catalyst to the resin, and mix well. This formula will normally harden in 30 minutes. Ten ounces of resin to 1 tsp. of catalyst. Use the same proportion for larger amounts.

Mix only as much as you are going to use within 30 minutes. The addition of more of the catalyst will cause a faster chemical reaction, therefore, setting up time will be reduced accordingly.

The filler is activated by the addition of a catalyst in proper proportions.

FILLER PREPARATION

Place the desired amount of the filler (powdered fiber glass) on a clean hard surface. Using a spatula or putty knife mix in the catalyst: (typical mixtures) 1/4 tsp. for a golf ball size lump, or 1 oz. of catalyst, to a 3 lb. 1 qt. can. If the putty-like filler hardens too quickly use less catalyst.

Wipe a thin coat of mixed material on the area to be repaired, assuring a good bond and then fill the entire hole with the filler mixture.

When the filler and catalyst are mixed as directed above, it will harden in about 10 minutes. For quicker hardening, use more catalyst while mixing. It is a good practice to mix a small quantity of the resin and catalyst, or the filler and catalyst, according to the basic formula, and note the hardening time required. The hardening time will vary according to temperatures and humidity conditions.

CAUTION: Never return mixed filler or resin to the stock can. Keep the can closed and in a cool place of storage. Do not take internally. Wash hands after using, and before smoking or eating.

REPAIRING HOLES IN PANELS

The following procedure is for use on the reverse side of panel, when accessible.

First clean the surface around the damaged area with a good commercial grease and wax remover. Remove all paint and primer with No. 80 grit paper, to expose plastic material at least 3 in. beyond the damaged area. Grind or file all cracked or splintered material away from the hole on both the inside and outside of the area to be repaired, Fig. 14-1.

Fig. 14-1. Grind or file edge of hole to remove splintered material.

On the inner surface of the repair area, remove any dirt, sound deadener, etc., from the damaged area. Scuff the area around the hole with coarse No. 80 grit paper to provide a good bonding surface. Bevel the outside edge of the area to be repaired about 30 deg. to permit better patch adhesion, and the inner edge to about 45 deg. as shown in Fig. 14-2.

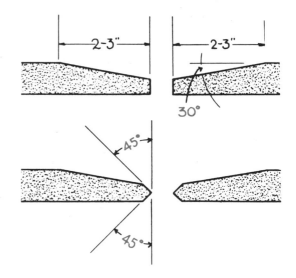

Fig. 14-2. Bevel surface of edge of hole.

Clean the repair surface well with mineral spirits, naphtha or a non-oily solvent.

Cut five pieces of fiber glass cloth large enough to cover the hole and the scuffed area. The amount may vary and the number of pieces should be determined by the thickness of the original panel. Prepare a mixture of resin and hardener (catalyst) following the mixture procedures previously outlined.

Using a small paint brush, saturate at least two layers of glass cloth with activated resin mix and apply to the inside or back surface of the repair area, making sure the cloth is in full contact with the scuffed area surrounding the hole.

Saturate three more layers of glass cloth with activated resin mix and apply to the outside surface, making certain that these layers are in complete contact with the inner layers, and in full contact with the scuffed outside repair area, Fig. 14-3.

Fig. 14-3. Apply fiber glass cloth and make saucer like depression.

After the layers of saturated glass cloth are in place make a saucer-like depression in them in order to increase the depth of the resin and glass putty-like repair material. Note: Immerse brush and all other tools in lacquer thinner immediately after use. Allow layer of saturated cloth to become tacky. To expedite hardening, external heat, preferably an infrared lamp, may be used. If external heat is used, do not heat area above 200 deg. F. Too much heat will distort the material.

Disk sand the patch area slightly below the contour of the panel, Fig. 14-4.

Fig. 14-4. Sand hardened patch slightly below contour of panel.

Mix patch material as outlined under Resin Preparation, and using a small spatula or putty knife, trowel this mix into the saucer-like depression in the repair area, leaving a sufficient mound of material to grind down smooth and flush when hardened. Before the patch begins to harden, waxed paper may be taped over the patch, then a rubber squeegee may be used to smooth out the patch, while keeping the patching material well above the surrounding contour of the panel. Allow patch to harden, Fig. 14-5.

Fig. 14-5. Apply putty-like patching material.

When patch if fully hardened, sand excess material down to basic contour, using No. 80 grit paper and a sanding block or pad. Finish sanding with No. 120 or finer grit paper.

Instead of applying fiber glass cloth on both sides of a hole, you can attach a bonding sheet of metal to inner side of hole with sheet metal screws, Fig. 14-6. Sand sheet metal and both inner and outer sides of hole to provide good adherence for repair material. Before fastening sheet metal, apply resin mix to both sides of rim of hole. Follow usual procedure for remainder of repair.

When inner side of hole is not accessible, apply fiber glass patch to outer side only. After usual cleaning and sanding operations, apply five layers of fiber glass cloth to outer side of hole. Before it dries, make a saucer-like depression to provide greater depth for resin and glass fiber repair material.

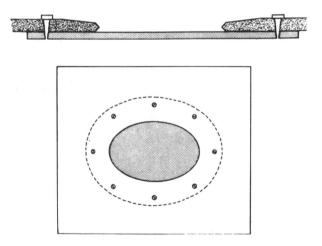

Fig. 14-6. Fasten bonding strip with sheet metal screws.

REPAIRING SPLIT OR CRACKED PANELS

Clean surface as previously described. Then, using a hacksaw blade, cut along break line and remove broken portion of panel. Remove dirt, etc., from inner surface of damaged area. Scuff area around hole with coarse No. 80 grit abrasive paper to provide a good bonding surface. Remove all cracked and fractured material along break, and bevel edge of break area approximately 30 deg. to permit better patch adhesion. Use C clamps or other suitable means to bring surfaces on each side of break into proper alignment. Clean repair surface well with solvent.

Cut three pieces of fiber glass cloth large enough to overlap repair area by about 2 in. Apply mixture of resin and hardener to layers of glass cloth and to inner surface of repair area. Make sure cloth is in full contact with scuffed area beyond break. Allow saturated cloth to cure. Then, mix patch material as outlined under RESIN PREPARATION.

Scuff break area with abrasive paper to provide a good bonding surface. Using a small spatula or putty knife, trowel mix into break area on outer surface, leaving sufficient material to grind down smooth and flush when hardened.

PANEL REPLACEMENT

Cut out damaged portion of panel with a hacksaw blade. Then, remove dirt and paint from both sides of panel about 2 to 3 in. back from patching line. Cut out section from service replacement panel. If section does not fit closely to break line, reshape panel to suit. Bevel attaching edges about 45 deg., so that a single V butt joint will be formed on finished surface when pieces are joined.

Align section of replacement panel to adjacent panel. If C clamps cannot be used, install 3/16 in. bolts and nuts with large washers on inner and outer surfaces of panels to hold them in alignment; or use bonding strips and sheet metal screws, Fig. 14-7. Clean repair surface well with non-oily solvent.

Cut three pieces of fiber glass cloth large enough to overlap entire length of joint area about 2 to 3 in.

Saturate three layers of glass cloth with activated resin mix and apply to inner surface of repair area. Make sure cloth is in full contact with scuffed area surrounding joined areas. Allow inner layers of saturated cloth to cure. Complete repair as previously given.

Fig. 14-7. Join panels with bonding strip and sheet metal screws.

REPAIRING SCRATCHES AND GOUGES

Starting with 1973 models, many automobiles are equipped with complete front end panels of fiber glass polyester. In addition, many rear end finishing panels, valence panels, fender extensions and specialty hoods are made of this particular material.

All types of damage to fiber glass polyester body parts can be repaired. The following materials are needed to handle the repair work: epoxy adhesive, polyester body filler, polyester resin, hardener and glazing putty. Figs. 14-8 to 14-17 apply to the repair of scratches and gouges. (All illustrations courtesy of Owens-Corning Fiberglass Corp.)

Fig. 14-8. Use a power drill with burr bit to rout length of scratch or gouge. Form a V groove tapered no more than 45 deg. Do not cut through laminate.

Fig. 14-9. Use 360 grit paper to remove flaky edges and feather painted surface back about 1/2 in. beyond damaged area. Clean surface with dry cloth or air.

Fig. 14-12. Apply and spread filler with a plastic squeegee. Remove all air bubbles. Allow filler to extend above original surface to allow for shrinkage.

Fig. 14-10. Mask undamaged surface, leaving a working area of approximately 5 in. around repair area.

Fig. 14-13. Let filler set until it is rubbery, but not fully hardened. Then, plane or file filler to original contour, but leave level slightly higher than original surface.

Fig. 14-11. Follow manufacturer's instruction and mix enough body filler on hard surface (Formica) to re-establish surface.

Fig. 14-14. Use a heat gun or heat lamp to shrink filler. Use a minimum temperature of 125 deg. F, keeping heat source at least 12 in. from surface.

Fig. 14-15. After filler has set, sand with 360 grit paper, using an orbital sander. Sand until surface is smooth and even with original surface.

Fig. 14-16. If filler has fine pinholes, apply a thin coating of glazing putty. If filler is pockmarked, do not use glazing putty. Instead, apply another layer of body filler and repeat refinishing steps.

RUSTPROOFING AND SOUNDPROOFING

There has been a considerable gain in the durability and lasting quality of automobile bodies in recent years. This marked improvement is the result of:

1. Better materials used in the manufacture of automobile bodies, together with increased use of rustproofing and sound deadening materials applied by the body manufacturer.
2. Better rustproofing and sound deadening materials and improvement in their application after the car is delivered to the car owner.

Fig. 14-17. Complete repair by cleaning with air. Then, spot prime, wet sand with 400 grit paper and paint.

In the case of improvement in the materials used in the manufacture of car bodies, some Fisher bodies (particularly GM X style bodies) are provided with special metals. These include one-side and two-side galvanized steel, Zincrometal, zinc-iron alloy and aluminum. These metals are found in doors, quarter panels, rear fenders, rocker panels, trunk lids, rear compartment floor pans, rear wheelhouses and many other critical points.

Zinc-rich preprimer paint is applied in specific areas where corrosion is most likely to occur. Also, the entire body is given a rustproof resistant primer either by spraying or submerging in a tank solution that is attracted to the bare metal through an electrical charge.

Wax coatings are sprayed into the bottom sections of doors, Fig. 14-18, door pillars, fenders, trunk lids and hatchback lids.

Also, on the GM X bodies, Plasisol and hot metal sealers are applied along exposed joints. Moisture-repellent asphaltic sound deadeners are sprayed inside wheel wells and doors.

Further, rustproofing is found in many other areas such as exterior moldings. Often, these are made of aluminum, plastic or bimetal material. To further reduce any tendency to rust, decorative parts such as moldings and name plates are no longer attached with clips and bolts (which required holes to be drilled in the panels). Now they are attached with modern adhesives.

Fig. 14-18. Using special equipment to apply rustproofing and sound deadening material to the interior of a door. (Stewart-Warner)

Fig. 14-18. Using special equipment to apply rustproofing and sound deadening material to the interior of a door. (Stewart-Warner)

IN-FIELD RUSTPROOFING

In the automotive service field, specialists with especially designed equipment are offering rustproofing and sound deadening services. Several organizations offer these services nationwide. Some also provide shine or polish service.

In order to reach the interior of some panels (such as doors) with the rustproofing material, special equipment, Fig. 14-18, is provided.

QUIZ - Chapter 14

1. A fiber glass body has high resistance to impact.
    True.
    False.
2. Fiber glass panels are not available for replacement.
    True.
    False.
3. The resin used in making fiber glass repairs may cause skin irritations.
    True.
    False.
4. Why is it advisable to use a belt sander when sanding fiber glass?
    It cuts faster.
    A vacuum attachment can be used to draw in the dust.
    Conforms to the curves of the body more accurately.

5. Catalyzed resin should not be left to stand too long, because -
    It dries and hardens quickly.
    Chemical action results in rapid heat buildup and is therefore a fire hazard.
    It evaporates quickly.
6. It is not necessary to clean the surface before applying fiber glass repairs.
    True.
    False.
7. After fiber glass patch has hardened, what grit abrasive should be used first?
    No. 80 grit.
    No. 180 grit.
    No. 16 grit.
8. When repairing a scratch or gouge on fiber glass, how would you shrink the applied filler?
    Apply ice.
    Allow it to stand for 24 hours.
    Use a heat gun.

Double-V Butt Weld

Multiple Bead Single-V Butt Weld

Multiple Bead Double-V Butt Weld

Corner Weld

Edge Welds

Fillet Weld

Lap Fillet Weld

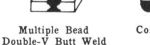

Types of welds that are used on plastic body panels.

Chapter 15

ALIGNING HOODS, DECK LIDS, PANELS

The accurate alignment of hoods, rear deck lids and panels is important, not only from the standpoint of appearance, but also unless correctly installed in relation to adjacent panels, hoods and deck lids will not close properly, and in addition will tend to squeak and rattle. In the case of rear deck lids, or trunk lids, there will also be a strong tendency toward rain and dust leakage.

In order to provide adjustment the hinges of such panels are usually provided with elongated holes, and in addition the position of latches are also made adjustable to insure proper operation. In many cases also, panels are adjusted by means of shims.

For correct installation of hoods, doors and deck lids, the clearance between these panels and adjacent panels should be the same on both sides, Fig. 15-1. Clearance should measure 5/32 in. In addition, the surfaces of each of these panels should be flush with adjacent panels.

Fig. 15-1. Spacing between doors and adjacent panels should be the same on both sides. (Chrysler Corp.)

If the sheet metal (fenders, hood, cowl, door) are not in proper alignment adjustments must be made. While the procedure on different makes of bodies varies somewhat, the adjustment of front fender and bumper on recent models of Fisher bodies is typical.

FISHER BODY ADJUSTMENTS

If the front end of the sheet metal assembly is too high, or too low, resulting in objectionably uneven vertical spacing between the front fenders and doors, it will be necessary to add shims at front support location, Fig. 15-2. Whenever shims are to be added or removed at the front support location, it will be necessary to loosen the lower rear attachment bolts, both at the shimming location, and at the inner skirt to body mount bracket.

Slight adjustment of fender to door spacing can be made by loosening the lower rear shimming bolts and also skirt body mount bracket and inserting a screwdriver between the rocker panel and fender to pry opening wider at lower edge. Or have helper lean on front fender to lessen gap at the bottom.

Rear height of the front fender is adjustable at rear location, Fig. 15-2. When shimming for rear height, it will be necessary to loosen lower rear attaching bolts, and the inner skirt to body mount bracket.

In and out adjustment of the lower rear edge of the front fender is accomplished by shimming at the two fender to body attaching bolts, Fig. 15-2.

The fender line should be flush with the rocker panel. Whenever adjustment is made at that location, the inner skirt to body mount bracket bolts must be loosened.

The bumper attaching bolt holes in frame cross member, anchor brackets, back bars, and bumper faceplate are slotted to permit movement of the bumper and permit proper alignment of adjacent parts.

The hood upper latch is adjustable and the procedure is to loosen the upper latch mounting bolts and tighten finger tight. Close the hood, causing the latch to shift to correct alignment. Then open hood and tighten bolts.

FENDER

SCREW
5-20 LB-FT

RADIATOR
SUPPORT

PANEL

Fig. 15-2. Illustrating adjustment points on typical Fisher body.

HOOD ADJUSTMENTS ON FISHER BODIES

Rear height of hood is determined on late model Fisher bodies by special washers between hinge and hood, Fig. 15-3. Removing or adding washers will shift rear of hood up or down with respect to hinge.

If the rear of the hood tends to flutter, it indicates too little tension. To increase tension add special washers between the hood and the hinges at the front bolts, Fig. 15-3.

Front height of the hood is determined by two adjustable rubber bumpers. However, the front of the hood may not contact these bumpers unless the hood latch is correctly adjusted.

When the hood to fender spacing is out of adjustment, minor adjustment can be made by means of slotted holes, to space the hood properly between the fenders, Fig. 15-3.

Fore and aft movement of the hood is allowed by slotted holes in the hinges. Before adjusting, scribe a reference line along the edge of each hinge flange. Then loosen the hinge to hood bolts and shift the hood from this line as required.

FENDER ADJUSTMENTS (FORD)

The fenders on recent model Ford built vehicles are mounted in such a manner that either fender can be shifted fore or aft to increase or reduce the amount of clearance between the forward edge of the door and the rear edge of the fender. When installing a fender, this alignment is accomplished when all the fenders and cap screws are loose. Shift the fender the required amount and while holding the fender in the desired position, tighten the fender bolts and cap screws. The proper amount of clearance between hood and fender is 5/32 in., Fig. 15-1.

If the fender is installed and only a limited amount of fore or aft adjustment is required, the following procedure is recommended:

1. Loosen three cap screws that secure fender to fender apron, Fig. 15-4.

2. Loosen three cap screws securing fender and lock dowel support.

3. Loosen cap screw at fender to cowl bracket.

4. Loosen cap screw connecting fender to rocker panel.

MOULDING-HOOD TOP ASSEMBLY
(NOSE SECTION)

HOOD ASSEMBLY

UPPER HOOD LATCH
ADJUST TO PROPERLY
SPACE HOOD BETWEEN
FENDERS HERE

RETAINER (6)

STAMPED
NUT

STAMPED NUT (12)

BOLT

BOLT

SPRING-HOOD HINGE (2)

HOOD HINGE ASSEMBLY

NUT-ANCHOR (4)

WASHER-SPECIAL (.060)
WASHER-SPECIAL (.120)
ADD AS REQUIRED
AT FRONT TO INCREASE HOOD PULL DOWN ON SHROUD
AT REAR TO DECREASE HOOD PULL DOWN ON SHROUD

MOULDING-
HOOD TOP

CLIP (12)

RETAINER (2)

HOOD
ASSEMBLY

HOOD HINGE
ASSEMBLY

BOLT ASSEMBLY

NUT
WASHER
STUD
BOLT
ASSEMBLY

OPTIONAL-(AT FRONT
LOCATION ONLY)

Fig. 15-3. Details of hood adjustments on Fisher body.

Fig. 15-4. Method of attaching fenders on Ford built bodies.

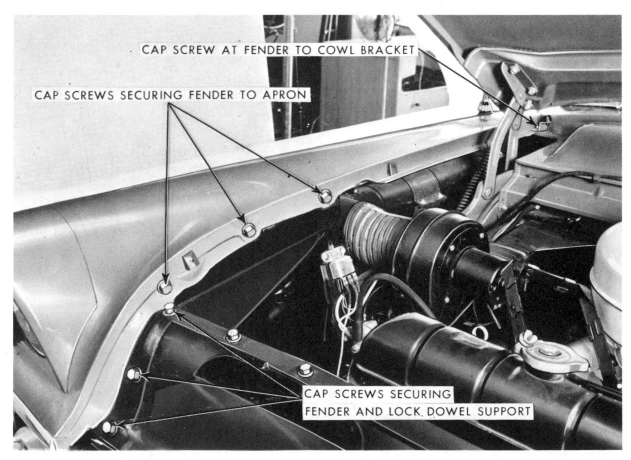

CAP SCREW AT FENDER TO COWL BRACKET

CAP SCREWS SECURING FENDER TO APRON

CAP SCREWS SECURING
FENDER AND LOCK DOWEL SUPPORT

5. From inside of car, remove cowl trim panel and loosen nut connecting front fender to cowl. Move fender fore or aft as required and while holding fender in desired position, tighten all cap screws and nuts.

To parallel the rear edge of fender with front edge of door the following procedure is recommended:

1. Underneath fender at rear, loosen 8 cap screws securing apron and deflector to body at dash to frame brace, apron and deflector to splash shield, and splash shield to body cowl side flange.

2. Loosen one cap screw at fender to cowl bracket, and one cap screw securing fender to body rocker panel.

3. Loosen the two attaching bolts located at bottom center of radiator support.

4. If more clearance is desired between fender and door at top, remove shims at radiator support. If more clearance is desired between the fender and door at bottom, add shims at radiator support.

The curve of the rear edge of the fender may be increased or reduced to bring it into conformity with the curvature of the door by inserting or removing shims between fender and cowl side panel, and between fender and rocker panel.

HOOD ADJUSTMENTS

The hood on recent model Ford and Maverick cars can be adjusted fore and aft and side to side by loosening the hood-to-hinge attaching screws, and repositioning the hood, Fig. 15-5. To raise or lower the hood, loosen the hinge-to-fender reinforcement attaching screws, and raise or lower the hood as necessary.

On Mustang and Torino models, the hood is provided with fore and aft, vertical and side-to-side adjustments and the following directions refer to the position of the hood when it is fully lowered. The elongated bolt slots in the hinge and hood provide the side-to-side and fore and aft adjustments, Fig. 15-6. The enlarged holes at the fender apron provide for up and down adjustments. Hood bumpers, located on the top left and top right surface of the radiator support, can be adjusted up and down to provide a level surface

Fig. 15-5. Hood hinge installation of recent model Ford cars.

alignment of the hood panel and the front fenders.

On Ford, Mustang and Thunderbird models the hood latch adjustment is as follows: Before adjusting the hood latch mechanism, make certain that the hood is properly aligned. The hood latch can be moved from side-to-side to align it with the hood latch hook and up and down to obtain a flush fit with the front fenders. Loosen the hood latch attaching bolts until they are just loose enough to move the latch. Move the latch from side-to-side to align it with the hood latch hook. Loosen the lock nuts on the two hood bumpers and lower the bumpers. Move the hood latch up or down as required to obtain a flush fit between the top of the hood and fenders when an upward pressure is applied to the front of the hood. Then tighten the hood latch attaching screws.

Fig. 15-6. Hood installation of recent Torino and Mustang cars.

Fig. 15-7. Details of hood latch, typical of Ford, Torino and Mustang.

Raise the two hood bumpers to eliminate any looseness at the front of the hood when closed. Then tighten the hood bumper nuts.

Adjustment of the Mustang and Torino hood latches is similar and differs only in detail. The Maverick and Torino hood latch is illustrated in Fig. 15-7.

TRUNK LID ADJUSTMENTS

To adjust compartment lid forward or rearward, or from side to side in body opening, loosen both hinge strap attaching bolts and adjust lid as required, then tighten bolts.

To adjust compartment lid at hinge area, up or down, install shims between lid inner panel and hinge straps as follows: To raise front edge of lid at hinge area, place shim between lid inner panel and forward portion of one or both hinge straps, at C, Fig. 15-7. To lower front edge of lid at hinge area, place shim between lid inner panel and rearward portion of one or both hinge straps at B, Fig. 15-8. Rear deck lid adjustment points on 1971 Fisher bodies are shown in Fig. 15-9, and are similar to the foregoing.

Fig. 15-8. Location of rear compartment lid adjustments.

© General Motors Corporation

Fig. 15-9. Mechanical pull down unit and hydraulic cylinder cable attachment, 1971 Cadillac style, also rear compartment lid adjustments.

QUIZ – Chapter 15

1. The position of hinges on deck lids is not adjustable.
   True.
   False.
2. On recent model Fisher bodies what means is provided for adjusting vertically the front end of the sheet metal assembly.
   Bolts in elongated holes.
   Shims.
   No adjustment provided.
3. How is rear height of hood on recent model Fisher bodies adjusted?
   Special washers between hinge and hood.
   Bolts and elongated holes.
   .005 in. shims.
4. Front fenders on recent model Ford Cars are adjustable, as to position, by what method?
   Elongated holes and bolts.
   Special washers.
5. What is the usual clearance between the hood and the fender?
   5/32 in.
   .001 in.
   .0025 in.
6. To correctly position the hood assembly on recent model Ford cars, how many adjustments are provided?
   Two.
   Three.
   Four.
   One.

Chapter 16
HOW TO
ADJUST DOORS

It is important to adjust car doors accurately so that they will close easily and without undue force being exerted. When doors are not correctly adjusted, they are difficult to close and will rattle when driven over a rough road. In addition, they are apt to leak excessive amounts of rain and dust.

When doors are correctly adjusted, the clearance between the door and the surrounding frame should be approximately 1/8 in. to 5/32 in. However, along the bottom edge 1/4 in. clearance is often provided.

Adjustments are provided so that the door can be moved up and down, fore and aft, in and out.

FISHER BODY DOORS

Typical front doors on recent model Fisher bodies are of the swing-out type with an integral door check on the top hinge assembly and a two-position hold open on the lower hinge. The hinges are attached to the front body hinge pillar and to the door assembly with bolts and anchor plates. Either of two methods can be used to remove the door from the body.

A. The door and hinge can be removed as an assembly from the body pillars.

B. The door can be removed from the hinge straps.

If door and hinges are to be removed from the body pillars, additional access may be obtained at lower hinge by loosening front fender lower rear attachment bolts. However, this may vary with different body designs.

Mark hinge locations on door or hinge pillar depending on method of removal being used.

With door properly supported, remove the bolts securing upper and lower hinges to front body hinge pillar or door hinge pillars, Fig. 16-1. With help, remove door from body.

To reinstall, reverse the procedure.

In or out, up or down adjustments are provided at door hinge pillars. Fore and aft adjustments are at the body hinge pillars.

On Fisher X style bodies (1980 Citation, Phoenix, Omega, Skylark), all front door hinges are of steel and are welded to the door and body hinge pillars. No adjustment is provided. However, a removable hinge pin allows removal of the door. Door side hinges are pierced to permit bolt-on installation into tapped anchor plates.

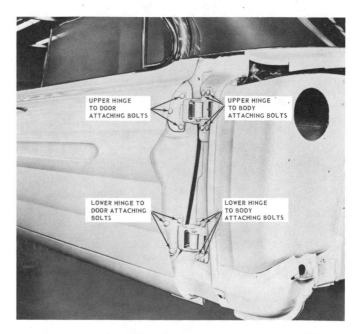

Fig. 16-1. Front door hinge attaching points on recent model Fisher body (Typical).

To remove doors on X style cars: First, remove the E ring, Fig. 16-1a, from lower end of both upper and lower hinge pins. (Cover with towel to prevent spring from flying out.) Disengage door hold-open spring from lower hinge assembly by prying upward against spring. Using a tapered tool, drive wedge between head of hinge pin and hinge, raising pin enough to force serrated shoulder out of the hinge. Support door at rear edge, remove loosened hinge pins and remove door assembly.

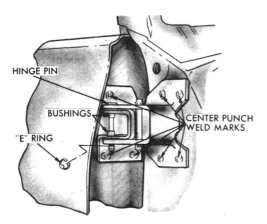

Fig. 16-1a. Details of front door hinge on Fisher X style bodies.

DOOR LOCK STRIKERS (FISHER)

The front and rear door lock striker on recent model Fisher bodies as installed on General Motors passenger cars consist of a single metal bolt and washer assembly that is threaded into a tapped, floating cage plate located in the body lock pillar, Fig. 16-2. With this design, the door is secured in the closed position when the door lock fork-bolt snaps over and engages the striker bolt.

The removal and installation procedure is as follows: Mark position of striker on body lock pillar, using a pencil. Procure a special tool or make a tool of the screw jack type and insert into the star shaped tool recess in the head of the striker bolt and remove striker, Fig. 16-2A.

To install, reverse the procedure. Make certain the striker is positioned within the pencil marks, touch up any unpainted surface on lock pillar adjacent to striker assembly.

Fig. 16-2. Lock to striker engagement on recent model Fisher bodies.

Torque striker bolt to 34-36 ft. lb.

Note: The door lock striker is an important attaching part in that it could affect the performance of vital components and systems, and/or could result in major repair expense. It must be replaced with one of the same part number or with an equivalent part if replacement becomes necessary. Do not use a replacement part of lesser quality or substitute design. Torque values must be used as specified during reassembly to assure proper retention of part.

When a door has been removed and reinstalled or realigned, the door should not be closed completely until a visual check is made to determine if lock fork-bolt will correctly engage striker.

Fig. 16-2A. Door lock striker installation on recent model Fisher bodies.

FRONT GUIDE CAM
ATTACHING SCREWS

UPPER HINGE TO DOOR
ATTACHING SCREWS

LOWER HINGE TO DOOR
ATTACHING SCREWS

LOWER ADJUSTING
STUD AND NUT

Fig. 16-3. Rear door hinges on recent model Fisher bodies (Typical).

To adjust striker up or down, in or out, loosen striker bolt and shift striker as required, then tighten striker.

To determine if striker fore and aft adjustment is necessary on recent model Fisher bodies, proceed as follows: First make sure door is properly aligned. Apply modeling clay or body caulking compound to lock bolt opening as shown in Fig. 16-2. Close door only as far as necessary for striker bolt to form impression in clay as shown in Fig. 16-2. Note: Do not close door completely. Complete closing may make clay removal very difficult.

Measure striker impressions as follows: Striker head should be centered fore and aft as shown, some tolerances are allowed. In any alignment, it is important that minimum dimensions as indicated in Fig. 16-2 be strictly maintained. Spacers are available to achieve the desired alignment.

REAR DOOR HINGES (FISHER)

Typical rear door hinges differ slightly from those described as used on the front doors. The rear door hinges are attached to the center pillar with two butt type hinges. The hinges are attached to the center pillar and door hinge pillar by screws and anchor plates, Fig. 16-3. The lower hinge incorporates an integral door check and hold open.

To remove: (On 4-door sports sedan models lower the door window). Clean off excess

Fig. 16-4. Front and rear door hinge installation on recent model Ford, Mustang, Maverick and Torino models.

sealer around each hinge strap and mark location on door hinge pillar, or center pillar, depending on whether hinge is being removed with door, or is being left on the pillar. On bodies equipped with electrically operated windows, it is necessary to remove the door trim assembly and water deflector. Then disconnect wiring from motor and remove conduit from door and harness from between door panels.

With door properly supported, move the three upper and lower attaching screws at door hinge pillar, or center pillar. On the four door sport sedan model, the rear door lower hinge to center pillar middle attaching bolt is also the rear door jamb switch. Be sure to disconnect wire before removing door. Door can then be removed.

When replacing the door, first with a scraper and mineral spirits, clean off the old sealing compound at hinge attaching areas. Take care not to soil adjacent trim material. Then apply a coat of heavy body sealer to attaching hinge straps. Lift door into position. Install screws loosely, align strap inside, scribe marks on pillar, and then tighten bolts. Check door for proper alignment. Install wiring harness.

In or out, or up and down, adjustments are provided at door hinge pillar. Fore and aft and slight up and down adjustments are provided at center pillar. When checking door for alignment, remove door lock striker from body pillar, and allow door to hang free on its hinges.

When performing in and out, or fore and aft adjustments, adjust one hinge at a time so that up and down adjustment is maintained.

Door should be adjusted so that when in the closed position its edges are evenly spaced around the door opening.

After performing any adjustment, the rear door window on four door sport sedan model should be checked for proper alignment with the side roof rail weatherstrip. In addition, door lock extension should be adjusted if necessary.

FORD DOOR ADJUSTMENTS

The door hinges on Ford cars provide sufficient adjustment latitude to correct most door misalignment conditions. The holes of the hinge and/or the hinge attaching points are enlarged or elongated to provide for door alignment, as shown in Fig. 16-4. Do not cover up poor door alignment with a latch striker adjustment.

Alignment procedure: Determine which hinge bolts must be loosened to move the door in the desired position. Remove the side cowl trim panel and/or door trim panel and hinge access covers, Fig. 16-4. Loosen the hinge bolts just enough to permit movement of the door with a padded pry bar. Move the door the distance estimated to be necessary. Tighten the hinge bolts and check the door fit. Repeat the operation until the desired fit is obtained. Check the strike plate alignment for proper door closing. On two door hardtop models, check the quarter glass to door glass fit. Adjust quarter glass if necessary.

Fig. 16-5. Door lock striker adjustment (Ford).

FORD LOCK STRIKER ADJUSTMENT

The striker pin can be adjusted laterally and vertically, as well as fore and aft. The lock striker should not be adjusted to correct door sag. The lock striker should be shimmed to get the clearance shown in Fig. 16-5, between the striker and the lock. To check this clearance, clean the lock jaws and the striker area and then apply a thin layer of dark grease to the lock strikers. As the door is closed and opened a measurable pattern will result. Move the striker assembly laterally to provide a flush fit at the door and the pillar or quarter panel.

CHRYSLER TYPE FRONT DOOR ADJUSTMENT

There are two general types of front door hinge attachments, as shown in Figs. 16-6 and 16-7. Up or down adjustment of the door

Fig. 16-6. One type of door hinge attachment as used on some Chrysler models.

Fig. 16-7. Details of door hinge attachment. The rear is shown at left and the front on the right (Chrysler).

can be made at the front pillar or in the door itself, as shown in Figs. 16-6 and 16-7. First, scribe a line around upper and lower hinge straps. Place a wood block on the lifting plate of a floor jack and position it under door (support door near center of balance when attaching bolts are loosened). Loosen upper and lower door hinge attaching bolts. Observing scribe mark, raise or lower jack until door is in desired position. Tighten attaching bolts and remove jack. Open and close door several times and inspect clearance around all edges of door. Repeat procedure until door is centered in opening.

The fore and aft adjustment of the front door is made as follows: With the door in the full open position (trim panel removed) scribe a line around upper and lower hinge straps. Place a wood block on lifting plate of floor jack and position it under outer end of door. Loosen door upper hinge attaching bolts only. Observe scribe marks and raise or lower door to desired position (raising outer end of door moves upper part of door forward when in closed position).

Tighten attaching bolts. Loosen door lower hinge attaching bolts and raise or lower door to desired position (lowering end of door moves lower part of door forward when in the closed position).

Tighten attaching bolts. Open and close door several times and inspect clearance around all door edges. Repeat procedure until door is centered in door opening.

ADJUST DOOR LOCK STRIKER

The in and out adjustment of the front door is made as follows: With the door in the full open position, place a wood block on lifting

plate of a floor jack and position it under outer edge of door. Loosen upper hinge to pillar attaching bolts. Raise or lower jack until upper part of door has moved in or out desired amount (raising the outer end of the door will move upper part of door into the door opening). Tighten upper hinge to pillar attaching bolts.

Loosen lower hinge to pillar attaching bolts. Raise or lower jack until lower part of door is in desired position (lowering jack moves door into door opening). Tighten attaching bolts.

Close door and observe alignment of door panel with body sill, fender, cowl and "B" post. Adjust door lock striker.

Fig. 16-8. Details of rear door hinge, Fury models.

CHRYSLER TYPE
REAR DOOR ADJUSTMENT

There are two general types of rear door hinge attachments. These are shown in Figs. 16-7 and 16-8. Up and down adjustment of the rear door is made as follows: With the rear door fully closed and front door open, scribe location of both upper and lower hinges on frame of door, Figs. 16-7 and 16-8. Then with the door slightly ajar, position floor jack under center of door. Loosen hinge to door attaching bolts. Observe scribe marks and raise or lower door to the desired position. Tighten attaching bolts. Close door and check alignment of door in opening. Adjust door lock striker.

To make the fore and aft adjustment, first remove "B" post trim panel and scribe around pillar post hinge plate. Loosen both upper

Fig. 16-9. One type of striker and rotor used on some Chrysler, Dodge and Plymouth models.

and lower pillar post hinge screws. With door slightly ajar, push door forward or back to desired position. Tighten pillar post hinge screws.

Close door and inspect alignment in door opening. Adjust door lock striker and install "B" post trim panel.

To adjust the rear door in or out, first scribe a mark on door around the door hinge plate. Loosen upper hinge attaching bolts. Grasp front edge of the door at the hinge and push door in or pull out to the desired position. Tighten hinge attaching bolts. Adjust one hinge at a time to prevent door dropping in door opening.

STRIKER AND ROTOR ADJUSTMENT

On doors with striker and rotor type of door striker, Fig. 16-9, the door strikers are attached to the pillars. Oversize holes permit up-and-down and in-and-out movement. Fore and aft adjustment is made by adding or removing shims between the striker

Fig. 16-10. Pin type of striker used on some Chrysler built cars.

and the post. The striker plate should be adjusted to lift the door slightly.

LATCH AND STRIKER PIN ADJUSTMENT

On cars with latch and striker pin construction such as the Valiant, the front door cannot be locked until the door is completely closed. The silent type door latch, Fig. 16-10, features a rubber isolation of the round striker pin on the door frame and those surfaces acting as stops inside the latch. The latch assembly is built into a sheet metal pocket on the door face. The striker pin is attached by a single screw which also allows for adjusting.

QUIZ - Chapter 16

1. What is the usual clearance between the door and the surrounding frame?
   - 3/8 in. to 1/2 in.
   - 1/8 to 5/32 in.
   - .005 to .010 in.
2. Adjustments are provided so car doors can be moved up and down, fore and aft, in and out.
   - True.
   - False.
3. Before removing door lock strikers on Fisher bodies, the usual procedure is to first mark the position of the striker on the body with a pencil.
   - True.
   - False.
4. Will door misalignment result from improper tightening of body bolts on Ford cars?
   - Yes.
   - No.
5. On Ford cars, should the lock striker be adjusted to correct door sag?
   - Yes.
   - No.
6. Up and down adjustment of the Chrysler door can be made at the front pillar.
   - True.
   - False.
7. On Chrysler doors with striker and rotor type of door striker, the door strikers are attached to the doors.
   - True.
   - False.

Chapter 17

DOOR HARDWARE SERVICE

Window regulators (devices to raise and lower windows), together with the various control handles and door locks, are generally classified as door hardware. The door striker plate is also considered door hardware, but this was discussed in the chapter relating to the adjustment of doors.

It is important that auto body service men become familiar with the various types of mechanisms used on present day cars. Typical job procedures will be discussed in this chapter.

ROUND ALL EDGES
1/64" RADIUS EXCEPT
ON UP-TURNED LIP

GRIND   BRAZING

MATERIAL: 1/8 INCH STEEL

Fig. 17-1. Details of tool for removing door and window regulator handles.

REMOVING DOOR INSIDE HANDLE (FISHER)

Door and inside quarter handles on Fisher bodies are retained by either screws or clips. On styles equipped with screw retained handles, the screws are either exposed or covered by a remote control cover plate. When a cover plate is used, it is generally held in place by short tabs and pressure, and can be removed by prying on the edge.

On styles with clip retained handles, the clip is either exposed when the arm rest is removed, or else is hidden by the handle. Exposed clips can be disengaged from remote control spindle with a screwdriver.

Clips hidden by a window regulator or remote control handles can be disengaged by depressing the door trim assembly sufficiently to permit inserting a forked tool between the handle and the plastic bearing plate. Then with the tool in the same plane as the inside handle, push tool to disengage clip, Fig. 17-1. Plier type tool, Fig. 17-2, can also be used for this purpose. Pull the handle inboard to remove from spindle.

ROLL SPRING OUT.
DO NOT FORCE!

Fig. 17-2. Plier type tool for removing door and window regulating handles.

To install ventilator and window regulator handles, engage retaining clip on handle. Position handle at same angle as opposite side handle and press handle outboard until clip engages regulator spindle. On remote control spindles, install handle in horizontal position.

When Fisher bodies are equipped with what is called a paddle handle, Fig. 17-3, the removal procedure is to remove the door arm rest, then remove handle-to-remote attaching bolt. The handle can then be removed from the door.

HOW TO REMOVE DOOR OUTSIDE HANDLES

Three basic types of door outside handles are used on Fisher bodies: lift bar, push button and pull out. See Figs. 17-4, 17-5

SECTION "A-A"

Fig. 17-3. Details of paddle-type handle used on some Fisher bodies.

and 17-5a. Removal and installation procedures are basically the same.

Raise door window and remove door trim. Detach enough of upper rear corner of inner panel water deflector to gain access to door outside handle attaching screws.

On "F" style bodies, remove rear guide upper bracket to inner panel and guide assembly attaching screws. Remove guide bracket

Fig. 17-4. Door outside handle of lift bar type.

Fig. 17-5. Removal of door handle of push button type.

from door. Then, working through access hole, disconnect door outside handle to lock push rod at handle assembly.

On all other styles, remove handle attaching screws (or nuts) through access hole and remove handle and gaskets from outside body. To install, reverse this procedure.

Fig. 17-5a. Details of door handle of pull out type.

FRONT DOOR LOCK CYLINDER (FISHER)

To remove door lock cylinder from recent Fisher bodies, first remove all door trim. Raise window to full "up" position and detach inner panel water deflector. If equipped with anti-theft system, disconnect wire at door guard beam. On "A" style bodies, disengage lock cylinder to lock connecting rod by disconnecting spring clip. With a screwdriver, slide lock cylinder retaining clip (on inboard side of outer door panel) forward until out of engagement. Remove lock cylinder, Fig. 17-6.

FRONT DOOR LOCK ASSEMBLY (FISHER)

Locks on recent model Fisher bodies are the rotary bolt type lock with a safety interlock feature. With the safety interlock feature it is important that the lock extension and housing engage properly in the door lock striker, and that, when necessary, striker emergency spacers of the proper thickness be used to obtain proper engagement.

To remove the front door lock assembly, first raise the window. Remove door trim assembly and detach inner panel water deflector. Through access hole, Fig. 17-4,

disengage spring clips securing lock cylinder rod, remote control connecting rod, and inside locking rod to lock and disengage rods from lock. On some body models it is necessary to remove door window rear glass run channel, lower attaching screw and loosen upper attaching screws on lock pillar facing of door and at top of door inner panel to permit removal of lock.

On other body models, from inside of door, remove rear glass run channel, lower attaching nut or screw, and pull channel forware to permit removal of lock.

Fig. 17-6. Removal of door lock cylinder. (Fisher bodies)

Remove door lock attaching screws from lock pillar facing of door, and remove lock assembly from door, Fig. 17-7.

To install, reverse removal procedure. Prior to installation, apply a ribbon of medium body sealer across face of lock frame. Check unit for proper operation and, if necessary, adjust glass run channel for proper alignment prior to installation of inner panel water deflector.

REAR DOOR LOCK ASSEMBLY (FISHER)

Locks are the rotary bolt type with safety interlock feature. With the safety lock feature, it is important that the lock extension engages properly in the door lock striker notch.

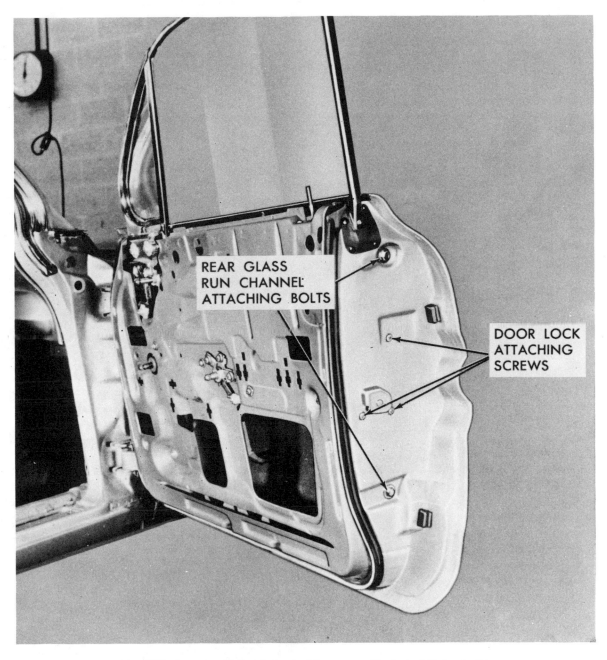

REAR GLASS
RUN CHANNEL
ATTACHING BOLTS

DOOR LOCK
ATTACHING
SCREWS

Fig. 17-7. Location of door lock attaching screws. Typical of Fisher bodies.

Where necessary, striker emergency spacers of the proper thickness can be used to obtain proper engagement. Typical removal procedure is as follows: Raise door window. Remove door trim assembly and detach inner panel water deflector. On most models through large access hole, remove screw securing lower end of glass run channel at door lock pillar, and raise end of channel to expose lock assembly.

Through access hole disengage spring clips and detach inside lock connecting rod and remote control connecting rod from lock assembly. At lock pillar facing, remove door lock attaching screws and remove lock assembly through access hole.

To install rear door lock, reverse removal procedure. Check all operations of door lock before installing door trim and inside hardware.

FRONT DOOR MECHANISMS (FISHER)

To remove and install front window regulator, Fig. 17-8, on Fisher X style bodies, first remove door trim assembly and inner panel water deflector. Secure window in full "up" position with pieces of cloth-backed body tape applied over door frame. Mark location and remove inner panel cam attaching screws, Fig. 17-8, and inner panel cam. On electric regulators, disconnect wiring harness at motor.

Drive out center pin and drill out four regulator attaching rivets with a 1/4 in. (6.3 mm) drill. Then, remove regulator.

Fig. 17-8. Details of front door hardware attachments on Fisher X style bodies: 1-Window regulator. 2-Glass run channel retainer. 3-Inside remote handle. 4-Window assembly. 5-Lower sash channel cam. 6-Outside handle. 7-Door lock. 8-Inner panel cam. 9-Inside locking rod. 10-Inside handle to lock connecting rod. 11-Power door actuator. 12-Down stop.

To remove the typical front door ventilator regulator on Fisher bodies, first raise the window. Remove door trim assembly and detach inner panel water deflector sufficiently to gain access to regulator attaching bolts, Fig. 17-9.

On styles equipped with electric ventilator regulators, disconnect regulator wires at connector. Remove ventilator T-shaft attaching bolt and ventilator regulator attaching bolt, Fig. 17-9. Disengage ventilator regulator shaft from ventilator T-shaft and re-

move regulator motor assembly from door through access hole.

To install reverse the procedure. Excessive play or flutter of ventilator at pivot shaft when ventilator is in the open position can be corrected by tightening ventilator T-shaft to regulator attaching bolt, Fig. 17-9. Bolts should be tightened carefully to avoid stripping threads in regulator spindle gear shaft.

To remove the front door ventilator on late model Fisher bodies, first remove the door trim assembly and detach inner panel water deflector. Lower the door window. Remove ventilator to door outer panel return flange attaching screw, Fig. 17-9. At front of ventilator assembly, break cement bond securing front door pillar sealing strip (at belt) to ventilator assembly.

Remove ventilator division channel lower adjusting stud and nut, Fig. 17-9. On styles with electrically operated ventilators, remove motor and ventilator assembly. Remove ventilator lower frame attaching bolt, and ventilator lower frame adjusting stud nut, Fig. 17-9. Remove ventilator regulator. Lift ventilator upward and remove from door.

Fig. 17-9. Details of ventilator hardware (Fisher).

To replace, reverse the procedure. Prior to installation, apply a bead of body caulking compound to door outer panel return flange along area contacted by ventilator assembly.

FRONT DOOR WINDOW ASSEMBLY (FISHER)

To remove front door window assembly on late model Fisher bodies, first raise the door window. Remove door trim assembly and detach inner panel water deflector. Through holes in inner panel, remove screw attaching window assembly front and rear stops to lower window shaft channel. Then lower window slightly and remove stops, Fig. 17-4.

Lower door window to expose window lower sash channel cam attaching screws. On styles equipped with electric window regulator, Fig. 17-10, disconnect wiring harness from motor connector. It may be necessary to loosen the ventilator frame and tilt it forward to facilitate removal of door window.

Remove window lower sash channel cam attaching screws and disengage cam from window sash channel. Then lift window assembly upward and remove from door. Do not operate motor after window assembly is disengaged as this will damage motor.

To install, reverse the procedure.

DOOR INSIDE HANDLE (FORD)

When removing the door inside handle on Ford cars, a plier type tool is usually employed, Fig. 17-2. The procedure is to press the trim panel inward to provide access to the door handle retaining clip. Engage the clip with pliers, Fig. 17-2. If such a tool is not available, you can improvise one by grinding a hook on the end of a hacksaw blade. Engage the clip with the hook and pull out the clip. The handle and spacer can then be pulled from the shaft.

When installing the handle, first install a retainer clip on the handle. Point the handle in a forward direction approximately 45 deg. above horizontal, and press the handle and clip into position until clip snaps into its groove on the remote control shaft.

Fig. 17-10. Door window regulator and motor assembly (Fisher bodies).

FRONT DOOR LOCK CYLINDER (FORD)

When a lock cylinder is replaced, both door lock cylinders and the ignition lock cylinder should be replaced in a set. This will avoid carrying an extra key which will fit only one lock.

Remove the trim panel and position the water shield away from the access holes. Disconnect the lock control-to-door lock cylinder rod at the lock cylinder arm. Remove the door lock cylinder retainer and remove the lock cylinder from the door. Transfer the lock cylinder arm to the new lock cylinder. Position the lock cylinder in the door, and install the lock cylinder retainer. Connect the lock control-to-door lock cylinder rod at the lock cylinder. Carefully position the water shield to the inner panel and install the trim panel.

DOOR OUTSIDE HANDLE

To remove the door outside handle on Ford and Mustang models, first remove the door trim panel and water shield. Remove the four screws attaching the door weatherstrip at the belt line. Disconnect the door latch actuator rod from the door outside handle, Fig. 17-11. Remove the two nuts retaining the handle to the door. Remove the door handle and the pad from the door. Transfer the actuator rod clip and the pad to the new handle, if the handle is to be replaced. Insert the handle into the door and install the two retaining nuts. Connect the door latch actuator rod to the door latch. Position the weatherstrip at the belt line and install the outside handle and the door latch. Check the operation of the handle and the door lock and

Fig. 17-11. Door outside handle. Typical of Ford, Mustang and Torino.

then install the water shield and door trim panel.

FRONT DOOR SERVICE ON PINTO

To replace front door glass on Pinto and Bobcat models, first remove the trim panel and water shield from the door. Lower the glass until the bracket rivets to the glass are visible at the access hole in the door inner panel. Use a drift punch to remove the center pins of the two rivets attaching the door glass to the glass bracket. Then remove the rivets by drilling the head from the rivet. Push the rivets from the

glass and bracket. Then, lift the glass from the door.

To remove the window regulator from recent model Pinto and Bobcat cars, first remove the trim panel, water shield and glass. Use a drift punch to remove the center pin from the regulator attaching rivets. Then, drill the head from each rivet and remove the rivets. Remove the nylon retainer from the drive arm, Fig. 17-12. Disengage the regulator arm from the glass bracket and remove the regulator from the door.

FORD WINDOW MECHANISM

Glass adjustment is minimal on vehicles with door frames since the glass is installed within the door weatherstrip run assembly on Fairmont and Zephyr models. On two door models, loosen the glass bracket lower guide and move the top edge of the glass inboard or outboard as required. On all other models, loosen the run and bracket assembly lower attaching nut for glass in-out adjustment, Fig. 17-13.

To remove the window mechanism on Zephyr and Fairmont (1978-1979 models), Fig. 17-13, place glass in full "up" position. Remove the glass run from the glass run

Fig. 17-12. Front door window mechanism on recent model Pinto and Bobcat cars.

retainer, taking care not to pinch the run at the belt and bottom of the glass. Remove the screw and washer assembly attaching the retainer to the door lock face. Remove the retainer from the end of the door frame. Take care when disengaging the retainer from the end of the door frame so that the glass run assembly is not pinched.

FORD WINDOW REGULATOR

To remove the window regulator on other 1978-1979 models, Fig. 17-13, first remove the door trim panel and water shield. Support glass in the "up" position. If equipped with electric windows (except T-bird and Continental), remove the center pin from the motor bracket to inner panel attaching rivet with a drift punch. Then, drill head from rivet and remove the rivet. Disconnect motor. Remove the center pin from the regulator attaching rivets with a drift punch. Drill the head from the regulator attaching rivet. Disengage the regulator arm from the glass bracket and remove regulator from the door.

REMOVING FRONT DOOR REGULATOR

On Ford and Mustang models with ventless glass (1971) the procedure for removing the front door regulator is as follows: Remove the door trim panel and water shield. Disconnect the window regulator arms from the glass channel and the door inner panel at the pivots assemblies. Disconnect the glass channel bracket from the glass channel. Disconnect the remote control rod from the door latch. Remove the rear weatherstrip cap. Remove the upper rear stop and remove the belt weatherstrip and molding from the door. Remove the window regulator attaching screws and remove the regulator from the door. To install the regulator, reverse the procedure.

To remove the front door regulator on 1971 Ford cars (not the ventless glass type) proceed as follows: Remove the door trim panel and water shields. Remove the retainer and nut attaching the glass channel bracket to the glass and prop the window in its up position, Fig. 17-14. Remove the equalizer bar bracket from the door. Remove the four regulator attaching bolts and remove the regulator.

Fig. 17-13. Fairmont and Zephyr door window mechanism on two door models. Close-ups at right provide detailed information.

Fig. 17-14. Ford front door window mechanism (typical).

DOOR HANDLES (CHRYSLER)

On some Chryslers (Dodge, Plymouth), the door inside handles and window regulator handles are fastened with Allen head screws. Removal of the screws permits the handle to be pulled from the shaft. On later models, a Phillips head screw holds the handle in place, Fig. 17-15.

Fig. 17-15. Removing door inside handle from Plymouth.

To remove the outside handle from front door, first place door handle in up position, remove door handle attaching nuts from mounting studs, Figs. 17-16 and 17-17, and

link from handle to lock. Lift handle up and remove from door.

To install handle into door opening, engage link from handle to lock. Attach retaining nuts and check operation of handle.

Fig. 17-16. Front door handle (Fury).

To remove outside handle of rear door, first open door and place glass in up position. Remove retainer from link at handle connector. Depress outside handle release button and remove link from handle connector. Remove nuts attaching handle to door and remove handle.

Fig. 17-17. Details of front door handle on Chrysler-Plymouth cars.

To install rear door handle, position handle in door and install mounting nuts. Depress handle button and position link over connector on handle. Install retainer over link and connector.

LOCK CYLINDER (CHRYSLER)

To remove lock cylinder on late model Chrysler and allied cars, place window in top position. Disconnect cylinder link, Figs. 17-18 and 17-19, from clip on lock lever (four door only) and from cylinder. On two door models disconnect lock link from clip on lock lever, remove link control bracket mounting screws and remove cylinder link from cylinder. Remove retainer from cylinder body and cylinder from door.

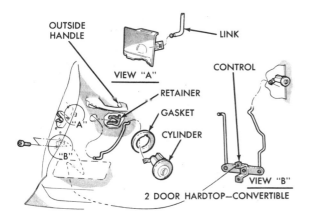

Fig. 17-18. One type of door lock used on Chrysler built cars.

To replace lock cylinder, position cylinder in door and install retainer on cylinder body. Connect the cylinder link to cylinder arm and to clip on lock lever (four door models).

Fig. 17-19. Type of door lock used on some Chrysler built cars.

On two door models connect cylinder link to cylinder, position link bracket on door face and install attaching screws. Connect lock link to lock.

ELECTRIC DOOR LOCKS (CHRYSLER)

Loosen the solenoid to mounting bracket screws. Push lock lever to down position and slide solenoid to full down position in mounting bracket. Raise lock lever to up position, extending solenoid rod to maximum position. Tighten solenoid to mounting bracket screws and test operation of the lock.

REAR DOOR REGULATOR (CHRYSLER)

Fig. 17-20 is typical of the rear door regulators used on Chrysler built cars. To replace this type of regulator which is attached to the door inner panel by screw and washer assemblies, support the glass assembly when removing the regulator. The roller on the regulator front arm is retained by a spring nut. Lubricate outboard side of regulator sector gear tooth contact area approximately 1/2 in. wide along entire length of arc and studs on front and rear arms before installing.

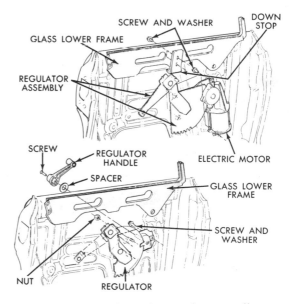

Fig. 17-20. Typical rear door regulator installation.

On some body models the rear door regulator installation is the same as that for front doors.

DOOR EMERGENCY OPENING PROCEDURE

If a door latch is inoperative on Ford cars and cannot be opened from either inside or outside of the vehicle, a latch actuating tool can be made, as shown in Figs. 17-21 and 17-22. The actuating tool can be made of 1/8 in. welding rod or its equivalent.

Fig. 17-21. Details of tool used to actuate door latch.

To actuate the latch, first lower the window glass of the inoperative door to its full down position. Insert the latch actuating tool in the glass opening at the rear edge of the door and engage the latch pawl lever, as shown in Fig. 17-22.

Apply a downward pressure on the latch pawl lever with the tool. This will open the door. When the door is open, inspect the latch assembly and rod attaching points to determine the cause of the trouble.

QUIZ - Chapter 17

1. How are door inside handles attached on recent model Fisher bodies?
   Retaining clip.
   Screw.
   Tapered pin.
2. On recent model Fisher bodies, is it necessary to remove the door trim assembly before removing the door outside handle?
   Yes.
   No.
3. Locks on recent model Fisher bodies are

Fig. 17-22. Releasing door latch with special tool.

of the rotary bolt type.
   True.
   False.
4. What type tool is usually used to remove the door inside handle on Ford cars?
   Adjustable wrench.
   Plier-type tool.
   Screwdriver.
   3/8 in. end wrench.
5. How is the vent glass regulator secured to the vent glass lower pivot on recent model Ford cars?
   Cap screw.
   Bolt and nut.
   Spring clip.
   Press fit.
6. How are door outside handles attached on recent model Chrysler built bodies?
   Screws requiring Allen type wrench.
   Spring clip.
   Stud and nut.

Chapter 18

REMOVING INTERIOR TRIM, WEATHERSTRIP, UPHOLSTERY

When it becomes necessary to do work on door hardware, replace door glass and remove dents in certain panels, including the roof, it is usually necessary to remove interior trim and/or upholstery. When there is rain and dust leakage around the doors it is usually necessary to replace the door weatherstrip.

This chapter discusses typical procedures for removing trim, weather strip and upholstery from current auto bodies.

REMOVING DOOR ARM REST ASSEMBLIES

Arm rests are attached to doors by means of screws located on the underside of the arm rest. Removal of these screws permits removal of the arm rest. A typical installation is shown in Fig. 18-1.

Fig. 18-1. Method of attaching arm rest assemblies to doors.

DOOR TRIM ASSEMBLIES (FISHER BODIES)

There are two basic types of door trim assemblies used on recent model Fisher bodies,

a one piece assembly and a two piece assembly. The one piece assembly in most installations hangs over the door inner panel across the top and is secured by clips or nails down the sides and by screws across the bottom. Fig. 18-2 is a composite illustration of the various types of door trim panel fasteners.

On the two piece trim, the upper portion hangs over the door inner panel across the top and is secured by trim nails and screws across the bottom. The lower portion is retained by screws across the top and by clips down the sides and across the bottom.

The removal and installation of the door trim assemblies on recent model Fisher

Fig. 18-2. Various types of door trim retention (Fisher body).

bodies is as follows: Remove door inside handles and door inside locking rod knob. Remove screws from door pull handles. On styles with remote control mirror assemblies remove remote mirror escutcheon and disengage mirror control cable from escutcheon. Also remove arm rests, remote control cover plates or other accessories that may be installed.

On cars equipped with two piece trim, remove attaching screws along upper edge of lower trim assembly. Then starting at lower corner, insert tool between door inner panel and trim assembly and disengage retaining clips from plastic cups down both sides and across bottom. On styles with courtesy lights in lower trim assembly, disconnect wire harness at lamp assembly. On some body styles it is necessary to remove all screws down both sides and across bottom of door trim pad. Then starting at a lower corner insert tool between door inner panel and trim assembly and carefully disengage retaining nails or clips from plastic cups inserted in door inner panel.

Fig. 18-3. Typical Ford door and window regulator handle construction.

To remove trim assembly, lift trim assembly upward and slide it slightly rearward to disengage it from door inner panel at belt line. On styles with electric switches located in trim assembly, disconnect wire harness and remove trim assembly from door.

To install door trim assemblies, reverse removal procedure.

On body styles with adjustable trim supports at belt line, the door trim assembly can be adjusted in or out so as not to restrict door window operation.

FORD DOOR TRIM PANELS

To remove the door trim panels on recent models of Ford, Maverick and Torino cars, the same basic procedure can be followed. Unscrew and remove the door latch control knob. Pry the window regulator retaining screw access covers from the window regulator handles, Fig. 18-3. Remove the handle retaining screw and the handle. Remove any screws which retain the trim panel to the inner panel such as the arm rest retaining screws and the molding screws. Remove the screw which retains the door remote control handle to the latch mechanism and remove the remote control handle.

Front Doors: Remove the remote control mirror bezel nut if so equipped. With a putty knife, pry the trim panel retaining clips, Fig. 18-4, loose from the door inner panel. If the door has power windows, disconnect the switch lead wires from the switch and remove the trim panel. If necessary carefully loosen the door water shield.

Installation: Place a daub of special sealer over each retaining clip to seal the retaining clips when they are pushed into the door. Also apply sealer around the door handles, window regulator shafts and other existing holes. Fasten the water shield to the inner panel with sealer. Be sure that the water shield is securely fastened to the door inner panel.

If the trim panel is to be replaced, transfer the power window switch, ornamentation (if so equipped), and the retaining clips from the old trim panel to the new one. Also transfer the door pull handle which is fastened by two pop rivets.

The door pull handle covers, Fig. 18-4, are cemented in place. To remove the door pull handle pop rivets, carefully pry the covers away from the handle. Position the pull handle to the new trim panel and install the pop rivets. Clean old cement from the covers with naptha. Use a 1 3/4 x 3/8 in. tape and cement

Fig. 18-4. Typical Ford, Mercury and Meteor door trim panel installation.

the covers back in place.

Position the trim panel to the door and connect the power window switch wires to the switch (if so equipped). Be sure that all the trim panel retaining clips are installed in the trim panel. Place the top edge of the trim panel over the trim panel upper brackets, and push the clips into place in the door

inner panel, Fig. 18-4. Position the door remote control handle to the latch mechanism and install the retaining screw.

Position the arm rest to the door and install the arm rest retaining screws.

Front Doors: Install the remote control bezel nut if so equipped.

Position the window regulator handles on

their shafts. Install the handle retaining screws and press the retaining screw access covers into place. With the windows closed, the handles should be positioned as shown in Fig. 18-3. Install the door latch control knob.

Mustang Models: To remove the door trim, first remove the retaining screw from the window regulator handle and remove the handle from the shaft, Fig. 18-3. Remove the two retaining screws from the arm rest assembly and remove the assembly. Remove the two retaining nuts and remove the door remote control handle from the door. Remove the trim panel retaining screws. With a putty knife, pry the trim panel retaining clips out of the door inner panel and remove the panel from the door. Carefully remove the water shield if necessary. When replacing the trim panel on the Mustang, follow the same instructions as given for the Ford.

FORD QUARTER TRIM PANEL REMOVAL

On Ford and Torino two door models, the removal procedure is as follows: Remove the

Fig. 18-5. Details of Ford quarter trim installation. Typical.

rear seat cushion and seat back from the vehicle. Remove the window regulator handle, if so equipped. Pry the handle retaining screw access cover from the handle and remove the retaining screw, Fig. 18-3. Remove any screws retaining the trim panel to the inner panel such as the arm rest retaining screws. On some models, the arm rest retaining screws are covered by an arm rest lower finish panel. For access to the screws, carefully pry the finish panel out of the arm rest. Remove the trim panel attaching screws. Then, unclip the trim panel retaining clips and pull the trim panel from the quarter panel, Fig. 18-5. Disconnect the power window switch wires, if so equipped from the switch. Installation is accomplished by reversing the procedure.

Fig. 18-6. Removing door trim from Plymouth bodies.

DOOR TRIM ASSEMBLIES (CHRYSLER)

To remove the door trim on recent model Chrysler bodies, first remove the inside handles and arm rests. Remove screws attaching trim panel to door inner panel. Then insert a wide-blade tool or screwdriver between the trim panel and the door frame next to the retaining clips, and snap out the retaining clips around the edge of the trim panel, Fig. 18-6. The trim panel can then be removed from the door.

To reinstall the door trim assembly, reverse the removal procedure.

HEADLINING ASSEMBLY (Fisher)

The one-piece, formed headlining on most Fisher bodies, including X style, consists of molded substrate covered with a foam and cloth or vinyl facing. On some Chevrolet Monza and Pontiac Sunbird models, the headlining is a scored and folded, grained perforated hardboard with an insulator cemented to the upper surface.

The headlining is held in place partly by retaining tabs located in the roof side rail, which engages recessed slots in both sides of the headlining assembly. Final attachment is accomplished when the interior molding and attaching screws that retain the sunshade brackets, dome lamp base, coat hooks and shoulder strap retainer covers are installed.

The one-piece construction requires the

Fig. 18-7. Installing headlining to substrate on late model Fisher bodies, including X style.

headlining to be serviced as a complete assembly. Front and rear station wagon headlining may be serviced separately.

To remove the headlining, first remove courtesy lamps, sunshade support brackets, coat hooks, upper quarter trim finishing panels, roof side rail moldings, windshield and back window garnish moldings, shoulder strap retainers, windshield side garnish moldings, roof-mounted assist straps and twin lift-off panel roof garnish moldings if present.

Next, disengage tabs or clips on each side of the headlining assembly from the attaching slots. Then, move the assembly rearward enough to provide clearance for the front portion of the assembly to unload through the front door. On some models, it should be unloaded through the back body opening.

The replacement headlining is available as two separate part assemblies. The headlining material is supplied separate from the foundation or trim panel. The trim panel is pre-pierced to accomodate attachments such as the sunshade, etc. To cement the headlining to the trim panel, proceed as follows:

Place the replacement headlining cover and trim panel on a clean work area. Place cover over trim panel, allowing it to overlap equally at all edges.

Place a protective cover over half the material and fold the other half back over the covering. See view A in Fig. 18-7. Using 3M vinyl trim adhesive or equivalent and a quart size pressure type spray gun, apply two medium coats of adhesive to both the surface of the panel (foundation) and the cover (material). See view B in Fig. 18-7. Allow the adhesive to dry for about three minutes.

With the aid of a helper, unfold the cover, stretch and align it with the outer edges. Then, using firm hand pressure, slick the adhesive applied surfaces together to effect a good bond. Avoid forming any wrinkles.

Repeat this procedure on the other half of the assembly.

Trim excess headlining cover, leaving about 6.3 mm (1/4 in.) of material extending beyond entire perimeter of the trim panel.

Using a sharp pointed knife, trim material away from the pre-pierced holes or openings in the trim panel, such as sunshade openings.

Complete elimination of solvent vapors from applied adhesive will require about 24 hours.

Load the rear portion of the headlining diagonally through the right front door opening or through the rear opening in the case of a station wagon. Care must be taken when handling the assembly as over flexing may result in damage.

Align headlining to roof inner panel with recessed slots positioned over retainers at side roof rail. Install side roof rail attaching clips.

Align headlining with cutouts for sunshades and dome lamp and install sunshade brackets and dome lamp base. Do not tighten brackets or dome lamp attaching screws completely until headlining is properly aligned at all other hardware attaching locations. Install all previously removed hardware and interior moldings.

REMOVING FORD HEADLINING

The procedure for removing the headlining on recent model Ford cars in general applies to all models. If some of the steps do not apply to the particular model being serviced, proceed to the next step.

First remove the sun visor and bracket assembly. Remove the windshield upper garnish molding. Note: Visor center clip attached. Remove the upper screw from the two windshield side garnish moldings and position the moldings away from the "A" pillar. Remove the shoulder strap assemblies and the shoulder strap retainers and coat hooks.

Remove the roof side center garnish moldings. On all 4-door sedans, first remove the center cap from the junction of the front and rear side moldings at the center pillar. On some 4-door sedans, there is also a joint cover at the rear quarter. On 2-door hardtops, there is one joint cover at the rear quarter.

Remove the rear seat cushion and back. Remove the right and left quarter panels. Remove the roof side rear trim covers (right and left). Remove the back window garnish moldings. Bend the retaining tabs and re-move the package tray and deadener. Bend up the tabs on all retaining strips and unhook the headlining from the tabs. Remove the dome light. Pry off the lens and remove four screws.

Remove the staples that fasten the headlining to the roof side retainer assemblies and around the back window.

Pull the headlining loose from the cemented area at the windshield header. Unhook the right and left retainers from the headlining rear support rod, disengage all support rods from the holes in the left and right roof rails and remove the headlining.

INSTALLING FORD HEADLINING

Installation: Unpack the new headlining and lay it out on a flat surface. Mark and trim the new headlining using the old one for a pattern.

Trim the listings on the new headlining to the approximate length of those used on the old lining. Remove the support rods from the old headlining and install them in the same relative rod listings of the new headlining. Roof headlining support rods are color coded at each end, Fig. 18-8. When ordering new rods be sure to note the color at each end of the rod. Position the headlining in the vehicle. To maintain the most driver headroom and wrinkle free headlining, insert the support rods into the upper holes in the left and lower holes in right roof rail except in the following cases. If the headlining is wrinkled (not taut enough) use the upper holes on both sides. If the headlining is too taut, use the lower holes on both sides.

Hook the rear retainers to the rear support rod. Staple the headlining to the retainer assemblies. Bend down the tabs on the retaining strips and hook the headlining to the tabs. Cement the headlining in place at the windshield header and trim the excess material.

Install the roof side rear trim covers, package tray, the rear window garnish moldings and quarter trim panels. Cut a hole in the headlining material for the dome light and install the lens and bezel. Install all garnish moldings, shoulder harness assembly, retainers and sun visors.

Fig. 18-8. Details of Ford station wagon headlining installation.

HEADLINING REPLACEMENT (CHRYSLER)

The headlining and quarter trim replacement procedure is similar for many Chrysler-built cars. The procedure for Fury, Monaco, Cordoba, Charger, Volare, Aspen, LeBaron and Diplomat models is as follows:

First, remove front seat shoulder belts at upper roof rail on 2-door models. Remove coat hooks, interior garnish moldings and dome light. Remove fasteners from upper quarter trim "C" pillar and silencer. Remove roof panel from vehicle. See Figs. 18-9 and 18-10.

To install the headlining and quarter trim, proceed as follows:

Install molding and retainer (Fury and Monaco models only) for roof side headling to roof side rail. Insert retaining clip into hole in windshield upper side frame rail.

Fig. 18-9. Details of Plymouth Fury and Monaco molded headlining.

Fig. 18-10. Hardboard headlining as installed on Volaré, Aspen, LeBaron and Diplomat models.

Install molded roof panel headlining into molding retainer assembly (Fury and Monaco only). Then, place molding into position, Fig. 18-9.

Index headlining to center line of vehicle, keeping in line with visor bracket attaching holes and dome light cutouts. Install fasteners to upper quarter trim "C" pillar. Then, install "C" pillar trim, inserting fasteners through silencer into quarter panel.

Install windshield and rear window garnish moldings. Install coat hooks, sun visors, dome light and safety belt attachments.

HEADLINING AND QUARTER TRIM (CHRYSLER)

Headlining and quarter trim work differs on late model Chrysler cars:

Disconnect starting battery. Remove upper belt mountings. Remove visors, moldings, hooks, and trim screws. Also, remove "C" pillar trim panel. Lower headlining and remove it from the vehicle. Also, remove the trim panel from the vehicle.

To install headlining and quarter trim: Install silencer to upper quarter trim

Fig. 18-11. Details of molded headlining and quarter trim on late model Chrysler cars.

panel. Install molded headlining panel, Fig. 18-11. On a bench, assemble applique to cover with lock nut and fastener. Install "C" pillar upper quarter trim panel with silencer to quarter panel and bracket with screws. Install assist strap over cover to quarter panel, using screws. Install interior trim hardware, such as lamp bezel, coat hooks, moldings, belt retainers. Reconnect starting battery.

Fig. 18-13. *Details of door weatherstrip as installed on Fisher bodies.*

Fig. 18-12. *Removing weatherstrip from Fisher bodies.*

FRONT AND REAR DOOR WEATHERSTRIP (FISHER)

Both front and rear door weatherstrips on recent model Fisher bodies use nylon fasteners to retain the door weatherstrip. The fasteners are a component part of the weatherstrip and secure the weatherstrip to the door by engaging piercings in the door panels. The serrations on the fastener retain the fastener in the piercing and also seal the openings from water entry, Figs. 18-12 and 18-13.

On closed styles, nylon fasteners are used below the belt line only. Weatherstrip adhesive retains the weatherstrip around the upper door frame. On all 1971 styles, in addition to the fastener, use weatherstrip adhesive at the belt line and down the front door pillar.

To disengage nylon fasteners from the door panel piercings use a tool illustrated in Fig. 18-12. This tool permits removal of the weatherstrip without damaging the serrations on the fasteners so that the weatherstrip can be reinstalled if desired.

Removal: On all hardtop and convertible styles remove door trim pad to gain access to weatherstrip fasteners hidden under trim assembly and remove fasteners. Use a flat-bladed tool to break cement bond between door and weatherstrip. On all 1971 styles, weatherstrip adhesive is used for a distance of 9 in. on door lock pillar and the entire length of the front door hinge pillar, Fig. 18-13. In addition, on closed styles, weatherstrip is retained by weatherstrip adhesive completely around door upper frame, Fig. 18-13. Use tool, Fig. 18-12, to disengage

Fig. 18-14. *Rear door weatherstrips (Fisher).*

Fig. 18-15. Rear door weatherstrip adhesion application (Fisher).

weatherstrip from door where weatherstrip is retained by nylon fasteners.

When replacing weatherstrip, make sure all nylon fasteners are in good condition and replace any that are damaged. Use adhesive in all areas where it was used originally.

On some older model Fisher bodies, weatherstrip attaching clips were used, Fig. 18-14. These clips fit into individual sealing plugs, along door bottoms and sides. Cement usage was limited to door lock pillar panels at belt line and at the lower corners of doors, Fig. 18-15. Cement, however, can be applied at any area where additional retention is required.

Also on some older Fisher bodies, the rear door weatherstrip is a one piece mechanically retained type. Mechanical retention consists of a series of weatherstrip attaching clips which fit into individual sealing plugs along door bottom and sides. The weatherstrip is also mechanically retained by nylon snap fasteners at belt line of hinge and lock pillar panels. In addition, some body styles have the rear door weatherstrip further retained by a single weatherstrip attaching clip, and screw at upper radius of lock pillar panel.

DOOR WEATHERSTRIP (CHRYSLER)

When replacing door weatherstrips on Chrysler-built cars, Fig. 18-16 and 18-17,

be sure to remove all of the old weatherstrip particles before installing the new strips. To make the installation on doors of sedans and station wagons: First, apply the lower half of the weatherstrip. Start at the hinge face at the belt line, Fig. 18-16. Work the fasteners into holes in the shut face of the door.

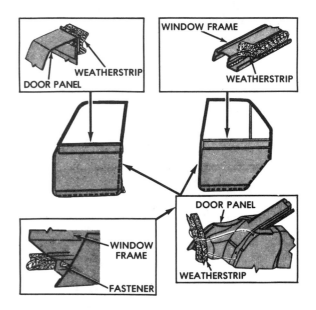

Fig. 18-16. Weatherstrip installation on Chrysler-built 4-door cars.

Apply a bead of adhesive to the weatherstrip seating area on upper and lower areas of door. Install upper half of weatherstrip on the door, indexing at upper corners. Work the weatherstrip from index points midway between them. Avoid puckering or stretching weatherstrip.

Fig. 18-17. Outer belt weatherstrip on Volaré, Aspen, LeBaron and Diplomat.

OUTER BELT WEATHERSTRIP

To replace the outer belt weatherstrip on Chrysler-built cars, first remove the trim panel and plastic air shield. Next, detach the glass from the glass lift plate by removing three nuts. Rest the glass in the bottom of the door. Then, remove the six weatherstrip attaching screws as shown in Fig. 18-17. Remove the weatherstrip.

To install the new weatherstrip: Secure it in place with the six screws. Fasten the glass to the glass lift plate and adjust to the opening. Install the plastic air shield and trim panel.

QUIZ - Chapter 18

1. How are door arm rests attached?
   Cap screws through door inner panel.
   Screws on underside of arm rest.
   Special type spring clips.
2. How is lower edge of door trim attached on most recent model Fisher bodies?
   By screws.
   Retaining nails.
   By grooved channel.
3. When removing door trim assemblies on recent model Ford cars is it necessary to remove garnish molding?

4. After removing inside handles and arm rests on recent model Chrysler bodies, how is the door trim panel removed?
   Use a screwdriver and snap out the retaining clips around edge of panel.
   Remove garnish molding and lift panel from retaining groove.
   Remove screws with Phillips type screwdriver.
5. On recent model Fisher bodies, how is the headlining made to conform to the contour of the roof?
   It is glued to the roof.
   By means of concealed listing wires.
6. Are roof lining support rods color coded on recent Ford models?
   Yes.
   No.
7. On recent model Chrysler built cars, how is the headlining attached to the windshield header?
   By means of small tacks.
   Listing wires.
   It is cemented in place.
8. What type fastener is used to attach the front door weatherstrip assembly on recent model Fisher bodies?
   Nylon component fasteners.
   Cement.
   Special adhesive tape.

Details of removal of front door power motor from late model Ford, Mercury, Lincoln Continental Mark VI. (Ford Motor Co.)

Chapter 19

DOOR WINDOW GLASS SERVICE

Replacement and adjustment of door windows form an important part of auto body work. Not only because it frequently is necessary to replace the glass, but also because adjustments are required. Often, for example, it is necessary to adjust the windows in order to eliminate rattles and to make sure the windows raise and lower smoothly and easily.

There are many different types of construction of window regulators. Various typical designs are described and illustrated in Chapters 16 and 17, and in the following pages. All should be studied to note their similarity as well as their differences.

Therefore, always remember that there will be detailed differences in design and repair procedures in different body models produced by a single manufacturer.

DOOR WINDOW ASSEMBLY (FISHER "A" COUPE)

The front window assembly installed on some Chevrolet, Pontiac and Oldsmobile models consists of solid tempered safety plate glass with bolt-on and riveted components. The lower sash channel cam (bolted to the glass) is removed during the window removal process. Fig. 19-1 identifies the window components and their assembly sequence. Specified installation torque is 72 ft. lb. (98 N·m). When replacing the glass, also replace the glass washers. See Fig. 19-1.

The stabilizer guide, shown at 14 in Fig. 19-1, is riveted to the glass at production. For service, this type installation requires a special hand rivet tool, along with parts

Fig. 19-1. Door window assembly as installed on Fisher A coupe styles. 1-Rear up-stop support. 2-Rear up-stop screw. 3-Rear up-stop support to glass nuts. 4-Rear up-stop. 5-Front up-stop. 6-Spanner bolt. 7-Bushing. 8-Washer. 9-Spanner nut. 10-Spacer. 11-Stabilizer button. 12-Rivet bushing. 13-Rivet retainer. 14-Stabilizer guide. 15-Rivet.

12, 13, and 15 in Fig. 19-1. The rivet bushing is held firmly to the glass by the rivet retainer. After glass removal, the bushing can be separated from the retainer, using a flat-bladed tool covered with cloth body tape.

CAUTION: Rivet bushings and rivet retainers must not be used when installing the stabilizer guide with bolt-on hardware. Otherwise, the glass may break when tightening the spanner nut.

If the hand rivet tool is not available, bolt the stabilizer guide to the glass. Special bushings, bolts and nut are required.

DOOR WINDOW ASSEMBLY (FISHER H AND X STYLES)

The door window assembly installed on Chevrolet Monza and Nova, Pontiac Phoenix and Sunbird, Oldsmobile Starfire and Omega, Buick Skylark and Skyhawk models consists of a frameless piece of solid tempered safety glass bonded to a lower sash channel. This channel also incorporates a lower sash channel cam. With this design, the door glass lower sash channel and cam should be removed from the door as a unit. Then, replacement glass is installed as a bench operation.

The inner panel cam, Fig. 19-2, can be adjusted to correctly position a cocked window assembly. To adjust down travel on most models, loosen stop, Fig. 19-2, and adjust glass to desired height at beltline. Position stop to contact glass (X styles) or regulator (H styles) and tighten attaching screw to 90 to 125 in. lb. (122 to 170 N·m) torque.

To remove and install the door window assembly on these H and X style Fisher bodies, first remove the door trim assembly, inner panel water deflector and door window inner belt sealing strip. Lower window to half-down position and remove inner panel cam, Fig. 19-2. For X style, remove front glass channel shown at 2 in Fig. 17-8. Lower front edge of glass and slide window lower sash channel cam off window regulator lift arm rollers. Remove window inboard of door upper frame.

To reinstall the assembly, reverse the removal procedure. Adjust window from correct alignment.

Fig. 19-2. Typical door of H and X style bodies. (Fisher Bodies)

REAR DOOR WINDOW ASSEMBLY (FISHER "A" SEDAN)

The rear door window assembly installed on Chevrolet Malibu, El Camino and Monte

Fig. 19-3. Rear door and hardware of Fisher A style body: 1-Outside handle assembly. 2-Door lock. 3-Inside handle to lock connecting rod. 4-Shoe. 5-Inside remote handle. 6-Power door lock. 7-Inside locking rod. 8-Trim support retainer. 9-Glass support clips. 10-Bell crank. 11-Bell crank to lock connecting rod. 12-Outside handle to lock connecting rod. 13-Door glass (stationary). 14-Inside locking rod knob. 15-Silencer.

Fig. 19-4. Rear door window hardware as installed on many recent model Fisher bodies.

Carlo, Pontiac LeMans and Grand Prix, Oldsmobile Cutlass, Buick Century and Regal consists of a frameless solid tempered safety plate glass window retained within the window opening with two beltline support clips. This window remains "fixed." The "A35" style has a removable vent window. It can be operated either manually or electrically.

Due to the fixed nature of the sedan window, no means of adjustment is provided. To remove this window: First, remove trim assembly and detach insulator pad (if so equipped) and inner panel water deflector. Remove two glass beltline support clips, Fig. 19-3. Slide glass straight down (glass suction cups may help) and remove from inboard side of door.

To reinstall, first spray silicone or liquid soap solution on glass run channel. Then, reverse removal procedure. Tighten attaching screws with hand screwdriver.

Older type rear doors, Fig. 19-4, are provided with wedge plates that are used to adjust the position of the windows.

To remove the rear door window illustrated in Fig. 19-4, manual and electric and

on four and six window sedans, first raise the door window. Remove door trim assembly and detach inner panel water deflector. Through access holes in door inner panel, remove screws fastening rear door window front and rear male wedge plates to window lower sash channel and remove wedge plates, Fig. 19-4.

Lower door window and remove lower sash channel cam attaching screws. On styles equipped with electric window regulators, disconnect harness electric feed plug from regulator motor at connector.

Carefully raise and remove window.

Fig. 19-5. Details of front door glass installation. (Chrysler Corp.)

CHRYSLER FRONT DOOR GLASS SERVICE

Vent wing adjustment: Fore-or-aft adjustment of the upper end of the vent wing, Fig. 19-5, is accomplished by moving the vent wing up or down. The assembly moves: upward or downward to relieve a binding condition of the door glass; rearward and upward to remove looseness.

Loosen vent wing to door face screws. Loosen adjusting screws at lower end of division channel. With glass raised, move entire vent wing assembly up or down until glass is free (not loose) in channel, and tighten screws. Insert a narrow blade screwdriver through opening in weatherseal, just ahead of lower pivot to turn adjusting screws.

Vent wing removal: Remove nut and washer from lower vent frame stud. Remove vent frame to door screws. With glass down, disengage lower frame stud from door bracket and remove window regulator arms from lift bracket. Slide glass out of channel. Disconnect outer belt weatherstrip for a short distance to provide clearance for division channel. Tilt top of vent frame toward rear and up out of door.

Vent wing installation: Place vent assembly into door. Move vent frame forward into position. Install attaching screws, but do not tighten. Position door glass in run channel and install regulator arms and clips. Position lower run channel adjusting stud into door bracket. Align window run channel.

Door glass adjustment: Lower glass. Move division channel far enough rearward to remove excessive looseness of glass without creating a binding condition. Tighten adjusting screws at lower end of channel. (It may be necessary to readjust lower end of channel to gain alignment of channel and rear glass run.) If necessary, adjust lower end of rear channel in or out. Adjust down-stop so top edge of glass is flush with top edge of glass opening in door.

Door glass removal: Remove vent wing. Loosen front run channel lower mounting screw. Move run channel forward and slide glass out of channel. Remove regulator arm from lift bracket channel. Remove glass from door. Push plug out of bracket rivet. Pinch expandable ends of rivet together and push rivet out of glass.

CHRYSLER TAIL GATE

Before making any glass adjustment, the tail gate on Chrysler station wagons must be properly aligned to the body opening. CAUTION: Do not close the tail gate as a tail gate with the glass in the "up" position during adjustment. Instead, open the tail gate as a gate and remove the inner trim panel cover. Then, close the tail gate.

Next, raise glass approximately 1/4 in. below weatherstrip. If top edge of glass is not parallel to weatherstrip, proceed as follows: Loosen corner window regulator

Fig. 19-6. Details of Chrysler station wagon tail gate.

mounting bolts. Twist regulator base to bring top edge of glass parallel to weatherstrip. Secure mounting bolts.

Raise glass all the way "up." Check for side fit; the glass should be centered in the body opening. If not, position the tail gate glass side-to-side when full "up" by means of an alignment bracket attached to the top of the right hand glass track. To adjust glass position: loosen the jam nut, and adjust the bracket sleeve nut. After sleeve nut adjustment is made, tighten jam nut.

Adjust the right and left up-stops to allow the glass (when in the full "up" position) to form a tight seal against the top weatherstrip. See that the glass does not raise too high, causing a sheet metal interference with the body when opened as a door.

Fig. 19-7. Tail gate remote control system installed on recent model Chrysler station wagons.

Fig. 19-8. Single tubular run front door window mechanism adjustment applies to 1973 to 1976 Ford, Thunderbird, Granada, Elite, Mustang, Montego, Mercury, Meteor, Monarch, Cougar, Continental and Lincoln Continental.

Open the tail gate as a gate and raise the glass about halfway "up" in the opening. Then, loosen the bolts that secure right and left glass runs.

To obtain glass seal at the roof, move the glass inboard or outboard as follows: Grasp bottom edge of glass and pull upward to bring top of glass away from the roof line; or push downward to bring glass closer to the roof line. Tighten lower glass run bolt. Repeat sealing operation on other side.

Close tail gate, raise glass carefully to full "up" position and check for glass seal at the roof. When proper in-and-out adjustment has been attained, open the tail gate and tighten all bolts, securing glass run channels. Close tail gate and check glass for ease of operation.

To remove tail gate glass, run glass to "down" position and remove inner trim panel cover. Run glass up and out of tail gate until

glass lift channel screws are visible in access holes. Remove glass lift channel attaching screws, Fig. 19-6, to disconnect glass from channel assembly, then remove alignment pin. Slide glass out of belt opening. Remove "T" nuts, gasket and rubber tubes from inside the gate. Remove slides from glass in four places, noting which slides have wedges, by removing the screws.

CHRYSLER TAIL GATE REMOTE CONTROL

Details of the Chrysler tail gate remote control are shown in Fig. 19-7. When replacing remote control: Assemble link, tail gate and door latch remote control to bracket on tail gate and door latch link guide. See Fig. 19-7. Install link and bracket through access hole in tail gate inside panel to attaching hole in panel. Secure with screw. Position tail gate and door latch in inside tail gate panel. Secure with screw and washer. Assemble link by inserting it into clip on lever of remote control.

Test operation of remote control unit.

FORD DOOR WINDOW MECHANISM

Separate steps are given for each adjustment on single, tubular run front window mechanisms, so that partial glass adjustments can be made. If a complete adjustment is required, follow instructions for indivisible adjustments in the order given. Remove door trim panel and watershield when making window mechanism adjustments.

Door glass position: It is necessary to reposition the glass in the opening if the glass has been removed or if major door hinge adjustments have been performed. To reposition glass, remove door trim and watershield. Then, loosen upper attaching screw, at A in Fig. 19-8, and reposition glass. Position upper guide and tighten upper run attaching screw after glass is removed to desired position.

Stabilizer adjustment: Stabilizers are used to support the glass at the belt line. To adjust, remove trim panel and, with glass up, push front stabilizer firmly against glass surface. Tighten attaching screw, at B in Fig. 19-8. Repeat procedure for rear stabilizer.

Glass in-out adjustment: The in-out adjustment is used to obtain a good seal with the weatherstrip at the top edge of the glass. This adjustment is made by repositioning the guides with respect to the glass bracket. To adjust the in-out position, loosen two lower guide attaching screws, at C in Fig. 19-8, and move top edge of glass inward or outward as needed to obtain a good seal with weatherstrip. Then, tighten lower guide attaching screws.

On right door, tighten lower guide rear screw first, then tighten front screw. After guide attaching screws have been tightened, again check glass-to-weather strip for a good seal. Readjust as needed.

Upper stop adjustment: The upper stop adjustments are used to limit the up travel of the glass to maintain a constant glass height when the glass is up. Check to be sure window is raised to full closed position. Make sure there is no interference when door is opened. Then, position up stop brackets down against glass stops and tighten stop bracket attaching screw, at D in Fig. 19-8. Use this procedure

Fig. 19-9. Typical Ford front door window mechanism.

for both front and rear stops.

Lower stop adjustment: The lower stop, Fig. 19-8, is used to control the depth the glass can be lowered into the door. To adjust, remove door trim panel. Loosen lower stop retaining screw, at E in Fig. 19-8, and lower glass until top edge is flush to 1/4 in. above outer panel. Then, lift stop against glass bracket and tighten retaining screw.

Glass removal: A special procedure is required to remove front door glass on Ford-built cars with single tubular run front window mechanisms. First, remove door trim panel and watershield. Remove screws attaching each glass stabilizer to inner panel and remove stabilizers, Fig. 19-9. Remove upper front and rear stop brackets from door inner panel. Use a drift punch to remove center pin from rivets attaching glass bracket to glass, Fig. 19-9. Then, use 1/4 in. drill to remove rivets by drilling head from rivet. Do not attempt to pry rivets out, since damage to window mechanism could result. Push rivets from glass and bracket. Move glass forward in door until rear upper stop is aligned with access notch in inner panel at belt line. Lift

rear of glass up and out of door. Then, move glass rearward until front upper stop is aligned with access hole and remove glass. Remove rivets from upper stops, following procedure for rivet removal. Then remove stops from glass.

Installation of door glass: Position upper stops of glass and install each stop on glass with 1/4 - 20 x 1 in. hex bolt and 1/4 - 20 nut and washer assembly. Torque-tighten nut 6 to 11 ft. lb. Insert glass into door, using the access notch for clearance of upper stops. Position glass to glass bracket and install three 1/4 - 20 x 1 in. bolts and three 1/4 - 20 nuts to attach glass to glass bracket. Torque-tighten nuts 6 to 11 ft. lb. Install stop brackets, Fig. 19-9. Install glass stabilizers and adjust glass, stabilizers and upper stops. Install watershield and trim.

Window regulator removal: Remove door trim panel and watershield and support glass in up position. Use a drift punch to remove center pin from regulator attaching rivets. Then, drill head from regulator attaching rivets with 1/4 in. drill. Disengage regulator arm from glass bracket and remove regu-

Fig. 19-10. Details of tailgate window mechanism used on
Ford, Mercury and Meteor.

lator from door.

Window regulator installation: Lubricate mechanism with polyethylene grease. Install nut and retainer mechanisms on regulator mounting plate and motor support bracket at rivet attaching holes. Position regulator in door and install screw and washers to attach regulator to inner panel. Tighten screws securely. Check operation of window mechanism.

FORD TAILGATE WINDOW GLASS ADJUSTMENT

All window adjustments except the in-out tilt adjustment must be performed with the trim panel removed. The tailgate window glass should be properly positioned within the glass opening to secure a good seal around the glass with the weatherstrip.

The top edge of the glass should be parallel to the top of the glass opening when the window is closed. To adjust, loosen each upper stop bracket attaching screw, at A in Fig. 19-10, and again check glass fit. If glass fit is not as specified, loosen four window regulator attaching bolts, at B in Fig. 19-10. Move glass until top edge is parallel with glass opening, then tighten glass regulator attaching bolts. After glass has been positioned in opening, move upper stop brackets down firmly against stops and tighten attaching screws.

Glass side-to-side position: The tailgate glass can be positioned side-to-side to obtain a good seal overlap with the side weatherstrips. To adjust, loosen two lower right guide-to-glass attaching screws, at C in Fig. 19-10. Then, move glass from side to side as necessary to obtain a good glass overlap with weatherstrip on each side of glass. Tighten glass attaching screws after glass has been moved to desired position.

Glass tilt in-and-out: To adjust, loosen glass run lower attaching screws, at D in Fig. 19-10. Then move lower ends forward or rearward as necessary to move glass top edge against weatherstrip to obtain a good seal. Tighten attaching screws.

To remove tailgate glass: Remove tailgate inside cover and watershield. Also remove tailgate inner panel lower access cover. Lower tailgate to down position and raise glass until glass brackets are accessible. Use a center punch to remove center pin from glass-to-glass bracket rivets. Then, drill rivet heads with a 1/4 in. drill and remove rivets. Disconnect wires from rear window defroster terminals, if so equipped. Slide glass from tailgate.

QUIZ - Chapter 19

1. What usually causes windows to stick so they cannot be raised or lowered?
   Lack of lubrication.
   Wrong type weatherstrip.
   Wrong type windlace.
   Misalignment.
2. On cars equipped with electric window regulators should the motor be disconnected from the circuit before removing window assemblies?
   Yes.
   No.
3. To remove the front door ventilator assembly on recent model Fisher bodies, it is not necessary to first remove the door trim assembly.
   True.
   False.
4. If major door hinge adjustments have been made, it is not necessary to adjust position of door glass.
   True.
   False.
5. When removing the glass from a Ford tailgate, first lower the tailgate, then raise the glass until the glass brackets are accessible.
   True.
   False.

Chapter 20
WINDSHIELD, REAR WINDOW REMOVAL, INSTALLATION

Windshields are frequently broken as a result of collision, flying gravel, and also as a result of strain from twisting of the car body. It is therefore, important for body repair men to be familiar with the different methods of removal and installation.

In general, modern windshields are held in position primarily with caulking compound and to a degree with garnish moldings and reveal moldings. The terms garnish and reveal are loosely used by manufacturers to identify the metal strips (chrome plated or painted) placed around the outer and inner edges of the windshield. Most General Motors' manuals refer to the molding used along the outer edge of the windshield as reveal moldings, Fig. 20-1, and that used on the inside edge as the garnish molding. Some other companies reverse this, while still others refer to both inner and outer moldings as garnish moldings, or simply molding.

REMOVING AND REPLACING MOLDINGS (FISHER)

Before removing the windshield glass or rear window glass from recent model Fisher bodies, it is necessary to remove all trim and hardware immediately adjacent to the glass being removed. This in the case of windshields would include reveal moldings, garnish moldings and windshield wiper arms.

The reveal molding, Fig. 20-1, around the windshield (and other stationary glass) is retained by clips which are attached to the body opening by welded-on studs or screws. A projection on the clip engages the reveal molding flange, retaining the molding between the clip and body metal, Fig. 20-2. To disengage a molding from the retaining clips, use a tool such as shown in Fig. 20-3.

Fig. 20-1. Typical windshield reveal molding on Fisher body.

Another method of attaching the reveal moldings is shown in Fig. 20-4. This method is used on Fisher bodies of recent manufacture on the Fisher B, C, D, E and F hardtop moldings. In this method the molding is retained by barbed clips. A thin flat bladed tool such as a putty knife must be inserted from the windshield side of molding to disengage barbed clips while lifting the molding.

In most cases, the garnish molding used on the inner face of the windshield consists

© General Motors Corporation

Fig. 20-2. A clip engages the reveal molding flange, on some Fisher bodies.

Fig. 20-3. Type of tool used to disengage retaining clips (Fisher).

of several pieces and is held in position by means of screws. The windshield reveal molding consists of several pieces as shown in Fig. 20-1. On some bodies the upper reveal moldings are held in position by clips and in others by screws as previously mentioned. The lower reveal molding on many bodies are secured to the upper shroud assembly by molding clip tabs.

Fig. 20-4. Barbed clips are used to retain the molding in some Fisher bodies of recent manufacture.

REMOVING AND REPLACING WINDSHIELD GLASS

The window removal procedure is the same for both the short and extended installation methods, with one exception. If the short method installation is to be used, more care must be taken during removal to make certain that an even, uniform bead of adhesive caulk material remains on the window opening to serve as a base for the replacement glass. Also make certain that glass lower spacers are not disturbed.

The removal procedure is as follows: First place protective coverings around area where glass is being removed. Remove all trim and hardware immediately adjacent to glass being removed.

On styles equipped with optional rear window electric defogger, disconnect wire harness connectors from glass. If same glass is to be reinstalled, tape electric leads to inside surface of glass to protect them during handling.

On styles equipped with radio antenna built into the windshield glass, disconnect antenna lead at lower center of windshield. If same windshield is to be reinstalled, fold and tape wire back onto outer surface of windshield to protect it during removal and reinstallation.

The windshield on all styles of Fisher bodies of recent manufacture is bonded to the body opening with either of two synthetic, self-curing rubber materials called polysulphide adhesive and urethane adhesive.

The back window and quarter windows are bonded to the body opening with polysulfide adhesive, urethane adhesive or butyl tape, which can be identified after molding removal by the absence of a rubber dam. Butyl tape also remains soft and does not cure to rubber.

To distinguish between urethane and polysulfide, cut a small piece of excess adhesive from the glass or opening. Stick the adhesive on a pointed metal tool and hold it over a flame. Polysulfide burns with a clear flame with a little white smoke and a strong odor of sulfur dioxide. Urethane material burns with a dirty flame with black smoke, but little odor.

To replace a window or windshield installed with either of these materials requires either partial or complete replacement of the adhesive material. Partial replacement of material is referred to as the "short method." Complete replacement is known as the "extended method."

Adhesive service kits containing the materials needed to install a windshield or stationary glass are available at car dealers and automotive paint wholesalers.

To replace a window installed with butyl tape, the extended method must be used.

Use a knife heated to 750 deg. F to remove urethane caulking; use a cold knife for polysulphide or butyl. Attach one end of steel music wire to a wood handle. With a long nose pliers, insert other end of wire through caulking and secure it to another handle, Fig. 20-5.

Fig. 20-6. One man method of cutting caulking material.

Fig. 20-5. Cutting the adhesive caulk material with the aid of a piece of steel music wire.

With the aid of a helper, carefully cut (pull wire) through caulking material around entire perimeter of windshield (or rear window as the case may be). If short method will be used to install new glass, hold wire close to inside plane of glass to prevent cutting an excessive amount of adhesive caulking from window opening. Keep tension on wire throughout cutting operation to prevent wire from kinking and breaking, Fig. 20-5. After the cutting of the caulking material has been completed, the glass can be lifted from the opening.

An optional method which can be performed by one man is illustrated in Fig. 20-6. In this method the cutting wire is pulled through upper and lower edges of glass at the same time. When using this method, insert one end of wire through caulking material at inner upper edge of glass and other end of wire through caulking material at inner lower edge. Attach handles to both wire ends outside of body.

If glass being removed is to be reinstalled, place it on a protected bench or holding fixture. Remove old caulking compound using a razor blade. Any remaining traces of caulk-

ing compound can be removed with toluene or thinner dampened cloth.

When cleaning laminated glass, avoid contacting edge of plastic laminate material (on edge of glass) with volatile cleaner. Contact may cause discoloration and deterioration of plastic laminate by "wicking" action. It is important that petroleum base solvent such as kerosene or gasoline NOT be used as the presence of oil will prevent adhesion of the caulking compound.

SHORT METHOD OF INSTALLING ADHESION CAULKED GLASS (FISHER)

The short method of glass installation can be used if original adhesion caulk material remaining on window opening flanges after glass removal can serve as a base for the replacement glass. If there is a substantial loss of adhesion between caulk material and body metal, opening must be reworked or refinished and the extended replacement method will be required.

Short Method Installation: Inspect reveal molding retaining clips. Replace or reshape clips which are bent away from body metal 1/32 in. or more.

Position glass in opening. If new glass is being installed, check relationship of glass to adhesive caulk material on pinch weld flange. Gaps in excess of 1/8 in. must be corrected by shimming or by applying more adhesive caulk material. If more caulk is needed, apply a smooth continuous bead around entire inside edge of glass. Material should be 1/16 to 3/16 in. in diameter, Fig. 20-7.

Fig. 20-7. Short method of applying adhesive material.

When glass is in proper position in opening, apply masking tape over each side edge of glass and adjacent to body pillar. Slit tape vertically at edge of glass. During installation, align tape on glass with tape on body to guide window into desired position.

Remove glass from opening. To speed clean-up after installation, apply 1 in. masking tape to inside of glass 1/4 in. inboard from edge, across top and down each side.

Use a commercial ammoniated cleaner to thoroughly clean surface of glass to which adhesive will be applied (edge of inside surface). Follow by cleaning with clean, water-dampened cloth. Dry glass with clean cloth.

Apply primer provided with urethane kit (primer requires thorough stirring and agitation before application). On windshields without embedded radio antenna, and other stationary glass, apply primer around perimeter of glass and 1/4 in. inboard on inner surface of windshield. Allow five minutes for primer to dry.

Apply a smooth, continuous bead of adhesive (1/8 to 3/16 in. dia.) over edge of glass where primer previously was applied. On windshields with embedded radio antenna, omit adhesive 4 in. each side of antenna pigtail.

With the aid of a helper, lift the glass into the opening. On back window installations it will be necessary to use suction cups to position glass in opening. Windshield glass can be positioned without the aid of carrying devices. As shown in Fig. 20-8, carry glass with one hand on inside of glass and one hand on outside. At opening, put glass in horizontal position. While one man holds glass in this position, second man can reach one arm around body pillar and support glass while other man assumes same position. Quarter window glass can be installed in the same manner.

Center glass at opening and place it on lower supports. Use tape guides previously installed to align glass in proper position. Press glass firmly to "wet out" and "set" adhesive caulking material. Use care to avoid excessive squeeze out of caulking, which would cause an

Fig. 20-8. Installation of windshield glass. Fisher method.

appearance problem.

Immediately water test car. Use a cold water spray, but do not direct a strong stream of water at the fresh adhesive material. If any leaks are found, paddle-in extra adhesive at the leak point, using a flat-bladed tool.

Cement a rubber spacer between right and left sides of glass body metal to assure that glass will remain centered while adhesive is drying. Complete job by replacing reveal molding and other trim. Also remove masking tape from glass.

EXTENDED METHOD OF INSTALLING ADHESIVE CAULKED GLASS (FISHER)

If, after removing glass, you find that adhesive material is damaged, or must be removed to permit refinishing of glass opening, or has insufficient adhesion to body material to serve as a base for replacement glass, it will be necessary to use the extended installation method. The procedure is as follows:

Remove screw retained lower glass supports on windshield. Using a sharp scraper or chisel, remove major portion of old caulking material from opening flanges around entire opening. It is not necessary that all traces of material be removed, but there should not be any mounds or loose pieces left.

Inspect reveal molding clips. If upper end of clip is bent away from the body metal more than 1/32 in., replace or reform clip.

Using black weatherstrip adhesive, or adhesive caulking material, cement rubber spacers to window opening pinch weld flanges, Fig. 20-9, location B. Spacers should be positioned to provide equal support around entire perimeter of glass.

'A' LOCATION   'B' LOCATION

Fig. 20-9. Showing location of spacers on window pinch weld flange (Fisher).

If weatherstrip adhesive is used, apply sufficient material to obtain a watertight seal beneath spacer, however, DO NOT allow excessive squeeze out. Weatherstrip adhesive is not compatible with replacement adhesive caulking compound and water leaks may develop at locations where these two materials are used together to form a seal.

Fig. 20-9, location A, illustrates rectangu-

lar spacers positioned in typical back window installations. Reinstall metal supports at lower edge of windshield glass (in lieu of two lower A spacers indicated in back window installation).

With aid of a helper, lift glass into position. On back window installations it will be necessary to use suction cups to position glass in opening. With one hand on each side of glass, put window in vertical position and support it on lower glass support spacers. While one man holds glass in this position, second man can reach one arm around body pillar and support glass while other man assumes same position. With glass positioned in opening, check relationship of glass to pinch weld flange around entire perimeter. Overlap of pinch weld flange should be equal with a minimum overlap of 3/16 in. Overlap across top of windshield may be corrected by repositioning lower metal support spacers. Overlap across top of back window may be varied by shimming or shaving lower glass support spacers.

Check relationship of glass contour to body opening. Gap space between glass and pinch weld flange should be no less that 1/8 in., nor more than 1/4 in. Correction can be made by repositioning flat spacers, or by applying more caulking material, by reworking pinch weld flange or by selecting another glass.

After final adjustments have been made and glass is in correct position, apply pieces of masking tape over edges of glass and body, depending on glass being installed. Tape on glass can be aligned with tape on body to guide glass into opening during final installation.

Remove glass from opening and apply one inch masking tape around inner surface of glass 1/4 in. inboard from outer edge. On windshield installations, apply tape to top and sides only. Do not use tape across bottom. Remove tape after glass installation to aid in cleanup and give a smooth even edge to adhesive material.

Using a sharp scraper, remove major portion of old adhesive from flanges around entire window opening. Scrape away all mounds and loose pieces. On butyl tape installations, remove all traces of material.

Thoroughly clean surface of glass to which adhesive will be applied (around edge of inside surface), using a commercial ammoniated cleaner. Follow by cleaning with clear water. Dry glass with a clean cloth. Apply primer supplied with urethane adhesive kit.

Use a caulking gun, Fig. 20-10, to apply a smooth, continuous bead of adhesive around inside edge of glass. Bead should be 3/8 in. high by 3/16 in. wide at base.

Since caulking material begins to cure within 15 minutes of exposure to air, install the glass quickly. Carefully position glass in opening, using tape guides previously applied. Guide the lower outer surface of glass along rear edge of front fenders to

Fig. 20-11. Details of electric knife, a specialty tool used to cut butyl tape.

permanent, watertight glass installation, observe the following procedure.

To remove the windshield or rear window: First place protective coverings over adjacent areas. Detach windshield wiper assemblies and/or moldings which would interfere with the removal of the glass. Then, using an electric knife as shown in Fig. 20-11, cut existing butyl tape as close to fence flange as possible and carefully remove the glass.

On older models, a fiber wedge is used to remove chrome trim around glass.

FOR EXTENDED METHOD, ENLARGE NOZZLE BY CUTTING-OUT MATERIAL WITHIN SCORE LINES

MASKING TAPE 1/4'' FROM GLASS EDGE

3/8''

ADHESIVE CAULKING MATERIAL

3/16''

Fig. 20-10. Application of adhesive material by Fisher extended method.

avoid smearing fresh adhesive material on instrument panel. Make sure glass is properly aligned. Apply light hand pressure to "wet out" adhesive material and obtain a bond to body opening.

Water test as previously described.

WINDSHIELD AND REAR WINDOW REMOVAL (CHRYSLER)

The windshield and rear window of recent model Chrysler cars are butyl adhesive sealed (cemented-in) types. Shortcut sealing methods should not be used. To insure a

PAINT BRUSH OR APPLICATOR

PANEL ROOF

PRIMER

.25 INCH.

PANEL-DECK UPPER

Fig. 20-12A. Method used to clean sheet metal surface on Chrysler cars prior to installing glass.

LACTOL SPIRITS

GLASS

GLASS

.30''

PRIMER

CHEESECLOTH OR OTHER SUITABLE APPLICATOR

CHEESECLOTH OR OTHER SUITABLE APPLICATOR

VIEW IN DIRECTION OF ARROW W

Fig. 20-12B. Applying primer to glass.

WINDSHIELD AND REAR WINDOW INSTALLATION (CHRYSLER)

To install a windshield or rear window in recent model Chrysler cars: Use solvent to clean foreign matter from the remains of the butyl tape from the fence flange. See Fig. 20-12A. Apply fence primer over the fence flange and remnants of the butyl tape, Fig. 20-12B, and allow to dry for 10 minutes. Then, starting at either side of the body

Fig. 20-12C. Butyl tape installed on Chrysler rear window. Windshield is similar.

opening, apply butyl tape to the fence with the tapered edge of the tape facing the reveal surface, as shown in Fig. 20-12C.

Then, using strong hand pressure, press the windshield or rear window into the opening. Inspect the installation carefully. If poor glass-to-butyl tape contact is noted, again apply pressure to areas where the glass is not seated properly. The bond width should be .025 in. (6.35 mm) or greater as evidenced by the amount of butyl tape observed through the glass.

Check to see if spacers are still in proper location.

WINDSHIELD SERVICE (FORD)

To remove a Ford windshield with a butyl seal, first remove the windshield wiper arms and then the windshield moldings. Using a special tool insert the blade under the edge of the glass, Fig. 20-13. Cut the butyl seal as close to the inside surface of the glass as possible. To cut the butyl at the lower corners of the windshield, move the handle of the tool as close to the corner as possible.

Fig. 20-13. Using a special tool to tape butyl seal from recent model Ford windshield.

Then rotate the blade downward to cut the corner butyl seal, Fig. 20-14. Remove the windshield from the vehicle, using the glass holding tool, Fig. 20-14.

To install a windshield in a recent model Ford with a butyl seal, first position the new windshield in the glass opening. Use the spacers provided with the special tool to prevent the glass from sticking to the butyl. Adjust the glass until it is properly seated. Mark the location of the glass.

Fig. 20-14. Cutting corner seal with special tool on recent model Ford windshields.

Remove the glass and thoroughly clean the inside edge. Apply the butyl bead on top and in the center of the existing butyl all around the glass opening. Start at the side opposite the original butyl splice. Do not stretch the butyl. Apply primer to the inside edge of the glass where it will contact the butyl, Fig. 20-15. Allow the primer to dry for 10 min.

Fig. 20-15. Installation of primer on Ford windshields using butyl type seal.

Position the glass in the glass opening and align the markings previously made. Press the glass firmly into the butyl seal, using only hand pressure to seat the glass in the sealing material.

Dull spots indicate areas where the glass is not contacting the seal. Additional pressure must be applied to correct this condition. The thickness of the glass-to-butyl seal must be a minimum of .180 in. Apply more pressure to the glass to obtain desired overlap.

Apply liquid butyl sealer around the outer edge of the glass to effect the final seal. When dry, check for leaks by making the water test. Remove excess primer. Clean glass and replace moldings.

To remove a Ford windshield with a weatherstrip type seal, first remove the glass outside moldings, Fig. 20-16. Then remove the windshield interior garnish moldings. Working with an assistant, push the glass and weatherstrip from the windshield opening as an assembly.

Clean all sealer from the glass and/or weatherstrip, if either unit is to be used again. Also clean all the sealer from the windshield opening.

Fig. 20-16. On Ford windshields with weatherstrip type seal the moldings are removed with a tool as shown.

To install a windshield with weatherstrip type seal: Check all the molding retainers. Repair or replace damaged retainers to insure adequate molding retention. Replace any missing or damaged weld studs with screws. Apply sealer in the glass groove of the weatherstrip. Position the weatherstrip on the windshield.

Fig. 20-17. Installing a draw cord, prior to installation of Ford windshield with weatherstrip type seal.

Insert a draw cord in the pinch weld opening of the weatherstrip all around the weatherstrip, Fig. 20-17, and overlap the cord about 18 in. at the lower center of the glass. Tape the ends of the cord to the glass as shown in Fig. 20-18.

Fig. 20-18. Draw cord installed.

Position the glass in the glass opening and align the markings previously made. Press the glass firmly into seal, using only hand pressure. Inspect the appearance of the glass. A dull spot indicates an area where the glass is not contacting the butyl seal. Use additional pressure to seal these areas. When installing a windshield, no more than 0.20 in. clearance should exist between the surface of the glass and the pinch weld flange.

From the outside of the vehicle, apply liquid butyl sealer around the outer edge of the glass. Allow the liquid butyl sealer to form a skin, then water test the glass seal for leaks. Remove the excess primer from the inside of the glass with a razor blade. Wipe the glass with a cloth dampened with naptha. Install the windshield moldings and windshield wiper arms.

GLASS POLISHING

Minor scratches on glass can be removed by polishing. A low speed polisher (600 to 1300 rpm) is used together with a wool felt polishing pad about 3 in. in diameter and 2 in. thick. Commercial polishes are available or cerium oxide can be used.

Fig. 20-19. Method of removing minor scratches from windshield glass.

FEATHERING-OUT MOTION

GUIDELINES

HOLD PAD FLAT AGAINST GLASS

Mix a small quantity of polish with water to obtain a creamy consistency. Draw a circle on opposite side of glass from scratches to act as a guide when polishing. Dip the polishing pad in the polish and use a moderate but steady pressure against the scratched area of the glass. Use less pressure on outer edges of scratched area.

Do not hold tool in one spot. Also less polishing can be done on windshield as drivers vision may be affected.

QUIZ - Chapter 20

1. A polysulfide adhesive is used to bond the windshield on some Fisher bodies.
   True.
   False.
2. Three types of adhesive are used on rear windows of Fisher bodies. Name one.
3. When removing an old windshield and installing the new one, which method of replacement requires the most care?
   Short method.
   Extended method.
4. To remove a windshield that is bonded with urethane adhesive, a cold knife is needed.
   True.
   False.
5. When a windshield does not have an embedded radio antenna, the primer should be applied all around the perimeter of the glass.
   True.
   False.
6. On a Fisher windshield that is installed with butyl tape, it is not necessary to remove all traces of tape.
   True.
   False.
7. How long does it take windshield caulking material to dry?
   15 minutes.
   30 minutes.
   60 minutes.
8. When polishing glass, should a low speed or high speed polisher be used?
   Low.
   High.
9. How soon should you water test a windshield sealed with urethane material?
   Immediately.
   Wait 15 minutes.

Chapter 21
POWER SEATS, WINDOWS, TOPS, TAIL GATES

Power seats, windows and tops are electrically operated. Therefore, it is important that the storage battery is fully charged to help insure satisfactory operation of the electrical units. Equally important is the condition of the wiring and electrical connections. Insulation must be good; all connections must be tight.

Electrical motors used to operate accessories are either series wound or multiple wound units. The series type motor should never be operated without a load. If it is, high rotational speeds will damage the motor.

Unless otherwise specified by the manufacturer, frictional surfaces of power seat transmissions should be lubricated with the type lubricant used on brake mechanisms. These frictional surfaces include gears, gear shaft, thrust washers, drive cables and adjuster tracks. See Figs. 21-1 and 21-2.

Fig. 21-1. Details of six-way power seat installed on Fisher A, B and C bodies: 1-Adjuster to seat attaching bolts. 2-Adjuster track rear covers. 3-Transmission and motor support attaching screws. 4-Motor relay. 5-Ground wire. 6-Transmission assembly. 7-Transmission stabilizer support. 8-Hole in seat frame for stabilizer support. 9-Horizontal drive cable (black). 10-Rear vertical drive cable (blue). 11-Front vertical drive cable (red).

FOUR-WAY SEAT (FORD)

Ford's four-way power seat mechanism provides: Fore and aft movement of the driver's (bucket or flight bench) seat; up and down movement of the front edge of the seat, resulting in a tilting action.

The power seat is driven by a dual electric motor, through two gear boxes and two flexible drive cables to provide the desired movement. A control switch is located on the driver's side in the left lower seat side shield. It controls the current to the motor.

To remove the seat track, first use the control switch to raise the seat and position it in the rearmost position. Then, remove the seat track rear attaching screws, Fig. 21-2. Remove the outboard seat track front attaching screw and inboard seat track attaching nuts. Disconnect the feed and switch wiring connectors. Remove the driver's seat assembly from the vehicle and place it on a clean work bench.

Installation of the seat track is accom-plished by reversing the procedure. Check operation of the seat.

FISHER BODY SIX-WAY SEATS

Trouble shooting suggestions on the Fisher Body six-way, power-operated seats are as follows: If horizontal movement is not smooth and works hard, check for lack of lubrication of the adjuster shoes and channels. Also inspect the adjuster horizontal gear. It may be too tight to the gear rack, or the adjuster shoes may be too tight in the upper channel. Details of the six-way seat are given in Fig. 21-1.

If there is looseness in the horizontal operation, the horizontal actuator may be incorrectly adjusted.

If one adjuster will not operate horizontally, the horizontal drive cable, may be disconnected, or the horizontal actuator may be inoperative.

If one adjuster will not operate vertically, the vertical drive cable may be disconnected,

CUSHION ASSEMBLY

384871S2 — SCREW 4 REQ'D. 14-22 Ft-Lb TORQUE

TO FRONT OF BODY

45341S36 — NUT AND WASHER 14-22 FT-LB TORQUE

DRIVER'S SIDE ONLY

Fig. 21-2. Seat and track installation of Ford four-way seat.

or the vertical gear nut may be inoperative.

If neither adjuster will operate vertically or horizontally, check the operation of the solenoid in the transmission.

POWER WINDOWS (FISHER)

The wiring harness for electrically operated windows on recent model Fisher bodies consists of four major sections, and in the 1971 models five sections. The crossover harness is installed beneath the instrument panel. The impact bar and reinforcements incorporated into some door construction reduces the accessibility for power wiring harness. Therefore if replacement of wiring harness should be necessary, attach a leader to the end of the harness before removal from the door. This will permit drawing the new harness into position.

TROUBLE SHOOTING

The following typical failures and corrections are provided as an aid in locating the cause of troubles.

If none of the windows operate, the trouble may be caused by a short or open circuit in the power feed circuit. When that occurs check operation of the circuit breaker. Also operation of ignition relay. Also check feed connection to power harness beneath instrument panel. Also check feed circuit wires for possible short or open circuit. On Cadillac styles only check window black-out switch.

If right rear window does not operate from master control switch on left door or from control switch on right rear door and left door window operates, there are four possible causes: (1) Short or open circuit between right rear door harness and power window front harness. (2) Short or open circuit in affected window control switch or window motor circuit. (3) Possible mechanical failure or bind in window channels. (4) Defective window motor. To correct these conditions, first check harness connectors beneath outer end of instrument panel for proper installation. Also check wires in power window front harness for possible open or short circuit. Also check operation of rear door window control switch. Also check cir-

Fig. 21-3. Checking feed circuit of Fisher power window.

cuit from window control switch to window motor for open or short circuit. Also check window regulator and channels for possible mechanical failure or bind. Also check operation or motor.

If right door windows will operate from left door master control switch but will not operate from right door control switch and left doors will operate, check for short circuit or open circuit in front harness feed wire circuit. Follow up feed wire in front harness for possible short or open circuit.

To check feed circuit continuity at circuit breaker: (1) Connect one test light lead to battery side of circuit breaker and ground other lead. If tester does not light, there is an open circuit or short circuit in feed circuit to breaker. (2) To check circuit breaker, disconnect the output feed wire (the wire opposite the power source feed to the breaker) from the breaker and with test light, check terminal from which wire was disconnected. If tester does not light, the circuit breaker is inoperative.

To check ignition relay assembly; with test light, check relay feed (orange/black wire). If tester does not light, there is an open or short circuit between relay and circuit breaker. Turn ignition switch on and with test light check output terminal of relay (red/white wire). If tester does not light; put test light on ignition relay terminal (pink or tan wire). If tester lights replace ignition relay. If tester does not light, locate short or open circuit along pink or tan wire. Also check fuse at dash panel.

To check for current at Master Control Switch, place ignition switch in "on" position. Connect one test lead to master window control switch feed terminal (red-white

Fig. 21-4. Left. Checking window control switch (Fisher). Fig. 21-4A. Right. Checking circuit between switch and motor of power window (Fisher Body).

stripe) of switch block and ground other test lead. If tester does not light, there is an open or short circuit between relay and master control switch.

To check feed circuit continuity at window control switch connect one test lead to feed terminal of switch block and ground other test lead to body metal, Fig. 21-3. If tester does not light there is an open or short circuit between switch and power source.

To check window control switch: Insert one end of a No. 12 gauge jumper wire to switch feed terminal and the other end to one of the motor leads terminal in the switch block. Repeat this check on the remaining motor lead terminal, Fig. 21-4. If window operates with jumper wire, but does not operate with switch, the switch is defective.

To check wires between door window switch and door window motor, disengage harness connector from window motor. The thumb release on the harness connector must be depressed before it can be disengaged from the motor. Insert one end of No. 12 gauge jumper wire to switch feed terminal and the other end to one of the motor lead terminals in the switch block, Fig. 21-4. With test light, check for current at motor harness connector terminal being tested. If tester does not light there is an open or a short circuit in the harness between the control switch and the motor connector, Fig. 21-4A. Also check other terminal.

POWER WINDOWS (FORD)

A wiring diagram of recent model Ford power windows is given in Fig. 21-5. Before making any of the following trouble checks, make sure battery is fully charged and turn ignition switch to accessory position:

The power window, power seat and convertible top electrical systems are connected through the same 20 amp. circuit breaker. If failure occurs in all systems at same time, 20 amp. circuit breaker is probably defective.

If all the windows do not operate, check to make sure that current is reaching the circuit breaker and if no voltage is available repair or replace the circuit breaker or wires leading to it.

If one window does not operate, operate the switch and listen for the noise of the motor running free. If the motor is running, it is loose and has pulled away from its coupling. Short out the ground circuit breaker of the inoperative window and operate the switch. If the motor runs, replace the circuit breaker.

If the window operates in one direction only, check the window operation with both switches. If window operates properly with one switch but not the other, check the switch and the red and yellow wires for voltage. Replace switch or wires as necessary.

If the window operates sluggishly check the regulator and window runs for excessive friction. Adjust the runs, repair and lubricate the regulator. Lubricate runs with silicone lubricant. Be sure to check for frayed insulation where wires may partially ground.

POWER TOP OPERATION (FISHER)

On recent model General Motors cars equipped with power operated tops, the hydraulic-electric unit consists of a 12 volt reversible type motor, a rotor-type pump, two hydraulic lift cylinders and upper and lower hydraulic hose assembly. The unit is installed in the body directly behind rear seat back, Fig. 21-6.

Fig. 21-7 illustrates and identifies the individual parts of the motor and pump assembly.

When servicing the motor assembly or pump end plate assembly, it is important that the small motor shaft "O" ring seal is properly installed over the motor armature shaft and into the pump and plate assembly prior to installing the pump rotor or the rotor shaft drive ball.

When the control switch is actuated to the up position, the battery feed wire is connected to the red motor lead and the motor and pump assembly operate to force the hydraulic fluid through the hoses to the lower ends of the double acting cylinders. The fluid presses piston rods upward, thus raising the

Fig. 21-5. Power window wiring diagram as used on some Ford cars.

top. The fluid in the top of the cylinders returns to the pump for recirculation to the bottom of the cylinders. When the control switch knob is actuated to the down position,

Fig. 21-6. Hydraulic-electric motor and pump assembly.

Fig. 21-7. Motor and pump disassembled.

the feed wire is connected to the dark green motor lead, and the motor and pump assembly operates in a reverse direction to force the hydraulic fluid through the hoses to the top of the cylinders. This forces the piston rod and the cylinders downward, thus lowering the top. The fluid in the bottom of the cylinders returns to the pump for recirculation to the top of the cylinder.

If there is a failure in the hydraulic electric system and the cause is not evident, the mechanical operation of the top should first be checked. If the folding top assembly appears to have a binding action, disconnect the top lift cylinder piston rods from the top linkage, and then manually raise and lower the top. The top should travel through its up-and-down cycle without any evidence of a binding action. If a binding action is noted when the top is being locked at the header, check the alignment of the door windows, ventilators and rear quarter windows with relation to the side roof rail weatherstrips.

Make adjustments necessary for correct top operation. If a failure continues to exist after a check for mechanical failure has been completed, the hydraulic-electric system should then be checked for electrical or hydraulic failures.

If a failure in the hydraulic-electric system continues to exist after the mechanical operation has been checked, the electrical system should be checked. A failure in the electrical system may be caused by a low battery, breaks in the wiring, faulty connections, mechanical failure of an electrical component, or wires or components shorting to one another or to body metal. Before beginning checking procedure, make sure the battery is in a fully charged condition.

To fill the hydraulic-electric reservoir, a filler plug adapter should be made as follows: Drill a quarter inch diameter hole through center of a spare reservoir filler plug. Install two inch length of metal tubing (1/4 in. OD by 3/16 in. ID) into center of filler plug and solder tubing on both sides of filler plug to form airtight connections.

Then to fill and bleed the reservoir, place the top in a raised position and remove folding top compartment bag material from rear seat back panel. Remove pump and water shield.

Place absorbent rags below reservoir at filler plug. Using a straight-blade screwdriver, slowly remove filler plug from reservoir.

When installing new or overhauled motor and pump assembly, as a bench operation, fill reservoir to specified level with hydraulic fluid. This operation is necessary as pump must be primed prior to operation to avoid drawing excessive amounts of air into hydraulic system.

Install filler plug adapter to reservoir and attach 4 or 5 in. length of 3/16-in. ID rubber tubing or hose to filler plug tubing.

Install opposite end of hose into a container of hydraulic brake fluid, Fig. 21-8. Note: Container should be placed in rear compartment area of body, below level of fluid in the reservoir. In addition, sufficient fluid must be available in container to avoid drawing air into hydraulic system.

Operate top to down or stacked position.

Fig. 21-8. Bleeding hydraulic system.

After top is fully lowered, continue to operate motor and pump assembly for approximately 20 seconds or until noise level of pump is noticeably reduced. Reduction in pump noise level indicates that hydraulic system is filling with fluid.

Operate top several times or until operation of top is consistently smooth in both up-and-down cycles.

With top in down position, remove filler plug tubing and remove filler plug adapter from reservoir. Check level of fluid in reservoir and reinstall original filler plug hole. The fluid level should be within 1/4 in. of lower edge of filler plug hole.

FORD ELECTRIC SUN ROOF

The Ford Sun Roof panel slides backward and forward on guide rails. It is actuated by a two-way electric motor at the center of the windshield header area, Fig. 21-9. The motor turns a drive assembly which, in turn, powers an output shaft that extends up into the cable drive housing. A pinion on the end of the output shaft drives flexible cables attached to the roof panel.

When the control switch is placed in the open position, the roof panel retracts down and rearwards. It moves from the flush, roof-mounted position on guide rails into a storage space located between the headlining and the stationary roof panel, exposing an opening over the front seat area.

When the control switch, Fig. 21-10, is actuated in the opposite direction, the sun roof panel moves forward in the guide rails. Near the end of the forward travel, the rear portion (lifting element) is started upward on two ramps, the lifters are actuated and the panel moves upward. This action positions the panel flush with the roof and seals it in the roof opening.

Fig. 21-9. Wiring system components of Granada and Monarch sun roof.

Fig. 21-10. Wiring schematic of Ford sun roof.

MANUAL OPERATION OF FORD SUN ROOF

The sun roof may be closed manually, if the electric power fails. Remove the auxiliary drive cover (located in middle of headlining close to front edge of roof opening). Grasp cover with fingers and pull downward. Then, remove hex-head screw which is visible when cover is removed. Use the hex-head end of the crank handle provided in the glove compartment. To close the roof panel, insert the screwdriver end of the crank handle into the socket in the auxiliary drive. Turn the crank handle clockwise to close the roof.

After performing these operations, remove the crank handle, reinstall the hex-head screw and auxiliary drive cover.

SWITCH TEST OF FORD SUN ROOF

To check the control switch on a Ford sun roof, first remove the switch from the vehicle. Then, connect the leads of an ohmmeter or self-powered test light to the terminals of the switch. Operate the switch in one direction and observe the result on the meter or test light. There should be continuity between the terminals. Likewise, with the switch operated in the opposite direction, there should be continuity between the terminals.

ADJUSTING FORD SUN ROOF PANELS

When preparing to adjust a Ford sun roof panel, first open the roof panel approximately three inches. Remove the three screws securing the headlining trim panel to the steel sliding roof panel at the center and front corners.

Slide the headlining panel forward approximately 1 in. to disengage it from the sliding panel mechanism. Disengage the plastic frontal piece from the vinyl cover trim panel. Deflect the frontal piece downward so the horizontal tabs are removed from the track mechanism. Repeat same procedure for trim panel. This will expose the guides and lifters. Reverse the pro-

Fig. 21-11. Dual acting tail gate hardware. (Fisher Body)

© General Motors Corporation

1. Outside handle
2. Gasket
3. Lock cylinder
4. Elec. feed block
5. Gasket
6. Lock cylinder retainer
7. Sash channel cam

8. Remote control con. rod
9. Left upper lock and hinge
10. Torque rod
11. Regulator, manual
12. Inside remote gate handle
13. Inside door handle and cable
14. Right upper lock

15. Right lower lock
16. Glass stabilizer
17. Lower glass run channels
18. Glass block-out rod
19. Regulator, electrical
20. Sealing strip
21. Remote control assembly
    (Gate operation)

cedure for installation.

If the roof panel does not rise into the roof opening during the closing cycle, open the roof panel to the full rearward position. Examine the ramps in the drainage channel to determine if they are properly aligned with the lifting elements at the rear of the panel.

The point where the lifting element makes contact with the ramp can be easily seen on the rearward slope of the ramp. Loosen the two screws until the ramp slides, then slide the ramp rearward or forward. Retighten the screws. Close the roof panel and not the lifting action of the panel. If necessary readjust the ramps until proper lifting action of the roof panel is obtained.

During cable replacement, lubricate the cables with vaseline. It is not necessary to lubricate the top surface of the guide rail covers or the slide tracks.

During regular maintenance, check to see that the two drainage holes at the front corners of the roof panel frame are open and free of any foreign material. If plugged, they can be cleaned with an air hose using low pressure.

DUAL ACTING TAIL GATE (FISHER)

The dual acting tail gate incorporates a unique hinge and locking arrangement that permits the tail gate to be operated in the conventional manner and, in addition, as a door. All wagons so equipped utilize either a manually or electrically operated window that can be lowered into the gate or raised into the back body opening.

Following parts replacement or realignment of the dual acting tail gate, Fig. 21-11, check all locks for synchronization.

THREE-WAY TAIL GATE (FISHER)

The three-way tail gate may be operated as a tail gate with the glass fully "down," or as a door with the glass "up" or "down." It uses an inside locking knob similar to the doors. The design of the locking rod knob prevents unlocking except from the outside with a key. If electric, it is controlled by a switch mounted in the front. The three-way tail gate, Fig. 21-12, is opened to the gate position with the glass "down" by means of an outside handle.

Fig. 21-12. Three-way tail gate (Fisher): 1-Striker, tail gate lock upper right side. 2-Tube assembly, tail gate window guide. 3-Rod assembly, tail gate lock cylinder-to-lock. 4-Rod assembly, tail gate lock-to-power actuator. 5-Weatherstrip assembly. 6-Handle assembly, tail gate outside. 7-Lock cylinder assembly. 8-Sealing strip assembly. 9-Tube assembly, tail gate window guide. 10-Weatherstrip assembly. 11-Lock assembly, tail gate upper hinge left side. 12-Plate assembly, tail gate window left side. 13-Bumper, tail gate window down stop. 14-Grommet, torque rod. 15-Regulator assembly, tail gate window electric. 16-Retainer assembly, tail gate belt trim support.

SYNCHRONIZATION CHECK AND PROCEDURE

The lock system on the dual acting tail gate is designed to perform the following two "block out" functions:

1. Allow the tail gate to be opened as a door and at the same time prevent accidental operation of the upper left lock (which allows the gate to be opened as a gate).

2. Allow the gate to be opened and closed as a tail gate and at the same time prevent accidental operation of the lower right lock (which allows the gate to be opened as a door).

The above "block out" functions are accomplished by levers in the upper right lock, Fig. 21-13. That illustration shows the upper right lock (in closed door position) and identifies the levers which perform block out functions.

To assure that the upper right lock levers perform the block out functions properly, the upper right lock and gate remote control must be synchronized with the rest of the tail gate system (lower right lock and upper left lock). This prevents accidental operation of either the upper left lock when the gate is opened as a door or accidental operation of the lower right lock when the gate is opened as a gate.

IMPORTANT: When servicing components, the locking system must be synchronized.

1. Synchronization check for lower right lock.
   A. Open tail gate as a gate (horizontal position). Take precautions to prevent damage if tail gate should become disengaged from the lower right lock by placing a protective support beneath the gate. Then grasp right inside lock release handle and pull upward until the gate is in the vertical position and close gate. Open gate as a door and close gate.
   B. Repeat above procedure (Step 1-A) five times. If tail gate lower right lock does not become disengaged, synchronization of lower right lock is correct. If tail gate becomes disengaged at lower right lock, reinstall gate on lower right lock and proceed with "synchronization" as described and illustrated.

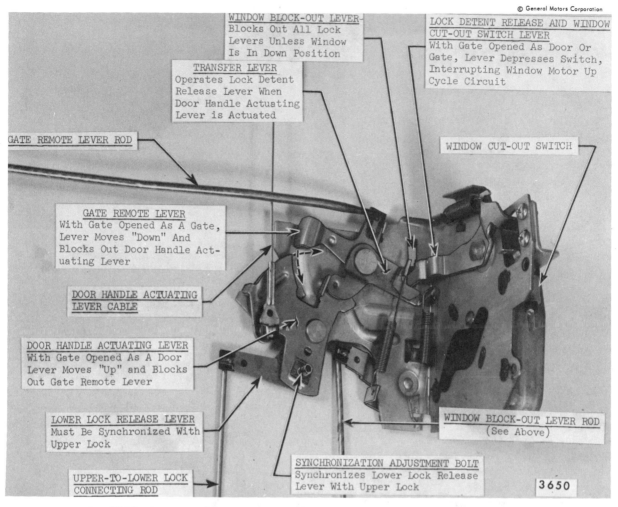

© General Motors Corporation

WINDOW BLOCK-OUT LEVER
Blocks Out All Lock
Levers Unless Window
Is In Down Position

LOCK DETENT RELEASE AND WINDOW CUT-OUT SWITCH LEVER
With Gate Opened As Door Or
Gate, Lever Depresses Switch,
Interrupting Window Motor Up
Cycle Circuit

TRANSFER LEVER
Operates Lock Detent
Release Lever When
Door Handle Actuating
Lever is Actuated

GATE REMOTE LEVER ROD

WINDOW CUT-OUT SWITCH

GATE REMOTE LEVER
With Gate Opened As A Gate,
Lever Moves "Down" And
Blocks Out Door Handle Act-
uating Lever

DOOR HANDLE ACTUATING LEVER CABLE

DOOR HANDLE ACTUATING LEVER
With Gate Opened As A Door
Lever Moves "Up" and Blocks
Out Gate Remote Lever

LOWER LOCK RELEASE LEVER
Must Be Synchronized With
Upper Lock

WINDOW BLOCK-OUT LEVER ROD
(See Above)

UPPER-TO-LOWER LOCK CONNECTING ROD

SYNCHRONIZATION ADJUSTMENT BOLT
Synchronizes Lower Lock Release
Lever With Upper Lock

3650

Fig. 21-13. Functions of levers in upper right lock on dual acting tail gate. (Fisher Body)

2. Synchronization check for upper right and left locks.
   A. Open tail gate as door.
      Important: Place a protective support under right side of gate in the event gate becomes disengaged from upper left lock.
   B. Operate center remote control handle (gate operation) with a moderately heavy pressure, then operate right inside lock release lever (door operation) in the same manner. Operate both handles at the same time.
   C. Close tail gate and repeat above operation (Step 2-A and B) five times. If tail gate upper left lock does not become disengaged, the upper locks are in synchronization. If tail gate becomes disengaged at the upper left lock, re-

install gate at upper left lock and proceed with "synchronization procedure" which follows.

LOCK SYNCHRONIZATION PROCEDURE

1. Open gate as a door then close securely. Open to "gate" (horizontal position).
2. Remove tail gate inner cover panel; carefully remove inner panel water deflector or detach water deflector sufficiently to gain access to gate remote control and door lock synchronization bolts. Remove right inner panel access hole cover.
3. Place tape over door lock handle to prevent accidental operation of lower right lock after upper locks have been manually locked as outlined below.

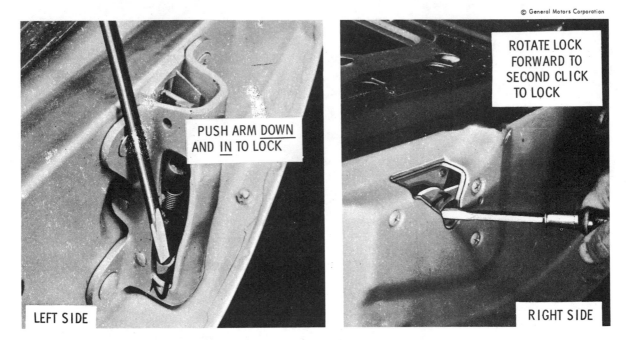

PUSH ARM DOWN AND IN TO LOCK

ROTATE LOCK FORWARD TO SECOND CLICK TO LOCK

LEFT SIDE

RIGHT SIDE

Fig. 21-14. Manual locking of upper right and upper left locks on a dual acting tail gate.
(Fisher Body)

4. Manually lock both upper right and upper left locks as shown in Fig. 21-14.

5. With all locks in locked position, visually check gate remote synchronization holes in gate remote control levers (center of gate as shown in Fig. 21-15). If holes line up, proceed with step 7. If the holes do not line up, loosen (turn to right approximately three turns) gate remote control synchronization bolt (this bolt has left hand threads). With synchronization bolt loose, check that there is no bind in remote levers. Align holes by inserting a cotter pin through alignment hole in both levers (Fig. 21-15). Then tighten synchronization bolt to 57-87 in. lb. Remove cotter pin.

6. With all locks in locked position and with the right lower lock securely engaged with the striker, loosen by approximately three turns, the door lock remote synchronization bolt at upper right lock, Fig. 21-15.

This adjustment is "self seeking" and should automatically synchronize the right upper and lower locks when the synchronizing bolt is loosened. However, to assure that the levers automatically assume their proper position, reach in through the access hole and hold lower-to-upper lock connecting rod FORWARD Fig. 21-15, while tightening door lock synchronization bolt to 76-116 in. lb. Make sure tab on door lock remote synchronization lever is properly engaged in hole.

Note: The action of loosening the lock synchronization bolt can readily unlock the right lower lock causing the right side of the gate to disengage from the striker. To help prevent this from occuring, reach through access hole and hole the upper-to-lower lock connecting rod, Fig. 21-15, FORWARD while loosening synchronization bolts.

If lower right lock should unlock and become disengaged from striker, lift right side of tail gate up and forward to reenagage lock with striker.

7. Unlock upper locks by actuating tail gate handle at center of gate.

8. Remove tape from door handle and close gate.

9. Perform lock synchronization checks, check window operation.

10. Reseal tail gate inner panel water deflector and install tail gate inner cover panel.

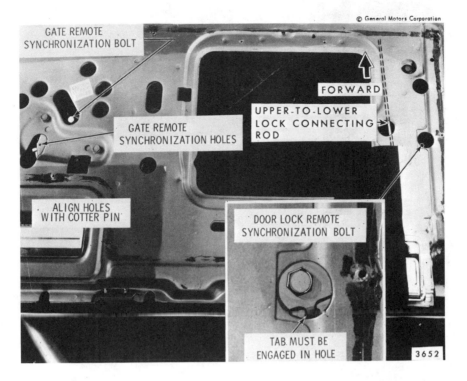

© General Motors Corporation

GATE REMOTE SYNCHRONIZATION BOLT

GATE REMOTE SYNCHRONIZATION HOLES

ALIGN HOLES WITH COTTER PIN

FORWARD

UPPER-TO-LOWER LOCK CONNECTING ROD

DOOR LOCK REMOTE SYNCHRONIZATION BOLT

TAB MUST BE ENGAGED IN HOLE

3652

Fig. 21-15. Dual acting tail gate lock synchronization check points. (Fisher Body)

QUIZ - Chapter 21

1. What is the first check to be made when trouble shooting power operated seats?
 Electric motor.
 Condition of starting battery.
 Wiring circuit.

2. What is the first step when removing the seat track on the Ford four-way seat?
 Raise the seat and position it in rearward position.
 Remove attaching bolts.
 Disconnect wiring connectors.

3. Where is the crossover harness on recent model Fisher power windows?
 Beneath the instrument panel.
 Under the seat.
 In back of the seat.

4. The power window, power seat and convertible top electrical systems are all connected through the same fuse.
 True.
 False.

5. The 12 volt motor used for operating the power top on a Fisher body is reversible.
 True.
 False.

6. Where is the motor which operates the Ford sun roof?
 Behind the instrument panel.
 At the center of the windshield header area.
 Between the roof and the headlining.

7. How many control switches are provided for the Fisher dual acting tail gate?
 One.
 Two.
 Three.
 Four.

Chapter 22
RECOVERING CONVERTIBLE TOPS
FABRIC ROOFS, WOODGRAIN OVERLAY

While the following description applies particularly to the method of removing and installing the fabric top on Ford convertible cars, it can also be used in general for other vehicles.

Fig. 22-1. Weatherstrip installation on convertible.

In the case of Ford cars the convertible top consists of the deck and two side quarters, bonded into one piece of material. The bonded seams eliminate the possibility of leaks, and also separation, due to thread deterioration. In most cases, it will be advantageous to replace the back curtain when replacing the top fabric.

To remove the top fabric, first place a protective cover across the deck, cowl and hood to prevent scratching the finish when replac-

ing the top.

Remove the rear seat cushion and seat back. Raise the top to gain access to the underside of the front bow. Remove the front weatherstrip retainer, Fig. 22-1, and the weatherstrip.

Remove the two front side rail weatherstrip retainers and the weatherstrips.

Remove the two center side rail and the two rear side rail weatherstrips. Remove the metal screw and washer that secures each end of the folding top compartment weld to the pivot bracket supports.

Starting at one end of the compartment, carefully pull the trim retainer out of the channel. Fold the trim over the seat area and quarter panel trim.

Remove the tip from each end of the molding on the rear bow. Carefully pull the molding out of the retainer. Pry the molding retainer off the bow.

Remove the bolts that attach the top and back curtain tacking strips to the body.

Remove the staples that secure the top material to the rear bow.

Carefully pull the top material free from the underside of each side rail. Remove the staples that secure the top material to the underside of the front bow. Carefully separate the top from the listings on number two and number three bows.

To install the new top fabric, first remove the tacking strips from the old top.

Staple them to the new top in the same location as they were on the old top. Fit the new top on the roof bows.

Working from the center outward, staple the top deck to the rear bow. Make sure that the rear sections of the slits are stapled to the bow before drawing and stapling the front portion of the slits.

Secure, and tighten the quarterdeck tacking strips to the body as required to align the listings with number two and number three bows.

Center the top material and pull it forward over the front bow to remove the wrinkles from the top deck and quarters. While the material is pulled over the front bow, make a reference mark on the material at the leading edge of the bow with a piece of chalk. The mark should extend the entire length of the bow.

Raise the top high enough to gain access to the underside of the front bow. Align the reference mark to the leading edge of the bow and staple the material in place.

Install the weatherstrip and the three retainers on the number one bow.

Secure the flaps to the underside of the side rail with trim cement. Trim the excess material from the flaps.

Install the rear, center and the front weatherstrips on the side rails so that the ends of the weatherstrip are in alignment of the side rail joints.

Tighten the quarterdeck packing strips as required to remove wrinkles from material and obtain a tight seal at the moldings. Install a piece of tape across the rear bow to cover the staples.

Install the molding retainer, molding and the two tips on the rear bow.

Secure the back curtain to the upper part of the zipper. Secure the back curtain packing strip in place with the attaching bolts. Tighten the bolts as required, working from the center outward.

Starting at one end of the folding top compartment, insert the trim retainer into the channel. Secure each end of the trim to the pivot bracket supports with a metal screw and washer.

Install the rear seat back and cushion. Cement the top material to the listings on number two and number three bows. Remove the protective covers from the deck and the hood and clean all chalk reference marks from the top material.

REPAIRING VINYL OUTSIDE ROOF MATERIAL

There are several types of vinyl material used as an outside cover for roofs. The following instructions apply particularly to the type of material used on many Ford cars.

To repair damage to vinyl material, certain tools and equipment are required: heat gun, soldering iron, transformer, hypodermic syringe, rubber cement pickup, abrasive cellulose sponge, vinyl top cleaner, vinyl top adhesive, vinyl paint spray gun.

Before proceeding with any repairs, carefully clean the vinyl roof with special cleaner. Use a scrub brush to remove all dirt that may be embedded in the graining.

CLEANING SCUFFS AND ABRASIONS

Connect the soldering iron to an electrical outlet and set the transformer at approximately 225 deg. F. Clean the soldering iron tip thoroughly with an abrasive pad. Then, lightly slide the soldering iron over the scuff marks, using short overlapping strokes until the frayed vinyl has fused into the surface.

If the scuff marks are deep enough to expose the cloth backing, it will be necessary to fill in with vinyl. This is accomplished by using the hot tip of the solder gun, Fig. 22-2, to strip off a small quantity of vinyl from a piece of scrap material. Carefully fill in the scuffed area as required, using short overlapping strokes.

The graining effect in the vinyl can be restored by carefully etching the pattern into the vinyl with the sharp tip of the soldering iron. The gloss created by the repair can be removed by spraying the area with liquid vinyl.

REPAIRING MINOR SURFACE CUTS

Connect the soldering gun and heat to 225 deg. F. Clean the tip and lightly slide the tip across the surface, using short strokes (1/4 in. or less) until the cut is covered with vinyl. Again go over the surface with the soldering tip to smooth out the surface. The graining effect can be produced with the sharp edge of the soldering tip.

Fig. 22-2. *Stripping and filling scuffed area with vinyl.*

REPAIRING MAJOR CUTS

Prepare the soldering iron as previously described. If damage is over 1 in. long, apply a light coat of adhesive, Fig. 22-3. It is not necessary to use cement if cut is over a padded area.

Fig. 22-3. *Types of major cuts in vinyl that are repairable.*

Start at the center of the cut and lightly slide the soldering iron across the cut surface, Fig. 22-4. Use short strokes (1/4 in. or less) until the cut is covered with vinyl. Again go over the cut lengthwise with the soldering tip to smooth out the surface. Restore the graining effect by etching the surface with the hot tip of the soldering iron. Shine can be eliminated by spraying with liquid vinyl.

Fig. 22-4. *Using a soldering iron to fuse a damaged area in vinyl.*

REPAIRING BUBBLES

Bubbles caused by trapped air can be corrected by expelling the air with the aid of a hypodermic needle, Fig. 22-5. It will be necessary to reactivate the adhesive under the vinyl after the air bubble has been dissipated. This is done by applying heat to the surface with the aid of a heat gun. To avoid overheating, hold the gun about 12 in. from the surface.

Fig. 22-5. *Using a hyperdermic needle to bleed air from a bubble in vinyl.*

REPAIRING WRINKLES

A wrinkle in vinyl usually has small radial folds with an excess of slack material that cannot be displaced without rearranging the material, Fig. 22-6. To correct this condition:

1. Partly or completely remove any moldings or ornamentation in immediate area.

2. Pull vinyl material free from roof panel up to bonded seam and along side drip rail for approximately 10 in.

3. Clean surface thoroughly of old adhesive.

4. Apply a thin film of adhesive to vinyl material and along drip rail.

5. Allow adhesive to air dry for several seconds.

6. Grasp material firmly, then draw taut until wrinkles are free, Fig. 22-6.

7. Fold material under drip rail flange.

8. Secure front edge of material with as many drive nails as needed to prevent material from slipping.

9. Apply sealer under drive nail to prevent a possible water leak.

10. Replace moldings.

Fig. 22-6. Correcting wrinkles at front corner.

REPAIRING LOOSENESS OF MATERIAL

Vinyl roof material sometimes becomes loose at padded areas of the roof. The proper repair for looseness is similar to the procedure suggested for the repair of wrinkles.

REPAIRING GAP BETWEEN VINYL AND MOLDING

In some instances, vinyl top material is too short to be concealed under the roof molding. This problem can be corrected by adjusting the molding or by stretching the material. If it is necessary to stretch the material,

use pop rivets to prevent the material from slipping back to its former position.

REPAIRING SEPARATED BONDED SEAM

Prepare the soldering iron in the usual manner. Insert the tip of the soldering iron at one end of the separated seam. Note the position of the curved tip of the soldering iron in Fig. 22-7. Slowly move the tip of the

Fig. 22-7. Applying heat to edge of bonded seam. By reversing tip of iron, heat can first be applied to underside of bonded seam.

iron across the underside of the seam. Follow up immediately by pressing the seam together with the fingers. Reverse the soldering iron and again slowly move the tip along the edge of the seam. Press into position. No paint touch up should be required.

WOOD GRAIN TRANSFER REPLACEMENT

These instructions apply to Chrysler-built cars, but also serve as a guide for applying wood grain transfers to other makes.

Clean all grease, oil and other foreign material from the body surface to which the wood grain overlay is to be applied. Then, sand all areas to be covered with the overlay, using No. 360 paper soaked in water or mineral spirits. Sand this area approximately 1/4 in. larger in all dimensions than the overlay, except when the overlay is turned at the door, etc., Fig. 22-8. Remove all metal and/or paint nibs prior to applying the overlay. Tack off all dust and dirt particles from the sanded areas.

Temperature: Do overlay work when air and application surfaces are between 70 and 90 deg. F. Below 70 deg. F., use heat lamps.

Fig. 22-8. Application of wood grain overlay.

Wetting Surface: Thoroughly mix two or three level teaspoons of mild powdered household detergent per gallon of clean warm (80 to 90 deg.) water in a non-rusting container.

Application: It is mandatory to remove the paper backing from the overlay and not the overlay from the backing as possible stretching or tearing will result.

Cut overlay 1/2 in. larger than the area to be covered and lay on a clean flat surface with the paper backing surface up. Hold overlay firmly and remove backing paper in a smooth 180 deg. motion. Under hot, humid conditions, a slight jerking motion will aid in the paper backing removal.

Thoroughly wet application surfaces of body and the adhesive surface of the overlay with the wetting solution and immediately apply overlay, grain side out, to the body. Adjust overlay so 1/2 in. of material shows beyond all edges and apply wetting solution to outer surface of overlay.

Follow details of application, Fig. 22-8. Flat Surfaces: Use a plastic squeegee with cloth sleeve, or Teflon coating, and pressurize all flat surfaces with firm, overlapping strokes to remove air bubbles, water wrinkles and to insure good adhesive contact. On vertical surfaces, pressurize and level off entire top edge first with a 3 x 4 in. squeegee, then work from top to bottom.

On horizontal surfaces, start at the center and work toward the edges using a 3 x 4 in. squeegee. Do not apply pressure to edges that will be wrapped around doors, fenders, gas cap areas or to compound curve areas.

Flange Areas: After being sure all metal and/or paint nibs and sanding residue have been removed, hand brush 3M Vinyl Adhesive 8064, or equivalent, to entire flange area with an even coverage. Note in Fig. 22-8, Section A-A is the break between front fender and front door; B-B is between doors; C-C is between rear door and rear fender. Minimum overlap for each flange area is 1/2 in.

Warm the unapplied overlay with a heat lamp. Avoid trapping air when turning the edge and wrap overlay around flange area. Press firmly with the fingers, making sure overlay overlaps the flange.

Using a single-edge razor blade, trim off all material extending beyond the flange.

Pressurize the flange area with a 2 in. rubber roller to be sure the overlay is well adhered to the metal surface.

Contoured Areas: Warm the unapplied overlay with a heat lamp, working on an area no more than 1/2 in. larger than the squeegee.

Using 3 x 4 in. plastic squeegee, pressurize and level off the small warmed area. Repeat warming and pressurizing until entire contoured surface is completely adhered and free of air, water and wrinkles.

Inspection: Upon completion of an area, inspect for blisters due to trapped air or water. All blisters should be worked out with squeegee, or punctured with a sharp needle and then pressurized until film adheres to the body surface. All edges must be adhered to the body surface.

TAPE STRIPING SERVICE

To remove tape striping from some Ford cars, first clean repair surfaces, adjacent panels and openings as required. Then, remove decal overlapping parts from affected panel. Remove decal by starting at one edge and peeling it from painted surface. Apply heat to decal to facilitate its removal. Do not use tools.

Remove adhesive from painted surfaces by wiping area with a rag saturated with special adhesive cleaner. Then scrape with squeegee. Exercise care when using solvents because of possible damage to painted surfaces. Rinse thoroughly with clean water.

DRY METHOD OF INSTALLATION

To install small or thin stripes by the dry method, first clean the painted surface with wax and silicone remover. Wipe surface with a clean cloth and let dry.

Position tape stripe to vehicle and align character lines and karats on tape stripe to contour of vehicle. Use masking tape to hold striping in place. Remove liner paper from stripe one-half distance of panel and tear off liner paper. The liner paper is removed by sharply bending edge of striping toward face with a flick of the fingernail. The liner then can be peeled from the striping.

Stretch the striping in place, but do not apply it to vehicle. Using squeegee (plastic), start from center of panel and press striping in place by moving toward end of panel. Do not use hands or fingers to smooth striping; this will create creases and air bubbles.

Peel off remainder of liner paper and press striping into place, using plastic squeegee. Remove premask by pulling at 180 deg. angle away from stripe. Inspect for bubbles.

Small nicks or scratches can be repaired with touch-up paints. Repair blisters or air bubbles by piercing them with a sharp needle at one end of bubble. Work trapped air out through pinhole with your thumb and, at the same time, press decal firmly against panel. If necessary, preheat panel slightly to soften adhesive and to remove wrinkles. Mold decal into recessed areas using 750 deg. F. (399 C) heat gun and a soft, clean cloth.

WET METHOD OF INSTALLATION

To install large decals by wet method, position decal to area to be striped in same manner described for dry installation.

Mix a teaspoon of standard dish washing detergent in one gallon of water. Fill a spray bottle with solution. Remove decal from vehicle and lay it on a flat area with liner paper up. Then, completely remove liner paper from decal.

Using detergent solution, wet pressure sensitive side of decal and area of vehicle to be striped. Reposition decal on vehicle, using squeegee and firm overlapping pressure. Begin at center of decal, squeegee toward sides, then toward front. If air bubbles appear, lift decal and reapply it.

After decal is in place and squeegeed, remove premask. Use heat gun (as in dry installation) to mold decal into recessed areas.

QUIZ - Chapter 22

1. When repairing damage to the vinyl on Ford car roofs, a transformer is used to control the temperature of the soldering iron. At what temperature should it be set?
2. When repairing a damaged vinyl top, it is often necessary to restore the graining effect of the surface. How is this accomplished?
     By installing a patch of new material.
     Stamping with a special formed die.
     Produced with sharp tip of soldering iron.
3. If a cut in vinyl is over a padded area, is it necessary to use cement when repairing the damage?
4. What is a hypodermic needle used for in the repair of damage to a vinyl top?
     To inject adhesive.
     As an aid in bleeding air from a bubble.
     To inject liquid vinyl into the material.
5. How is the material on a Ford convertible top secured to the rear bow?
     Sheet metal screws.
     Staples.
     Blind rivets.
6. When using a heat gun to apply striping to recessed areas of a car body, what temperature should be used?

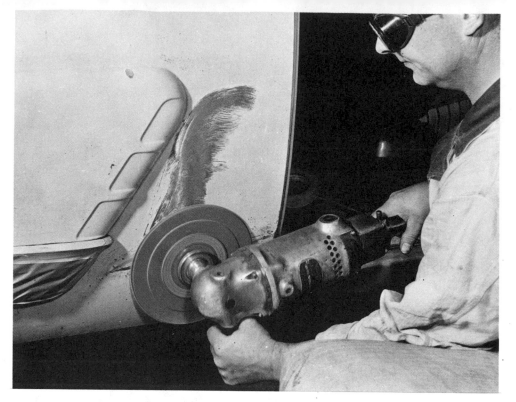

Fig. 23-1. Using disk grinder to remove paint.

Chapter 23

PAINT REMOVAL

On most cases it is necessary to remove all the paint from a vehicle before repainting only when the original paint is in poor condition. This is because the original paint has poor adhesion and tends to flake off.

There are several different methods used to remove paints including:

1. Sandblasting.
2. Hot caustic solution with pressure equipment.
3. Paint remover.
4. Power sanding equipment.

The method used depends largely on the quantity of work and personal preference. When there are a large number of vehicles to be completely refinished, and the supply of such work is steady, either sandblasting or hot caustic is usually selected.

Sandblasting, as the name applies, uses air pressure to direct a stream of sand against the painted surface. The force is such that the sand chips or blasts off the paint from the surface, leaving the bare metal exposed. The sand also makes tiny indentations in the surface of the metal, and in that way provides good adherence for the new paint.

Sandblasting leaves the raw metal exposed and unless the metal is painted promptly rusting soon takes place.

Sandblasting should be performed in an area where the dust does not get out to the rest of the shop. Particular care should be taken that such work is not done close to a painting area, and the mechanics doing the sandblasting should use respirators and goggles.

The hot caustic process is also a popular means of removing all paint from vehicles. This is also known as the flow on, or steam spray method. This process of paint removal uses steam under pressure to spray a hot caustic solution of a special paint removing compound on the surface of the auto body. Chrome and other decorative parts should be removed before the caustic spray is used. Parts which are not removed should be carefully masked so they are protected from the action of the caustic.

In operation, the hot chemical solution is first sprayed on the painted surfaces. After it has remained on the vehicle a sufficient time to loosen the paint, the paint is flushed off by hot steam. Every care must be taken to remove all traces of the chemical. If any remains, the newly applied paint will not adhere to the surface.

After the chemical remover and old paint have been flushed off, and all crevices blown out with compressed air, the surface is then treated with a metal conditioner to prevent rusting.

Paint removing compounds, because of cost, are not used extensively in removing paint from auto bodies. Detailed instructions vary with the make of remover, and the instructions of the manufacturer should be carefully followed. In general, the liquid paint remover is applied with a brush, and after it has remained on the surface a sufficient length of time, the paint will have been loosened and is scraped off with a putty knife. All traces of the remover must be removed from the surface before the car is painted.

REMOVING PAINT WITH A DISK GRINDER

The use of a disk grinder, Fig. 23-1, for removing old paint is probably the most popular method and is used extensively by auto body shops. It is used not only when the paint from the entire vehicle is to be removed, but is also used when only small areas and single panels are to be repainted.

If the original paint is in good condition, without cracks, blisters, or other blemishes,

it is not necessary to remove all the paint before refinishing. When the original paint is smooth, all that is necessary is a light sanding.

The old finish can be removed with No. 16 open-coat disk on a conventional rotary grinder. The exposed metal should be finished with No. 50, and then No. 220 grit paper. If only a portion of the panel is being refinished all edges of the paint film should be feathered, that is, tapered back, Fig. 23-2. This tapering

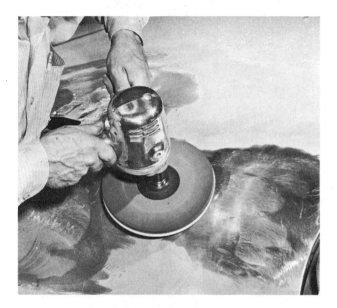

Fig. 23-2. Featheredging with disk sander.

back of the original paint is known as featheredging, and simply means that the finish adjoining the surface to be sprayed is sanded so as to eliminate any sharp edge. To do this, first use No. 320 grit paper and finish with No. 400 grit paper.

PAINT REMOVAL

Before starting to remove paint from a car body in preparing to apply refinishing coats, first determine what type of paint is on the vehicle. Then, sand it to produce the type of surface that will provide good adherence for the new paint, whatever it might be.

As mentioned earlier in this text, there are several satisfactory methods of determining what type of paint is on the surface.

There is very little original type lacquer

(nitrocellulose) being used. Many paint suppliers do not carry it, or they stock it in black only. However, if a vehicle has been finished in nitrocellulose, and it is to be refinished with nitrocellulose lacquer or enamel, only light sanding is required.

If you want to refinish a car that originally

Greatly enlarged scratch in an old finish showing insoluble outer-layer.

The solvents in the fresh coat of lacquer cause swelling in the freshly exposed parts of the scratch.

The swelling recedes after all of the solvents have evaporated and the new finish shrinks leaving furrows similar to the old scratches.

Fig. 23-3. As lacquer dries, it shrinks into cracks as shown in these illustrations.

was finished with acrylic lacquer, acrylic enamel or enamel, proceed as follows:

1. Wash surface with water.

2. Clean with a special solvent.

3. Sand with 240 grit paper or treated paper no coarser than 320 grit.

4. If the surface is in poor condition and may have poor adherence, sand it to bare metal, then treat it with a special solvent designed for use on bare metal.

For several years after 1958, a super enamel was used by some manufacturers. This was a very hard finish and required a thorough sanding to provide good adhesion of the new coating.

It is essential that a smooth surface be provided for the primer surfacer. Modern primer surfaces and glazing putties will fill almost any rough surface, but much time and material can be saved, if the metal is quite smooth before the material is applied.

A good practice is to use three or four

grades of paper from coarse to fine and to take off most of the ridges left by the coarser papers. In other words, start with a No. 16 paper and follow through with a No. 50 close-coated disk and finally sand with No. 220 paper. Featheredge the area with No. 320 and final finish with No. 400 grit paper.

It must be remembered, particularly when spraying lacquer, that as the thinner in the lacquer evaporates, the lacquer shrinks into the cracks and depressions left by sanding, then the cracks become quite visible, Fig. 23-3.

QUIZ - Chapter 23

1. Sandblasting is used to remove the paint from what areas of an automobile body?

Rear deck, top and hood.

Doors and quarter panels.

Entire vehicle.

2. What is the method used most for removing paint from an auto body in auto body shops?

Sandblasting.

Hot caustic solution.

Chemical paint remover.

Disk grinder.

3. If the original paint is in good condition is it ordinarily necessary to remove all the paint before refinishing?

Yes.

No.

4. If the original finish is acrylic lacquer a great deal of sanding is needed before refinishing.

True.

False.

5. The super enamels used in recent years are very soft.

True.

False.

6. The super enamel used in recent years requires a great deal of sanding before refinishing.

True.

False.

7. More cars are being finished with nitrocellulose lacquer.

Yes.

No.

Chapter 24

STEPS IN MASKING

When painting an automobile it is important to cover and protect certain areas from paint overspray while adjacent areas are being painted. Areas to be protected are covered with masking paper, which is attached to the auto body by means of masking tape.

Fig. 24-1. Stand designed to speed dispensing of masking paper.

Manufacturers of masking tape and paper have devoted much time and expense to improve their products and their research has produced products which materially reduce the time and costs required to mask a vehicle.

Good quality masking paper will not permit any paint to penetrate or seep through to the panel it is protecting. The paper should be capable of withstanding rough handling. It must also have a slight amount of stretch which is needed when masking along curved edges. At the same time there must be no possibility of the paper scratching newly painted surfaces.

Tape must adhere easily to painted and unpainted surfaces, chrome, stainless steel, aluminum and other materials. Equally important, none of the tape adhesives must remain on the surface after the tape is removed. Quality tape must also retain its adherent qualities when it is drenched during wet sanding operations.

Special dispensers are available which speed up the preparation of the masking paper and tape for application. See Figs. 24-1, and 24-5. As the paper is pulled from the roll, the tape is automatically applied to the edge of the paper, one-half of the width of the tape is applied to the edge of the paper, while the remaining half is free so it can be applied to the car body to hold the paper in position.

PRECAUTIONS WHILE MASKING

Masking tape should be applied only to clean, dry surfaces. Such surfaces must be free from silicone polish, rubber lubricants, dust, rust, etc.

Unless masking curved surfaces, tape should not be stretched. Simply lay it on the surface and press down, making sure that the edges of the tape are adhering to the surface, not just the center. Unless the edges of the tape are adhering to the panel, water from sanding operations, or paint spray will seep under the tape and free it from the panel.

Fig. 24-2. Method of masking door handles.

Fig. 24-3. Masking decorative emblem.

Fig. 24-4. Chrome trim strips are easily masked.

Tape manufacturers caution against applying or removing tape at temperatures below 50 deg. F. Masking paper and tape should not be removed until the newly applied paint is dry (no longer sticky). When removing tape it should be pulled directly outward at an angle of 90 deg.

Masking tape should be stored in a cool place and never placed on a hot radiator or other hot surface.

MASKING TRIM AND HARDWARE

When masking chrome trim, door handles and similar ornamentation, no paper is required, only masking tape. Select a tape of sufficient width to cover the parts as completely as possible. In Fig. 24-2, tape of

1 in. width is being applied to the door handle. In this instance, the tape is applied to the upper area of the handle. The second piece will be used to cover the lower side and at the same time slightly overlap the tape which was first applied.

A small ornamental light is being masked in Fig. 24-3. In this case, the base of the light is first covered with tape, then the front and back faces. Finally, as shown, tape is wound around the outer circumference, which also helps seal the edges of the tape on front and rear faces.

To mask a side view mirror, some shops use a small paper or plastic bag. It is placed over the mirror, then taped to secure it in place and cover the base of the unit.

MASKING MOLDING AND BEADING

Chrome beading, molding and similar trim can be quickly and effectively masked by using masking tape of the correct width. By having tape of the correct width, the entire surface can be masked with a single strip of tape. Fig. 24-4 shows the operation being performed on front door molding strip. This is typical of the procedure to be used on other moldings.

Masking the weatherstripping on doors is simple, Fig. 24-5, and it makes a good job look better. To help the masking tape stick to the rubber weatherstrip, first apply clear lacquer.

Fig. 24-5. By selecting correct width tape, job of masking weatherstrip is quick and easy.

MASKING WINDSHIELD

Two or three sheets of masking paper are needed to successfully mask a windshield on a modern car. The number of sheets is dependent on the height of the windshield and also on the width of paper that is available.

Fig. 24-6. *Pulling off a sheet of masking paper to mask the windshield.*

Figs. 24-6 and 24-7 show the step-by-step procedure. It will be noted that the lower portion of the windshield is covered first. In that way any water will run down over the masking paper and will not reach the covered area. Other large areas can be masked by using the same method. After the windshield is completely covered, apply tape so that each edge of the paper is taped down.

MASKING A PANEL

When masking a panel for a two-tone paint job, as in Fig. 24-8, select paper which is slightly wider than the panel to be masked. Attach tape to one edge, and apply upper edge to car body. Then crease paper to needed width and tape into position.

Fig. 24-8. *Masking a panel with paper and tape.*

MASKING WINDOWS

The procedure for masking a window is shown in Fig. 24-9. First apply paper to

Fig. 24-7. *Masking of windshield is completed by covering lapped edges of masking paper with tape.*

lower area, and then to the upper. When two sheets are in position, run a length of tape on the overlapping edge to completely seal it.

Fig. 24-9. *When masking a window, lower area is first covered, then upper.*

MASKING UPHOLSTERY

When painting the inside of a door jamb it is necessary to protect the upholstery from overspray. Use a narrow strip of masking paper approximately 10 ft. long. Starting at the outside lower corner, continue around the door in a single operation. Follow the same procedure on the door frame, Fig. 24-10. Place a piece of masking paper over the seat, seat edge, and seat back.

MASKING HEADLIGHTS

Headlights vary in shape and size, but the same basic masking procedure is used for all of them. Usually, masking paper 6 in. to 8 in. wide is all that is needed.

Cut a piece of masking paper that will go approximately three quarters the distance around the light. Start applying the taped

Fig. 24-10. *Method of masking door and door frame.*

paper on one side, then continue until the first sheet of paper is installed. Next, apply the second piece so that a "funnel" of paper surrounds the light, Fig. 24-11. Then, fold the paper over the front of the light and hold it in position with strips of masking tape, Fig. 24-12.

Small areas, such as safety marker lights on the side of the fenders are easily masked by using various widths of tape. In most cases, 2 in. wide tape is all that is needed.

For the rocker panels, either masking tape or 3 in. wide masking paper will do the job.

When masking bumpers, 9 or 12 in. masking paper will do an effective job. The same treatment can be used on grilles but, in general wider paper is needed.

Letters and emblems may present a problem which is most easily solved by using masking tape of narrow widths (1/8 or 1/4 in.).

Long, narrow tail lights can be masked by using 3 or 6 in. masking paper and 3/4 in. tape.

Fig. 24-12. Complete headlamp masking by folding paper over lamps and taping folds in place.

bunching and wrinkling. This is the way it is done: First cut a piece of masking paper the desired length. Next make a pleat about 1/4 in. deep by crimping both edges. The pleat should extend the full width of the apron. Continue pleating the full length of the apron, making a pleat every 2 to 4 in. Apply the apron to the surface. Then after pleated apron is

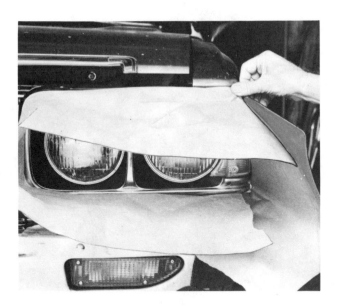

Fig. 24-11. After taping masking paper around headlamps, overlap it with a second piece of paper to form a cone.

MASKING WHEELS

When it is necessary to mask a circular surface, it is advisable to first pleat an apron. This will make it easier to follow the curved contour and will prevent the apron from

Fig. 24-13. Masking a tire prior to painting the wheel.

securely in place, fold the untaped edge so it will catch the overspray. This pleating method can be used to good advantage on wheels as shown in Fig. 24-13.

FRONT END MASKING

Masking a car with large areas of chrome on the front end can be most quickly accomplished by using wide paper. Each car re-quires different treatment. The masking pro-cedure for a sports car is shown in Figs. 24-14 and 24-15. The operation is started at one side of the vehicle, and the tape on the edge of the masking paper is applied to the edge of the chrome area. At the inner edge of the headlamp, the paper is folded as shown in Fig. 24-14. The masking is then carried over to the other headlamp by way of the grille; or, the headlamps, grille and bumper are masked separately, Fig. 24-15.

Fig. 24-14. Masking up front includes grille, bumper and headlamps. (3M Co., Automotive Trades Div.)

MASKING ANTENNAS

Radio antennas can be most quickly masked by using a length of carbdoard tubing which is slipped over the antenna and then taped around the bottom. If such tubing is not avail-able, make a long sleeve of masking paper, taping the edges together. Then slip them over the antenna and tape the bottom as shown in Fig. 24-16.

Fig. 24-15. Side of car masking technique. (3M Co., Automotive Trades Div.)

Fig. 24-16. Masking a radio antenna.

QUIZ - Chapter 24

1. Good quality masking paper will permit paint to seep through to the panel beneath.
    True.
    False.
2. A masking paper dispenser will automatically apply masking tape to the edge of the paper.
    True.
    False.
3. Should masking paper be applied to damp surfaces?
    Yes.
    No.
4. Tape manufacturers caution against applying masking tape below what temperature?
    75 deg. F.
    50 deg. F.
    32 deg. F.
    20 deg. F.
5. Where should masking paper be stored?
    In refrigerator.
    In a cool place.
    On heated radiator.
6. When masking a windshield, how many pieces of masking paper should you use?
    One.
    Two.
    Three.
7. When masking a wheel, or similar circular area, what procedure should be followed?
    Cut the paper in a circular form to fit the area.
    Pleat the paper into an apron.
8. How should a radio antenna be masked?
    Make a sleeve of masking paper.
    Wind the masking paper in a spiral manner around the antenna.

Chapter 25

PAINTING MATERIALS

Acrylic lacquer, acrylic enamel, urethane enamel and synthetic enamel are used in the refinishing field. Refinishing with nitrocellulose lacquer is decreasing rapidly.

In addition to these finishing coatings, other painting materials include thinners, primers, surfacers, reducers, solvents, sealers and metal conditioners.

Automotive paints are composed of volatiles and film-forming material. The volatile material (thinner) evaporates; film-forming material provides color and protection. Lacquers dry from the outside-in, enamels dry from inside-out.

Basically, the main purpose of the volatile material is to act as a solvent for the nonvolatile material. The nonvolatile (film-forming) material is made of binders and pigment. The binder acts as a carrying medium for the pigment and gives body, toughness and gloss to the film.

ACRYLIC LACQUER

Acrylic lacquer dries by evaporation of the volatile material. Since it remains more or less soluble, the new coat of acrylic lacquer will bond or unite with the old.

Acrylic lacquer is considered to be a general purpose finish since it can be used as a spot repair for both acrylic lacquer and baked enamel finishes. It also can be used for panel repairs and complete paint jobs. Acrylic lacquers require some compounding or polishing.

ACRYLIC ENAMEL

Acrylic enamel consists of a solvent blend of binder and pigment materials. This also

applies to synthetic enamel which, in the past, was used extensively as a refinishing material. Acrylic enamel does not require compounding or polishing.

Acrylic enamels dry in two stages: by evaporation of the solvents and by oxidation of the binder (same as synthetic enamel). Oxidation is the change in the binder that results when it combines with oxides of the air.

URETHANE ENAMEL

Urethane enamels used in automotive refinishing provide a hard, tile-like finish, high gloss, improved flow and appearance, good adhesion and flexibility. Urethane enamel dries slower than acrylic enamel, but faster than synthetic enamel.

SYNTHETIC ENAMEL

Synthetic enamels dry by evaporation and oxidation. Thoroughly dry synthetic enamel is not soluble in ordinary solvents. In today's refinishing field, synthetic enamels are used primarily on commercial vehicles.

COMPARISON OF COSTS

Acrylic lacquer is more easily applied than acrylic enamel. However, acrylic lacquer requires several top coats and, therefore, more application time. The necessary compounding also takes time.

As a result, the cost of completely refinishing a vehicle with acrylic lacquer is somewhat higher than with acrylic enamel or synthetic enamel. Material costs for synthetic enamel jobs are slightly less than for acrylic enamel or acrylic lacquer. The cost of applying urethane enamel is, in general, slightly higher than other materials.

CATALIZED ACRYLIC ENAMEL

A recent development in automotive refinishing is the catalized acrylic enamel system, which produces a tile-like premium finish. This finish is extremely durable and highly resistant to chemicals.

PRIMER SURFACERS - PRIMERS

Before the color or finish coat (top coat) Fig. 25-1, is sprayed on the vehicle, a coat known as the primer surfacer is applied.

Fig. 25-1. The primer surfacer is intended for adhesion and fills small depressions and cracks in the sheet metal.

Primer surfacers provide adhesion to the metal and fill slight imperfections in the metal surface. When thoroughly dry, sand down the primer surfacer coats to a smooth, flat surface. If not dry, shrinking of the primer over cracks will produce an uneven surface.

There are two general types of primer surfacers: One is a lacquer-base product with fast drying characteristics. The other is a synthetic-base product of slower drying properties. Generally, it is not advisable to use a synthetic-base primer surfacer under a lacquer finish for refinishing work. Follow the manufacturer's instructions. Use a primer surfacer that will provide good adhesion for the color coat to follow.

For adhesion to special surfaces, manufacturers provide materials generally known as primers, to distinguish them from the primer surfacers, Fig. 25-2. For example when painting aluminum, a zinc chromate primer is used. If the surface to be painted is galvanized, a zinc dust primer is usually recommended.

Primers are intended for adhesion, and do only a small amount of filling imperfections in the metal. Where the metal requires filling, a primer surfacer should be used, applying it directly on the metal under normal conditions, but over a primer if a special primer is required.

Fig. 25-2. The primer forms a bond between the sheet metal of the body and the top coat.

SEALERS

Sealers are used for sealing down sand scratches when recoating a lacquer or acrylic surface. Bleeder sealer is used for sealing reds, maroons, etc., so that they will not "bleed" or show through the new coat. Sealers are formulated from resins, and when dry are not easily soluble in the common solvents. They act as a shield for material over which they are sprayed by preventing the penetration of the solvents that are used in the final coats.

METALLICS

Both lacquers and enamels come in all colors of the rainbow and appear to have the same color value regardless of the angle from which they are viewed. However, to give the paint a "luminous" quality, small metallic flakes (usually aluminum) are mixed with the paint. These flakes are often of different sizes and such paint is known as metallic paint. When viewed from different angles, the color shade seems to vary. The reason for the apparent variation in shade is that the metallic flakes are all at different angles in the paint and consequently reflect the light differently.

These metallic paints are very popular, but present a problem to the painter when attempting to get the same shade and reflective quality.

THINNERS AND REDUCERS

Thinners and reducers are solvents used to thin or reduce paints to the correct viscosity for spraying. Thinners are used for lacquer and acrylic products, while reducers are used for synthetic base resins. In general, they are not interchangeable.

The best results are obtained with the refinish material when it is thinned with a reducer or thinner designed specifically for the material being sprayed.

Some manufacturers provide special thinner for use under conditions of different spraying temperatures.

PUTTY

For deep nicks or scratches there are materials known as putties. Such material is used when the nicks or scratches are too deep to be filled by the primer surfacer. Putty, while of the same general consistency as the familiar glazer's putty, has an entirely different composition, usually being made of the same basic materials as the primer surfacer, but heavier in solids. Some manufacturers provide one type of putty for lacquers and another for enamels.

WAX, POLISH AND GREASE REMOVERS

Before spraying any primer surfacer or color coats, it is essential that all wax and grease be removed from the area to be sprayed. This is important, as the adhesion of any paint film to the surface depends first on whether or not the surface is absolutely clean. By clean, we mean not only physically clean, but chemically clean as well. The slightest film of oil, grease, wax, rust, or moisture will prevent paint from adhering to the surface. Wax and grease removers are solvent type materials that will dissolve partly oxidized waxes and greases that are imbedded in the old finish. A final wipe off with a clean rag saturated with wax and grease remover will insure against the new coat peeling.

Most polishes and waxes used today contain silicone resin. This is more difficult to remove than conventional polishes. When paint is applied to a surface on which silicone is present, the paint will tend to crawl and leave craters or "fish eyes." In addition, there will be poor adhesion of the new paint to the surface.

Special preparations have been prepared for removing waxes and polishes containing silicone products.

METAL CONDITIONER

When auto bodies are stripped to the bare metal before repainting, rust will form quickly. In order to prevent the formation of such rust, make sure that the metal is chemically clean and also etch the surface so there will be better adhesion of the new paint. Manufacturers have prepared metal conditioner and rust inhibitors. Such materials also prevent the formation of rust.

TACK RAG

A tack rag is a special piece of cheesecloth that has been dipped in a thin nondrying varnish and then wrung out. It is kept in a container so that the varnish will not harden, but will remain tacky. The tack rag is used to wipe a surface to remove all dust just before spraying the color coat.

RUBBING COMPOUNDS

Rubbing compounds or pastes, are mild abrasives and are used to polish lacquer and acrylic lacquer surfaces. Rubbing compounds will impart a higher than normal lustre to finished surfaces. Rubbing compounds are available for hand rubbing and machine polishing.

LACQUER? ENAMEL? ACRYLIC?

When refinishing a car, the question arises as to what type of refinishing material should be used. In general, less trouble is experienced if the same type of material is used for refinishing as was used originally.

Prior to 1955 all Ford, Chrysler, Studebaker and American Motors cars used standard baked enamel. During 1956 through 1958 those same cars, in some instances, used

Fig. 25-3. Some of the painting materials used in a typical auto paint shop.

super-enamel and, in 1959-1964, those cars were finished at the factory in super-enamel. In 1965, acrylic enamel was adopted for Ford, Chrysler-built cars and American Motors.

General Motors used nitrocellulose lacquer exclusively prior to 1955. Starting in 1956, some GM cars were finished in acrylic lacquer and, by 1959, acrylic lacquer was used exclusively. In 1973, a water-based paint was used on some Chevrolet models and, in 1976, acrylic enamel was used on some Chevrolet models.

Today most cars are refinished in either synthetic enamel, acrylic enamel or acrylic lacquer. In only a few cases is nitrocellulose lacquer used and then only when there is little drying time. Nitrocellulose lacquer is also used often for retouching small scratches and nicks such as occur on the edges of door panels and fenders. In such cases a small striping brush is used to apply the lacquer. But the spots must be small enough that no sanding or priming is needed. It should also be understood the color match to the original finish will not be perfect under such conditions.

Acrylic lacquer is recommended for use in all cars which were originally finished in lacquer. If acrylic lacquer is used over enamel, a sealer should be applied over the enamel. Further in that connection, complete panels, never a portion of a panel should be sprayed.

When spraying acrylic lacquer, old nitrocellulose lacquer and enamel lacquer, a surface in good condition need not be sanded before applying the finish coat, but the surface should be thoroughly cleaned. If acrylic lacquer is applied over a synthetic enamel surface, the surface must be cleaned and sanded to achieve the necessary adhesion.

When repairing or refinishing over acrylic enamels, the surface must be thoroughly cleaned and sanded to provide the necessary adhesion and resist peeling and chipping.

Synthetic enamels are recommended for use on all cars which were originally painted with enamel. Complete panels should be refinished when enamel is used for repair because of the difficulty of spotting in with enamel without leaving a ring around the spot. Enamel can also be used over lacquer finished cars.

The choice of top coat whether synthetic

enamel, nitrocellulose lacquer, acrylic lacquer, acrylic enamel or urethane enamel depends mostly on whether the vehicle is being completely refinished or partly refinished, and on personal preference.

In general, it is advisable to refinish with the same material that was used on the car originally. In that way, many difficulties such as lifting and poor adherence are avoided.

Some painters prefer to use acrylic lacquer. Others prefer acrylic enamel since compounding is not required. Others will use synthetic enamel because of lower costs. When an especially striking appearance is desired, many shops prefer the newer urethane enamels.

Desirable qualities of acrylic lacquer and acrylic enamel are durability, gloss, gloss retention and hardness.

DETERMINING TYPE OF OLD FINISH

Before applying any paint to an old finish it is important to determine whether the old finish is acrylic lacquer, lacquer, alkyd enamel or acrylic enamel. There are several ways of making such a determination and the easiest method, provided the vehicle has not been repainted is to consult a paint manufacturer's production book which will list the type of paint used by each manufacturer.

Another method which is used particularly when the type of finish material is not known is to use one of the special compounds which the larger paint manufacturers have for that purpose. The procedure is rub a small area with the special compound. The compound will dissolve lacquer very quickly and acrylic lacquer with considerable rubbing. Alkyd enamel and acrylic enamel will not be dissolved.

To distinguish between nitrocellulose lacquer and acrylic lacquer, rub a small area with silicone polish remover. Acrylic lacquer will rub off with this method, while conventional nitrocellulose lacquer will not be affected.

QUIZ - Chapter 25

1. What characterizes the volatile material in automotive paint?

Coloring material.
It evaporates quickly.
2. Acrylic lacquers have been in use on General Motors cars since what year?
1957.
1958.
1959.
1960.
3. Synthetic enamels dry in what manner?
Evaporation only.
Evaporation and polymerization.
Polymerization only.
4. The major advantage of acrylic lacquer over nitrocellulose lacquer is superior gloss retention.
True.
False.
5. Lacquers are said to dry from the outside in.
True.
False.
6. To tell whether a car is finished with nitrocellulose lacquer or with acrylic lacquer, what procedure should be used?
Rub surface with thinner.
Rub surface with silicone polish remover.
Rub surface with rubbing compound.
7. Primer surfacers are used to provide adhesion.
True.
False.
8. What is the purpose of a bleeder sealer?
To prevent reds and maroons from bleeding through following coats.
To seal off scratches.
Provide adhesion on rusted surfaces.
9. What is the purpose of a tack rag?
It is used to wipe off dust from the surface immediately before spraying.
Special rag used for holding upholstery tacks.
Special cloth used to wipe off spray gun.
10. Is acrylic lacquer recommended for use on cars originally finished with lacquer?
Yes.
No.
11. Name four popular automotive refinishing materials.
12. Which once popular refinishing material has practically fallen out of use?
Synthetic enamel.
Nitrocellulose lacquer.

Chapter 26
PREPARING SURFACE
FOR PAINT

Before any paint is applied to an automobile it is important that the surface be prepared correctly. It must be smooth, clean and dry.

In many cases it is not necessary to remove the original finish, but it must be determined that the old finish has good adhesion, and that rust has not developed under the paint. A method of checking the adhesion is to sand through the finish and featheredge a small spot, Fig. 26-1. If the thin edge of the paint does not crumble or break, it is reasonable to assume there is no rust under that particular area. However, it is important to make such a check at several critical points of the vehicle: Along the lower edge of the doors, the rocker panels, and the area below the lower edge of the deck lid. Developing rust can usually be detected by a roughness and pitting of the surface. The paint over such areas must be removed down to the bare metal.

REMOVE WAX AND POLISH

All traces of wax, polish and grease must be removed. A specially blended wax and grease remover should be used to remove all traces of such foreign matter. Gasoline should not be used, as this often contains materials which will prevent good adhesion of the new paint. Reducers should never be used to clean up the surface, particularly when the car has been finished with acrylic lacquer, as acrylic will absorb reducer into the paint film and blistering and lifting will result.

When applying and removing the wax and grease remover, always use new, clean wiping cloths. Cloths that have been laundered often still contain a certain amount of grease or other materials that would be harmful and prevent good paint adherence.

The paint is usually removed by grinding, Fig. 26-2. First a No. 16 open-coat disk is used. This is followed by a No. 50 and then a No. 220 disk. All edges are then feathered with No. 320 and then No. 400 grit paper.

Some painters prefer to use an orbital type sander, claiming that there is less chance of gouging than with non-orbital types. A 240 grit paper usually is used. If the original finish is acrylic lacquer, sanding can be held to a minimum. In the case of acrylic enamel, the surface must be thoroughly sanded using No. 400 grit paper. Some manufacturers state their particular type of acrylic lacquer may be applied directly over the original acrylic lacquer; others state a sealer should be applied first.

If synthetic or acrylic enamel is applied over acrylic lacquer, a special sealer should be applied. The super-enamels used as original equipment on some makes of vehicles since 1958 are extremely hard and require thorough sanding to provide good adhesion

Fig. 26-1. Featheredging to check adherence of paint.

for the new paint. Putting enamel over old enamel will cover small sand scratches provided the final sanding has been done with No. 360 or finer grit abrasive.

Fig. 26-2. Illustrating how edge of paint is tapered back or featheredged.

Nitrocellulose lacquer will tend to show sand scratches in enamel unless the final sanding has been done with No. 400 grit abrasive. To reduce the sand scratches and reduce compounding of the new lacquer finish, a sealer is used, but it is necessary to refinish the entire panel.

Primer coats should not be applied until the bare metal has been treated with special metal conditioner to prevent future rusting. The etching action of metal conditioners produces maximum paint adherence.

Modern primer surfacers and glazing putties will fill almost any rough surface, but much time and material will be saved if the metal is quite smooth before such materials are applied.

After the surface has been cleaned and prepared for painting care must be exercised that the surface is not touched with hands, gloves or in any other manner. Checking the surface for smoothness by rubbing your hands over it should not be done before the final cleaning. Your hands always have a certain amount of oil on them, even after washing, and this is sufficient to destroy the durability, adherence and appearance of the new finish.

SPOT REPAIRS

When repairing small scratches and/or imperfections, only a small area requires treatment. Water wash and follow by washing with solvent. Then, featheredge repair area. Do not cut through primer if damage is minor. Lightly "wet sand" any rough surface, then featheredge to a smooth taper. Refinish.

For deep damage, featheredge and apply several coats of primer surfacer. When dry, sand surface and blend top coats into original finish.

If damage is extensive, or it there is excessive fading of original paint, refinish entire panel. Water wash panel. Then, wash with solvent, sand, featheredge and prime surface. When primer is dry, apply top coat of either acrylic lacquer or acrylic enamel. NOTE: Use paper towels (not shop towels) when using wax and silicone remover.

PAINTING FLEXIBLE PLASTIC PARTS

Flexible plastic parts, such as urethane body panels and bumpers, cannot be painted with ordinary acrylic lacquer or acrylic enamel methods. However, special acrylic lacquers with flexible additives are available. Urethane paints and materials are especially made with a flexible conditioner, so the cured film will flex without cracking. Urethane enamels are also available.

Follow manufacturer's recommendations for adding materials to flexible parts. First, clean surface with a special cleaner. Then, hand sand it with 240 grit treated paper. Reclean surface with special cleaner and apply a primer coat. Next, apply a double coat of special primer, and complete the job with a color coat. NOTE: Wear a respirator when applying urethane enamel.

Heat lamps help dry paint, but plastic parts must be shielded from excessive heat.

REFINISHING PLASTIC TRIM PARTS

Many interior body parts are now made of plastic. In general, there are three different types of plastic being used for interior parts. In the case of Fisher bodies installed on General Motors cars, the three types of plastic are known as:
1. ABS plastic.
2. Polypropylene plastic.
3. Vinyl plastic.

Vinyl plastic is used primarily for seat cushions and seat backs. Vinyl plastic parts should not be refinished. However, you should be able to determine which plastic part is which plastic material. For example, you must be able to distinguish ABS plastic from polypropylene. Different materials and procedures are used when repainting such parts.

DETERMINING TYPE OF PLASTIC

Polypropylene plastic is used in the majority of interior trim installations. To determine whether a part is made of ABS plastic or polypropylene, cut a small sliver from a hidden back side of the part. Place this sliver on a noncombustible surface and ignite it. Little, if any, smoke will come from the burning of polypropylene. ABS plastic, on the other hand, burns with a highly visible black smoke.

To determine if a part is made of vinyl plastic, heat a copper wire in a suitable flame until the wire glows and turns red. Touch the heated wire to the normally hidden side of the vinyl plastic so as to retain some of the plastic on the hot wire. Then, hold the wire with the retained plastic in the flame. The color of the flame should be green to turquoise blue if the plastic is of the polypropylene type.

PROCEDURE FOR PAINTING POLYPROPYLENE PARTS

A special primer designed for use on polypropylene parts is required. The proper procedure is to first wash the part with a cleaning solvent, following the instructions on the container. Then, apply a thin coat of primer to the polypropylene. Be sure the application of the primer includes all edges. Allow the primer to flash dry for one minute minimum, ten minutes maximum. During the flash period, apply conventional interior acrylic lacquer as required. Allow the part to dry before reinstalling it.

PROCEDURE FOR PAINTING HARD ABS PLASTIC PARTS

No primer is required when refinishing hard ABS plastic parts. Conventional acrylic lacquer or enamel adheres well to hard ABS plastic parts. The proper procedure is to first thoroughly wash the part with a paint finish cleaning solvent. Then, apply conventional interior lacquer or enamel. Apply only enough color for proper hiding to avoid washout or grain effect.

PAINTING SOFT VINYL AND FLEXIBLE ABS PARTS

The outer cover of flexible instrument panel cover assemblies and padded door trim assemblies frequently are made of ABS plastic modified with vinyl. The soft cushion padding under ABS covers usually is urethane foam plastic.

The paint system used for vinyl and plastic ABS of the flexible type involves the use of interior vinyl color and a clear vinyl top coat. No primer or primer sealer is required.

The proper procedure is to first wash the part with a vinyl cleaning and preparation solvent. Using a clean, lint-free cloth, wipe off cleaner while it is still wet. Then, apply interior vinyl color in wet coats, allowing enough flash time between coats. Apply only enough color for proper hiding. Before color flashed completely, apply one wet double coat of vinyl clear top coat. Use top coat of appropriate gloss level to match adjacent area.

REFINISHING METAL REPLACEMENT PARTS

Metal service replacement parts provided for Fisher bodies are painted with black, high-bake factory primer. For proper adhesion of color coats in service, the following procedure is recommended: First, wash the replacement part with cleaning solvent. Then, scuff-sand lightly with 500 grit paper. This is a dry sanding operation. Rewash the part.

Apply a high grade sealer, following the manufacturer's instructions. If necessary, apply primer-surfacer and sand smooth. Apply color coats as required.

Before replacing exterior parts or assemblies, check the condition of paint on all covered or hidden interior panels. If powder or scale rust is found in such areas, proceed as follows:

Remove rust with suitable wire brush, abrasive or liquid rust removing agent. Wash with detergent, then rinse and dry.

Apply a heavy coating of anti-corrosion compound to all cleaned hidden surfaces before installing the exterior replacement part. Also apply anti-corrosion compound to

Fig. 26-3. Applying rustproofing material to interior of a tail gate. (Stewart-Warner Corp.)

all inner surfaces of exterior body parts being installed.

Remember that rust causes premature vehicle failure. Surface rust caused by paint film failure can be seen immediately and repaired promptly. Any rust in unseen critical areas that are left unprotected spreads quickly. Special equipment is needed to apply rust proofing material, Fig. 26-3.

QUIZ - Chapter 26

1. Gasoline may be used to remove traces of wax and grease from the surface.
    True.
    False.

2. Is a cloth that has been laundered satisfactory for removing wax and grease from the surface to be painted?
    Yes.
    No.

3. What grit abrasive should be used for featheredging?

4. If acrylic enamel is applied over acrylic lacquer, a special sealer should be applied.
    True.
    False.

5. Which paint usually is used as a top coat when repairing scratches?
    Acrylic enamel.
    Acrylic lacquer.
    Either acrylic enamel or acrylic lacquer.

Chapter 27

PREPARING PAINT, MATCHING COLORS

Fig. 27-1. Color of original paint is indicated on tag on dash panel or on door frame. (AMC)

A very important part of painting an automobile is the selection and preparation of the paint. Selecting the correct color is particularly important when only a panel or portion of a panel is being repainted. In addition to selecting the correct color so that it will match the color of the rest of the vehicle and meet the desires of the car owner, it is also important that the paint be thoroughly mixed and thinned to the proper consistency for spraying.

COLOR IDENTIFICATION

To aid the automobile body painter, each type and color of paint is given an identifying number. This number appears on a tag under the hood. See Figs. 27-1 and 27-2. In some instances, it is mounted on the door frame. Information on these colors with identifying names and numbers is published by the paint manufacturer, and is supplied to auto body refinishers and paint suppliers in what are generally known as paint chip books. Fig. 27-3, shows a page from one of those books. As a result, the body refinisher has

only to note the paint number on the tag on the vehicle and use this number to order identical colors, when refinishing the vehicle.

PREPARING THE PAINT

Many paint failures are caused by improper mixing of the paint before spraying. Heavy pigments give color, opacity and specific performance properties to the paint. Some pigments weight seven or eight times as much as the liquid part of the paint. Because of this weight, they will settle to the bottom of

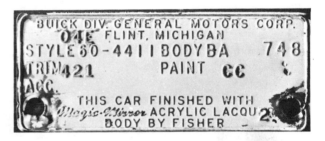

Fig. 27-2. Another type of tag giving color of original paint.

the container. This is particularly true of whites, chrome yellow, chrome orange, chrome green, red and yellow iron oxides. Most other pigments are light and fluffy and have little or no tendency to settle.

The consistency or viscosity of the liquid part of the paint has a great deal to do with the rate of settling. If its viscosity is high (a heavy consistency) the rate of settling will be slower. Heavy pigments will settle out of straight thinners in a few minutes. Careful judgment in thinning only sufficient material to do the job and discarding the small amount that is not used is a practice followed by many experienced painters.

Fig. 27-3. Typical page from color code book showing colors used on one make of vehicle in one year.

If a color which contains one or more of the heavy pigments is thinned to spraying consistency, and is allowed to stand 10 to 15 minutes without being stirred, it will settle enough in that time to be off-color when sprayed.

Factory-mixed lacquers and enamels are carefully proportioned at the factory to give the desired color, but it is important that they be carefully stirred before using. A good practice is, after a can of paint has been thoroughly stirred, is to empty it into the gun cup, wash the can clean with a little thinner and add this to the gun cup. In that way it will be sure that all of the pigment and solid matters will have been thoroughly mixed.

If the paint has been in inventory for an extended period and has settled out hard, the liquid part should be poured off and the solid part thoroughly broken up. Then pour back the liquid part and stir vigorously.

A clean spatula or a one inch wide clean wooden or plastic stirring paddle should be used for stirring. Above all, the implement must be clean and free from dirt, grease and other paint. Do not use a screwdriver or other tool for stirring.

Commercially mixed automotive paints are usually shipped at a high rate of viscosity as practical to aid in slowing down the rate of settling. It is, therefore, necessary to add thinners or reducer in order to obtain a viscosity that can be properly sprayed. A power driven shaker should be used for mixing paint whenever possible, Fig. 27-4.

When adding thinner or reducer, it should always be added slowly and stirred in at the same time. Adding thinner quickly may result in "seedy" looking paint jobs.

Each paint manufacturer has specific recommendations covering the amount of thinner, or reducer, to be added to lacquer, enamel, or acrylic. The amount to be added in some cases varies with the individual color. For example: One paint manufacturer recommends 1-1/2 parts thinner to one part of lacquer color. For enamel the same manufacturer recommends 4 parts of color to one of reducer. All manufacturers have particular recommendations for their products.

There are many different types of thinners available. Some are slower drying than others, some prevent moisture blush, and are designed for use on excessively damp, humid days. Others are for normal conditions. Whatever type is selected, the manufacturer's instructions should be carefully followed.

Fig. 27-4. Paint must be thoroughly mixed before spraying. Paint can is clamped in power mixer, which features an agitator at left and an electric motor at right.

COLOR MATCHING

Color matching is one of the most difficult jobs a painter has to do. Since women usually have a keener color perception than men, it pays to check with a woman when a difficult color matching job occurs.

If the entire vehicle has to be repainted, there is relatively no problem with color matching since the color prepared by the paint manufacturer closely matches the paint chips in the paint catalog. But in many cases only small areas of the car are to be painted. Then matching the color of the rest of the vehicle becomes a major problem if the original color has faded as the result of weather conditions. Some colors fade lighter, others become darker as they weather. Yellow, for example, fades quite rapidly. If the yellow fades from a cream, it usually becomes lighter. If the yellow fades from a green component of blue and yellow, the color usually becomes darker. To those who are not experienced in colors, and tones of colors, it comes as a surprise to learn that there are many different shades of black and also of white.

Every color weathers a little differently than any other color, depending upon its pigment composition. It has been found on occasion that if cars are parked always in the same position and location, the finish will fade more on one side of the vehicle than on the other. In general, the color on cars that are stored in a garage will change less than those that are always parked outside. Those cars operated in hot climates will fade more than those in colder areas. Also those cars which are rubbed and polished a lot generally fade more than those which are not polished.

Weathering and coloring change is most rapid during the first few months after the car has been painted, and then the rate of change slows considerably.

In order to provide customer satisfaction, many paint shops tint colors to match the weathered color on the car.

Although the ability to match colors is mostly a matter of experience, it must be emphasized that anyone with poor color perception cannot do such work successfully. Statisticians tell us that one man in 12 is partly or totally color blind. Men with normal color perception will find that with patience, observation and experience, they can do a good job of color matching.

For tinting work a number of single pigment colors are needed. Such colors must be uniform in tinting strength, and should be in lacquers, acrylic and enamel, as these three types will not mix satisfactorily.

Paint manufacturers supply such basic single pigment colors designed especially for auto painters as an aid in matching colors. Some thirty basic colors are available in each type of material, but for most work the following nine single pigment colors are sufficient:

White
Black Weak
Blue
Black Strong
Rich Brown
Green
Oxide Yellow
Oxide Red
Burnt Sienna

The art of knowing how tinting colors will behave in hundreds of different combinations is a matter of practice and experience. Each color has what is known as mass tone and tint tone. The mass tone can be judged from the color as it appears in the can, or as it is indicated on the painted panel. The tint tone of a color is a shade resulting from mixing a small amount of color with a large amount of white. A dark green mass tone, for example, will often give a blue tint tone. Some maroons have a violet or purple tint tone. Usually adding white to dark green does not give light green, or adding white to maroon does not produce light red. Small additions of tinting color will tint according to their tint tone, while large additions influence color according to their mass tone.

Polychromatic (multicolored) colors are particularly difficult to tint because they often have what is known as flop. That is the color looks different from an angle than it does straight on. When looking directly into the color, the tint tones have the greatest effect, while at an angle the mass tones show the most.

Paint manufacturers provide equipment designed to aid and simplify matching colors. One type of equipment is shown in Fig. 27-5.

When tinting a color some device must always be used for measuring the quantities being used, and a list of colors and amount used on each paint job should be kept. A lot of paint will be saved, if only a small amount is tinted initially. Remember that color tone will change as it dries, and in general the tint should be kept in the light side until a final dried match is determined. And color should always be checked in the daylight as well as artificial light. When a refinished color matches in one light, but not in another, it usually indicates that the same pigments were not used in the refinish material as in the original material.

MATCHING COLORS WITH SPRAY GUN

It is important to remember that the strength or tone of a color is affected by the manner in which it is sprayed. Spraying technique can change the color considerably. This is particularly true when high polychromatic colors (that is colors with high metallic content are sprayed).

Too great a distance between the gun and the surface of the work will produce a dry spray and tend to lighten the color, Fig. 27-6. A wet spray, produced by holding the gun too close to the work will darken the color. Insufficient air pressure will also darken the color. The type of thinner may affect the color tone.

The number of coats applied will also affect the color or shade. Most colors, particularly pastel colors, will produce a lighter shade by spraying an excessive number of coats, and darker shades will be the result if a lesser number of coats are applied. As a general rule the thickness of automotive finishes is .004 in. The undercoat will be .002 in. thick, and the color coat .002 in. thick. To obtain a good color match, the film thickness of the refinish paint should be the same as the original.

The following method may be used to check for difference in color. First use a rubbing compound to clean an area of the original finish. Select an area that can be viewed from several different angles to observe the

Fig. 27-5. Supplies and equipment used to accurately match colors and mix paint.

light reflection. A good spot is a lower corner of the trunk lid, as it can be raised or lowered to permit easier viewing for light reflection. Rubbing compound should be used because it has enough abrasive action to cut through wax

Normal spray 6" to 8"   Dry spray.
Air pressure 40 to 45 lbs.   Too far away 10" to 12"
at the gun.   Too much air pressure.

Fig. 27-6. Note how excess air pressure and holding the spray gun too far from the surface affects color of paint.

and oxidized finish, and brings out the true shade of the existing color. Then clean the area with a wax and grease remover, to remove any traces of oil left by the rubbing compound. Do not let the cleaner dry, but wipe it dry with clean (not laundered) cloth. With the area clean, take a piece of masking paper about 18 in. square and cut a 2 in. hole in the center. Place this hole over the cleaned area and hold the masking paper in position with masking tape, Fig. 27-7. Now with the correct color correctly reduced and with the right air pressure, spray the 2 in. hole in the normal manner. Remove the masking paper and allow the sprayed area to dry. The newly finished area can be accurately compared with the original finish.

Fig. 27-7. *Spraying a restricted area helps determine accuracy of paint match.*

Because there can be a difference in gloss between the compounded area and the newly sprayed test patch, it may be desirable to wet the area with cleaner's naphtha. If there is a color shade difference between the original finish and the test patch, it then becomes necessary to determine which way the color is off, and how much.

First decide which way the color is off. If still in doubt as to which way the tinting should progress, take a small amount of the reduced color and start by adding a darker or lighter shade, and note the result. After the lighter or darker problem has been solved, the proper tinting color can be chosen to further the tinting process.

It is always a good idea to start by taking a small amount of reduced color in case you over-tint. Any time any one color is added to excess, it throws the entire color formula out of balance. To compensate for it, a corresponding amount of each of the colors that it takes to make up the original, should be added to bring the color back to its original shade.

This is impractical, however, and the easiest thing to do is to use some of the original material that was held back. Only a drop or two of base color should be added at a time. Also it should be remembered that contrasting colors change the shade more quickly than colors of a close hue.

The chart, Fig. 27-8, can be used as a guide when tinting.

Now by deciding which way the color should go, and by use of the tinting chart, the tinting color is selected and added to a small amount of the reduced color. This in turn is sprayed just to one side and overlapping over the first test patch. This process is repeated until an exact match is obtained.

In general, metallic colors can be tinted in the same manner as solid colors, with the exception of dealing with the metallic effect. These colors must definitely be viewed from different angles when checking the test patches to insure getting the same light reflection quality from the metallic particles disbursed through the paint film. In viewing a comparison patch against the original finish, with the light at your back, look directly into the test patch color. If it appears too dark, it needs more metallic tinting material. If the patch is too light, it has too much metallic and needs some of all the other colors used in formulating the shade.

Now look at the patch from an oblique angle. In that way you get away from the distraction of the reflection of the metallic particles and allow the eye to see the basic shade. This color may be tinted using the same procedure as described for a solid color. Keep in mind it should not be attempted to make a large amount of color change in a metallic shade, particularly in the so-called "high glamour" colors. They are formulated with a high content of clear material in order to make the material more transparent and thereby allow more of the reflecting metallic particles to be seen.

So with a high percentage of clear, it stands to reason there is very little color pigment in this type of material. Therefore, just a small amount of tinting color is needed to make a decided change in shade. Also in these "high glamour" colors, there are usually not less than two kinds or sizes of metallic particles. This makes it difficult to know what kind or how much to add to a given color when more metallic is needed to change the effect for a better match. Medium metallic tends to lighten a color "face on," but has little effect on the angle view. Fine metallic lightens a color from the angle view. Coarse metallic lightens a color "face on," but less than medium or fine metallic. Coarse metallic is used mainly in high glamour colors.

Some custom colors are very difficult to duplicate. One is a metallic color in which the metallic particles are not aluminum flakes. In some cases gilt or bronze powder is used.

Another type of finish that is difficult to

COLOR	IF COLOR TOO STRONG ADD	IF COLOR TOO LIGHT ADD	IF COLOR TOO GREEN ADD	IF COLOR TOO RED ADD	IF COLOR TOO YELLOW ADD	IF COLOR TOO BLUE ADD	IF COLOR TOO "DIRTY" ADD
Gray	White	Black	Mix White and Oxide Red	Medium Green	Mix White and touch of Indo Blue	Mix Med. Yellow and either Cadmium Red or Oxide Red	Mix White and either Blue Toner or Indo Blue
Blue	White	Blue or Blue Toner or Indo Blue	Deep Maroon	Medium Green	Deep Maroon	Mix Med. Yellow and either Cadmium Red or Oxide Red	Mix White and Blue Toner
Green	White or Yellow	Medium Green or Blue or Blue Toner		Mix Blue Toner and Med. Yellow and Medium Green	Blue Toner	Mix Med. Yellow and either Cadmium Red or Oxide Red	Mix Med. Yellow and Blue Toner
Red	Mix White and Cadmium Red	Oxide Red or Light Maroon			Light Maroon	Oxide Red	Mix Light Maroon and Touch of White
Maroon	Light Maroon or Cadmium Red	Deep Maroon			Deep Maroon	Light Maroon or Oxide Red or Medium Yellow	Mix Deep Maroon and touch of White
Yellow	White or Medium Yellow	Ferrite Yellow or Medium Yellow	Mix White and touch of Cadmium Red	Mix White and Light Green	White		Mix White and Medium Yellow
Orange	Medium Yellow	Cadmium Red or Orange	Mix Cadmium Red and Medium Yellow	Medium Yellow	Cadmium Red or Toluidine Red		Mix Med. Yellow and either Cadmium Red or Toluidine Red
Ivory	White	Ferrite Yellow or Medium Yellow	Orange or touch of Cadmium Red	Mix White and Light Green	White		Mix White and touch of either Ferrite Yellow or Medium Yellow
Brown	Mix White and either Orange or Burnt Sienna	Mix Black and Medium Yellow and Oxide Red	Oxide Red or Burnt Sienna	Mix Light Green and Burnt Sienna (Add White if Necessary)	Mix Oxide Red and Black		Mix Ferrite Yellow and Oxide Red and touch of either Orange or Burnt Sienna
Cream	White	Ferrite Yellow or Medium Yellow	Mix White and either Orange or Cadmium Red	Mix Medium Yellow and White (Add Light Green if necessary)	White		Mix White and touch of either Ferrite Yellow or Medium Yellow
Tan	White	Burnt Sienna or Mix Ferrite Yellow and Black	Cadmium Red or Toluidine Red (Add White if necessary)	Mix White and Touch of Light Green	Mix White and either Cadmium Red or Toluidine Red		Mix White and either Oxide Red or Ferrite Yellow

GLAMOUR COLOR	IF COLOR TOO GREEN ADD	IF COLOR TOO BLUE ADD	IF COLOR TOO "DIRTY" ADD
Blue	Indo Blue or Deep Maroon	Green Toner	Blue Toner and touch of White
Green	Blue Toner	Old Gold	Touch of White
Brown	Burnt Sienna and Light Maroon	Old Gold or Burnt Sienna	Burnt Sienna or Old Gold
Maroon		Burnt Sienna or Light Maroon	Cadmium Red

CAUTION: A few drops of shading color may be enough, especially when the fresh color is too yellow, blue, green or red. Occasionally, two shading steps are needed for an accurate match. Glamour colors are very sensitive. Be very careful toning colors with these bases: Old Gold Toner, Blue Toner, Green Toner, Indo Blue.

If the color contains not more than 20 parts of the glamour color base, use the regular tinting instructions. If the color contains more than 20 parts of the glamour color base, follow the instructions in the small chart.

If necessary, add polychrome base, a very small amount at a time, to maintain brilliance.

Fig. 27-8. Chart which may be used as a guide when tinting.

match is the "candy apple" finish. This attractive colorful finish has an amazing appearance of depth as obtained by spraying many coats of tinted clear material (usually a rich maroon or lime green) over a metallic base coat. The base coat often used resembles burnished brass. The clear material has just enough color to give a definite cast or shade and as much as twenty-five coats of it may have been sprayed over the base coat to give an illusion of depth.

Acrylic and conventional lacquer are tinted to the desired shade in the same manner as just described. However, because acrylic has greater durability and does not fade as readily as lacquer, matching colors is not so great a problem. Colors in enamel are more difficult to match because it takes so long for the enamel to dry in order to compare the new color with the original.

QUIZ - Chapter 27

1. How can you determine the color used to finish the vehicle originally?
    Comparing with color code books.
    Noting color code number placed on tag on vehicle.
    Read owner's manual.

2. It is not necessary to thoroughly stir the paint before using.
    True.
    False.
3. When adding thinner or reducer, it should be added as quickly as possible.
    True.
    False.
4. All colors fade lighter.
    True.
    False.
5. When is color change most rapid?
    First few months after painting.
    After car is a year old.
6. Polychromatic colors are easy to tint.
    True.
    False.
7. Can spraying technique affect the tone of the color being sprayed?
    Yes.
    No.
8. Will the number of coats being sprayed affect the color or shade?
    Yes.
    No.
9. What is the approximate thickness of automotive finishes?
    .010 in.
    .002 in.
    .004 in.
    .005 in.

Showing the location of heat shields made necessary by the use of catalytic converters. Converter temperatures are in excess of 1000 deg. F. (538 °C). Location of heat shields varies with different cars (Chrysler shown). Heat shields MUST NOT be painted.

Chapter 28
SPRAY PAINTING EQUIPMENT

Fig. 28-1. Using spray gun to paint a car.

Automotive vehicles, both passenger car and commercial, are painted with a spray gun, Fig. 28-1. By using such equipment, the paint is applied evenly and without any brush strokes to mar the appearance and smoothness of the finished surface. However, skill and care are required in the operation of the spray gun, in order to obtain good results.

Fig. 28-2. Spray gun used for painting cars.

THE SPRAY GUN

The paint spray gun, Fig. 28-2, is a device which uses air pressure to atomize sprayable material and apply it to a surface. Air and paint enter the gun through separate passages and are mixed and ejected at the air cap in a controlled pattern, Fig. 28-3. Adjustments are provided to control the air pressure and the amount of paint being sprayed.

Fig. 28-3. Shape of spray from spray gun.

There are two basic types of paint spraying equipment. One type, Figs. 28-1 and 28-4, has the gun and paint container forming a single unit, while the other type has the paint container separate from the spray gun, Fig. 28-5.

These two basic types can be further divided into bleeder and nonbleeder, external and internal mix, and pressure, gravity or suction feed guns.

The spray gun designed without an air valve is known as a bleeder type gun. Air passes through the gun at all times, preventing pres-

Fig. 28-4. *Using spray gun with paint cup attached.*

Fig. 28-5. *Spray gun with paint in separate container.*

sure build-up in the air line, and is, used with small air compressors of limited capacity and pressure. No pressure controlling device such as an unloader, or pressure switch, is provided. The trigger controls only the flow of paint in this type gun.

A nonbleeder type gun is equipped with an air valve which shuts off the air when the trigger is released. In this type gun, the trigger controls both the air and the flow of paint.

A spray gun that mixes and atomizes air and paint outside the air cap is known as an external mix gun, Fig. 28-6. This type of gun can be used for spraying all types of fluid materials, and is the type best suited for spraying fast drying materials, such as lacquers.

An internal mix gun mixes air and material inside the cap before expelling them, Fig. 28-7. This type of gun is used for spraying slow drying materials, not containing any abrasive. It is frequently used for spraying flat wall paint or outside house paint.

A suction feed gun utilizes a stream of compressed air to create a vacuum so that paint is forced from an attaching container. This type gun is usually limited to containers of one quart capacity, and is easily identified by the fluid tip extending slightly beyond the air cap, Fig. 28-8. Such guns are used primarily when there are many color changes and small amounts of paint, such as is the case when refinishing an automobile.

A spray gun with an air cap is not necessarily designed to create a vacuum. In the case of a pressure feed gun, Fig. 28-9, the fluid tip is generally flush with the air cap

Fig. 28-6. *External mix gun.*

Fig. 28-7. *Internal mix gun mixes air and material inside the cap.*

Fig. 28-8. *Suction feed gun.*

Fig. 28-9. *Pressure feed gun.*

and material is forced to the gun by air pressure from a tank, cup or pump. This type of gun is used extensively when large amounts of the same color are to be sprayed such as production finishing of automobiles.

Other types of spray guns are available for production finishing of various types and are usually adaptations of some of the previously described guns. Such guns are usually automatic in their operation and are mounted on special fixtures and movable conveyors.

DETAILS OF SPRAY GUNS

A typical spray gun such as is used in the refinishing of automobiles is shown in Fig. 28-10. The principal parts of this DeVilbiss Spray Gun are: Air Cap A, Fluid Tip B, Fluid Needle C, Trigger D, Fluid Adjustment Screw E, Air Valve F, Spreader Adjustment G, Gun Body H.

As shown in Fig. 28-10, the air cap is located at the front of the gun and directs the compressed air into the material stream to atomize it and form it into a spray. The cross section of this spray is called the spray pattern, Fig. 28-3. There are various style caps producing different sizes and shapes of patterns for all types of applications. Air caps are either of the external or internal mix types.

SELECTING THE AIR CAP

There are two types of air caps: External and Internal Mix Types. The external mix caps, Fig. 28-6, are used with either suction or pressure feed and eject air through one or more holes to atomize the paint. External mix caps may have from one to as many as four orifices for production spraying.

The internal mix caps, Fig. 28-7, mix air and material inside the gun before ejecting them through a single slot or round orifice and are used only with pressure feed, and consequently are used primarily for spraying heavy viscous (sticky) materials.

Multiple jet caps have the advantage of providing better atomization for such materials and synthetics and heavy body lacquers. Also higher pressures can be used on more viscous materials with less danger of

Fig. 28-10. Details of typical spray gun as used in auto paint shop, A—Air cap, B—Fluid tip, C—Fluid needle, D—Trigger, E—Fluid adjustment screw, F—Air valve, G—Spreader adjustment valve.

distorting the spray pattern. For materials that can be sprayed at lower pressures, multiple jet caps provide better atomization with less air.

FLUID TIP

The nozzle directly behind the air cap is known as the fluid tip. It meters and directs the paint into the air streams. The fluid tip forms a seat for the fluid needle which shuts off the flow of material. Fluid tips are available in a variety of nozzle sizes and the larger the nozzle, the greater the amount of material that can be sprayed. Sizes range from .086 in. to .110 in. The size can be identified by a letter or dimension stamped on the fluid tip and needle. Sizes ranging from .070 in. to .041 in. are most frequently used for automobile spray painting. To obtain a given rate of fluid flow, pressure feed setups operate with smaller tips than suction feed. Tips and needles must always be the same size. For suction feed guns, such as are usually used when repainting automobiles, a nozzle size of .041 in. is often used.

SPREADER ADJUSTMENT VALVE

To control the air to the air horn, a spreader adjustment valve, Fig. 28-10, is provided. By this means the size of the spray pattern is controlled.

FLUID NEEDLE ADJUSTMENT

The fluid needle adjustment controls the travel of the fluid needle, and in that way permits more or less material to pass through the fluid tip.

CARE OF PAINT SPRAY GUN

Paint spray guns should be cleaned immediately after use. If this is not done, the paint will dry in the nozzles making cleaning exceedingly difficult.

To clean a suction feed gun and cup, first loosen the cup from the gun and while the paint tube is still in the cup, unscrew the air cap about two or three turns. Hold a cloth over the air cap and pull the trigger. Air diverted into the fluid passageways forces material back into the container, Fig. 28-11.

Fig. 28-11. *Material is forced back into container, when cloth is held over air cap and trigger is pulled.*

Fig. 28-12. *Solvent is being sprayed through gun to flush out fluid passages.*

Next empty cup of material and replace with a small quantity of clean solvent. Spray solvent through the gun to flush out fluid passages, Fig. 28-12. Wipe off the gun with a solvent soaked rag or, if necessary, use a fibre bristle brush moistened with thinner and scrub the gun. Then remove the air cap and clean as follows: The air cap should be removed from the gun and cleaned by simply immersing in clean solvent and then drying by blowing it off with compressed air. If small holes become clogged, soak the cap in solvent. If reaming out the hole is still necessary, use a wooden match stick, a broom straw, or other similar material. A wire or nail should not be used as this may permanently damage the cap.

A pressure feed system is cleaned by following this procedure: Back up the air pressure regulator adjusting screw on the tank, release pressure from the tank by means of a relief valve, or safety valve. Loosen spray gun air cap ring three turns. Hold a cloth over air cap and pull trigger to force material back into tank, Fig. 28-13. Remove fluid hose from gun and attach it to a hose cleaner, A, Fig. 28-13. Run air and solvent through the hose and fluid tube on the tank. Dry hose with compressed air. Clean air cap and tip as described in connection with suction type guns. Clean out tank and reassemble for future use.

A hose cleaner is a device which forces

Fig. 28-13. *Holding cloth over cap and pulling trigger, forces material back into tank.*

air and solvent through fluid hose and guns, cleaning them of paint residue.

Spray guns should never be immersed in solvent. Such a practice allows sludge and dirt to collect in the air passages of the gun. Such accumulations will then be blown on the surface being sprayed the next time the gun is used. Solvents also remove lubricants and dry out the packings of the spray gun.

Caustic alkaline solutions should never be used to clean spray guns, because they will corrode the aluminum and die cast parts of which spray guns are made.

Spray guns require occasional lubrication. The fluid needle packing A, Fig. 28-14, air valve packing B, and the trigger bearing screw C, require a drop or two of light oil occasionally. The fluid needle D should be coated with petrolatum.

Fig. 28-14. *Points requiring lubrication, A—Fluid needle packing, B—Air valve packing, C—Trigger bearing screw.*

PRESSURE AND SUCTION FEED GUN

Most auto paint shops are equipped with the suction feed type spray guns in which the spray gun is attached directly to the cup, Fig. 28-4. However, when painting any surface except a vertical surface, it is necessary to hold the gun at an angle with the result the applied thickness of paint will be uneven. The suction feed gun employs a partial vacuum created by the air stream just outside the fluid tip of the spray gun. Paint in

the attached cup is therefore under atmospheric pressure via a vent hole in the top of the cup cover. This pressure forces the paint

Fig. 28-15. *Spray gun and separate paint container.*

up the fluid tube into the path of the air jets, and in that way becomes atomized.

However, if the gun and its container are tilted (as would be necessary when painting the top or the hood) paint would flow over the vent hole and air pressure will no longer reach the paint to force it up the fluid tube. Another disadvantage is the same air flow that atomizes and sprays the paint is used to operate the syphon. In many cases the amount of air pressure required to operate the syphon is greater than that needed to atomize the paint. This is particularly true when painting large areas. With the fluid adjustment wide open for maximum pattern size, the atomization pressure could be 25 to 35 lbs. higher than needed.

In addition, the amount of paint that can be sprayed is limited to about 12 oz. per minute.

To overcome these disadvantages, many

paint shops are turning to pressure feed systems, such as shown in Fig. 28-5. In this type system, paint is fed from a pressurized tank that is separate from the gun, Fig. 28-15. Atomization here is fed through the gun in the same manner as suction feed. The advantage of this system is that the gun is not dependent

Fig. 28-16. Details of a two-stage, four cylinder air compressor. Each large cylinder is paired off with and is connected to a small cylinder by way of twin intercoolers. A—Outlet valve. B—Inlet valve. C—High-pressure cylinder. D—Crankcase. E—Crankshaft. F—Piston. G—Connecting rod. H—Air filter mounted on top of twin intercooler.

upon atomization air pressure, and consequently the air pressure can be set at its proper level without affecting the flow of paint. Paint flow can be adjusted independently with the fluid adjusting screw without changing atomization air pressure. In other words, two separate controls are provided, one for air and the other for fluid. The paint is in a container separate from the gun, which leaves the gun free of the weight and restricting size of the cup. Most important, it leaves the gun free so that it can be used at any angle. Also more paint can be applied in the same amount of time.

However, more skill is required to use a pressure feed system than a suction or syphon system. The reason is that the greater paint flow requires faster and fewer passes of the gun to prevent flooding and consequent sagging of the paint.

TYPES OF COMPRESSORS

The compressors used for spray painting are of two basic types known as single-stage and two-stage compressors.

A single-stage compressor has only a single cylinder and provides pressures up to 100 psi (pounds per square inch). A two-stage compressor, Figs. 28-16 and 28-17, pairs two cylinders of unequal size with an intercooler between the two cylinders. It is

Fig. 28-17. Complete air compressor and storage tank.

used for pressures of over 100 psi. In the two-stage compressor, air is compressed first in the larger of the two cylinders, this is the low-pressure cylinder, and as a result of being compressed the temperature of the air is increased. From the low-pressure cylinder the air passes into an intercooler where its temperature is reduced. Then it passes to the smaller cylinder where it is further compressed and then forced into the storage tank.

COMPRESSOR SIZE

Compressors must be of adequate size to supply all the requirements of the shop. If the air compressor is for the paint department only, the air requirements would include air for the spray guns, pneumatic lifts, pneumatic fender hammers, vacuum cleaner. If the same compressor is to be used to supply the air for the entire shop, then all of the tools and equipment must be included. The amount of air needed to operate the various types of shop tools and equipment is as follows:

For example, from Chart No. 1, determine the average free air consumption required to operate all the tools in the department, or a shop. Spray guns require 8.5 cu. ft. per minute. If three guns are being used, the total

CHART NO. 1

Quantity	Type Device	Air Pres. Range	Avg. Free Air Cons.	Total Avg. Air
	Air Filter Cleaner	70-100	3.0	
	Air Hammer	70-100	16.5	
	Body Polisher	70-100	2.0	
	Body Sander	70-100	5.0	
	Brake Tester	70-100	3.5	
	Carbon Remover	70-100	3.0	
	Car Rocker	120-150	5.75	
	Car Washer	70-100	8.5	
	Dusting Gun (Blow gun)	70-100	2.5	
	Engine Cleaner	70-100	5.0	
	Fender Hammer	70-100	8.75	
	Grease Gun (high pressure)	120-150	3.0	
	Hoist (one ton)	70-100	1.0	
	*Hydraulic Lift	145-175	5.25	
	Paint Spray Gun (production)	70-100	8.5	
	Paint Spray Gun (touch-up)	70-100	2.25	
	Pneu. Garage Door	120-150	2.0	
	Radiator Tester	70-100	1.0	
	Rim Stripper	120-150	6.0	
	Spark Plug Cleaner	70-100	5.0	
	Spark Plug Tester	70-100	.5	
	Spray Gun (Undercoating)	70-100	19.0	
	Spring Oiler	70-100	3.75	
	Tire Changer	120-150	1.0	
	Tire Inflation Line	120-150	1.5	
	Tire Spreader	120-150	1.0	
	Trans. & Diff. Flusher	70-100	3.0	
	Vacuum Cleaner	120-150	6.5	

*For 8000 lbs. capacity. Add .65 cfm for each additional 1000 lbs. cap.

CHART NO. 2

Compressor Pressures per Square inch		COLUMN A Average Service Station or Garage Use Free Air Consumption in Cubic Feet per Minute of Total Equipment	COLUMN B Continuous Operation Free Air Consumption Free Air Consumption Cubic Feet per Minute of Total Equipment	COM-PRESSOR Horse-power
Cut-in	Cut-out			
		10.6- 13.6	3.1- 3.9	1
80	100	13.7- 20.3	4.0- 5.8	1-1/2
		20.4- 26.6	5.9- 7.6	2
		30.5- 46.2	8.8-13.2	3
		46.3- 60.0	13.3-20.0	5
		60.1- 73.0	20.1-29.2	7-1/2
100	125	73.1-100.0	29.3-40.0	10
		100.0-125.0	40.1-50.0	15
		up to - 3.8	up to - 1.1	1/2
		3.9- 7.3	1.2- 2.1	3/4
120	150	7.4- 10.1	2.2- 2.9	1
		10.2- 15.0	3.0- 4.3	1-1/2
		15.1- 20.00	4.4- 5.7	2
		up to - 11.9	up to - 3.4	1
		12.0- 18.5	3.5- 5.3	1-1/2
		18.6- 24.2	5.4- 6.9	2
		24.3- 36.4	7.0-10.4	3
140	175	36.5- 51.0	10.5-17.0	5
		51.1- 66.0	17.1-26.4	7-1/2
		66.1- 88.2	26.5-35.3	10
		88.3-120.0	35.4-48.0	15

will be three times 8.5, or 25.5 cfm. After all the needs of the shop have been totaled, note the highest pressure required for any of the tools or equipment. Then using Chart No. 2, select the pressure range capable of meeting the maximum pressure requirements. Within that range, locate the line indicating the air consumption adequate for the shop requirement. On the same line, in the next column, is the size of the compressor needed.

For suction feed guns, the compressor should deliver a minimum of 11.5 cfm and for pressure feed guns it should deliver 14 cfm. A compressor of the preceding size is adequate in shops where the gun is used intermittently, as the unit will have time to cool off during periods when the gun is not being used. When the spraying operation is continuous, a compressor of one-third higher capacity is required.

CARE OF COMPRESSORS

The crankcase of the air compressor should be filled to the proper level with a good grade of motor oil. Most manufacturers specify S.A.E. 10 for most conditions, and S.A.E. 20

Fig. 28-18. Type of transformer or regulator.

for temperatures above 100 deg. F. Oil level should be checked at least once each week and the oil changed every three months. Electric motor bearings should be oiled monthly unless they are of the grease-packed type.

Belt tension should be maintained so that there is no slippage. Cooling fins on compressor and intercooler should be kept clean and free of dust. The air cleaner on the air intake should be cleaned weekly, or oftener, if the compressor is located in a dusty area. The drain cock on the air storage tank should be opened monthly to drain any condensed moisture that may be present. To insure the operation of the safety valve, it should be operated by hand once each week.

AIR FOR PAINTING

In order for the finished painted surface to be smooth and without defects, it is essential that the compressed air supplied to the spray gun be cleaned and free from all dirt, moisture and oil. Also air pressure must be maintained between 80 and 100 lb.

In order to supply such clean air, and maintain the desired pressure, many paint shops provide a separate compressor used for painting only, Fig. 28-17. Another compressor being provided to supply other needs of the shop. The compressor used for painting should always be maintained in top-notch condition. In addition to using a special compressor for spraying paint, the system is provided with an air transformer and/or oil and moisture separators.

AIR TRANSFORMER

The air transformer, Fig. 28-18, as designed for use with spray painting equipment, is able to maintain the pressure of air supply to the spray gun within narrow limits and also prevent oil, dirt and water from entering the air lines, which would spoil the paint job.

A high quality air transformer will maintain air pressure within three-quarter pound variation for each ten pound fluctuation in the main line, and will also extract oil, water, and other foreign materials.

Various types of filter elements are used to filter out all foreign matter from the line.

In addition to having the filter elements of the replaceable type, drain cocks are provided, so that oil and moisture can be easily drained from the system.

Air transformers without cleaners are also available. When transformers of that type are used, it is necessary to use individual oil, dirt, and moisture separators.

In operation the air transformer catches dirt, oil and moisture. It does this by means of baffles, centrifugal force, expansion chambers, impingement plates, and filters. The transformers allow only clean, dry air to emerge from the outlets. The air regulating valves provide positive control, insuring uniform regulated pressure. Gauges indicate air pressure, and valves provide outlets for hose lines to the spray guns and other equipment. The drain valve provides for elimination for accumulated sludge, dirt and moisture.

LOCATING COMPRESSORS AND TRANSFORMER

It is advisable to place the air compressor and air transformer as close to the paint spray booth as possible. In that way the air lines are kept short. This will reduce the amount of moisture condensing in the pipes.

The transformer should be installed in the paint booth for convenience in reading gauges and operating the valves. In addition, it should be installed at least 25 ft. from the compressor.

Piping should be as direct as possible. If a large number of fittings are used, large size pipe should be installed to help overcome the excessive pressure drop. The take-off for the transformer should be from the top of the line as shown at C, Fig. 28-19. Piping should slope toward the compressor, or a drain leg D, Fig. 28-19, should be installed at the end of the air line, or at the end of each branch, to provide for drainage of moisture from the air line. Valves at the lower end of the drain leg should be opened each morning to drain any accumulated condensation, and the drain cock on the transformer should also be opened daily in order to drain the unit.

Fig. 28-19. Air piping should be direct and takeoffs should be made from the top of the line.

Piping from compressor to transformer must be of sufficient size for the volume of air passed. Pipe size recommendations being as follows:

MINIMUM PIPE SIZE RECOMMENDATIONS

COMPRESSING OUTFIT		MAIN AIR LINE	
SIZE	CAPACITY	LENGTH	SIZE
1-1/2 & 2 H.P.	6 to 9 C.F.M.	Over 50 ft.	3/4"
3 & 5 H.P.	12 to 20 C.F.M.	Up to 200 ft. Over 200 ft.	3/4" 1"
5 to 10 H.P.	20 to 40 C.F.M.	Up to 100 ft. Over 100 to 200 ft. Over 200 ft.	3/4" 1" 1-1/4"
10 to 15 H.P.	40 to 60 C.F.M.	Up to 100 ft. Over 100 to 200 ft. Over 200 ft.	1" 1-1/4" 1-1/2"

HOSE SIZE

It is important to use hose of adequate size when connecting the spray gun to the air transformer. Resistance to the flow of air or paint, as the case may be, increases rapidly as the diameter of the hose decreases.

For maintenance refinishing of automobiles, two types of hose are used: Air hose and paint hose. Air hose usually has a red rubber cover, although on small low pressure systems the hose may be black and orange braid covered. The paint or fluid hose is black or brown.

For automotive refinishing the fluid hose used for large guns is usually 1/2 in. or 3/8 in. inside diameter. For small guns, such as are used with 1/4 and 1/3 HP compressor outfit, 5/16 in. inside diameter hose is generally used. For spraying underbody coatings, 3/4 in. inside diameter hose is specified.

The air hose from compressor or transformer to the spray gun is usually 5/16 in. ID hose. Hose of 1/4 in. inside diameter may be used for small guns provided the hose length does not exceed 12 ft.

If a pressure feed tank is used, 7/16 in. inside diameter air hose is used from the compressor to the pressure feed tank on large units, and 5/16 in. inside diameter on small units.

PRESSURE DROP

Pressure drop is the loss of air pressure due to friction between the source of air and point of usage. This loss can become quite serious particularly on long distances and when small diameter hose is used. The following table should be consulted to determine pressure drop when locating compressor and transformer, and when purchasing hose.

tion, built to confine an exhaust overspray and fumes resulting from spray painting or similar operations.

There are two major reasons for placing vehicles in a spray booth while they are being painted.

1. Dust is excluded and in that way will not settle on the vehicle while the paint is being applied, nor while it is drying.

2. Paint booths are provided with exhaust fans which force out the paint odors and thereby reduce fire hazards, and also greatly improve working conditions for the painter, which in turn results in less sickness and lost time.

Painting materials and fumes are highly flammable, and when spraying is done on the open shop floor, where sparks from welding are common, fire may result.

If a commercial booth is not available, a room approximately 0 ft. high, 14 ft. wide and 25 ft. long may be used. Adequate lighting to eliminate all shadows should be provided. an exhaust fan capable of maintaining air movement of 100 linear feet per minute throughout the area is also necessary. A filtered air intake is another requirement. To prevent contamination of the newly painted vehicle, the air spray may be used as a drying area. Or, another clean, dry, enclosed area should be provided.

TABLE OF AIR PRESSURE DROP

AIR PRESSURE DROP AT SPRAY GUN

SIZE OF AIR HOSE INSIDE DIAMETER	5-FOOT LENGTH	10-FOOT LENGTH	15-FOOT LENGTH	20-FOOT LENGTH	25-FOOT LENGTH	50-FOOT LENGTH
1/4-inch	Lbs.	Lbs.	Lbs.	Lbs.	Lbs.	Lbs.
At 40 lbs. pressure	6	8	9-1/2	11	12-3/4	24
At 50 lbs. pressure	7-1/2	10	12	14	16	28
At 60 lbs. pressure	9	12-1/2	14-1/2	16-3/4	19	31
At 70 lbs. pressure	10-3/4	14-1/2	17	19-1/2	22-1/2	34
At 80 lbs. pressure	12-1/4	16-1/2	19-1/2	22-1/2	25-1/2	37
At 90 lbs. pressure	14	18-3/4	22	25-1/4	29	39-1/2
5/16-inch						
At 40 lbs. pressure	2-1/4	2-3/4	3-1/4	3-1/2	4	8-1/2
At 50 lbs. pressure	3	3-1/2	4	4-1/2	5	10
At 60 lbs. pressure	3-3/4	4-1/2	5	5-1/2	6	11-1/2
At 70 lbs. pressure	4-1/2	5-1/4	6	6-3/4	7-1/4	13
At 80 lbs. pressure	5-1/2	6-1/4	7	8	8-3/4	14-1/2
At 90 lbs. pressure	6-1/2	7-1/2	8-1/2	9-1/2	10-1/2	16

SPRAY BOOTHS

A spray booth is a compartment, room or enclosure, generally of fireproof construc-

In many cities fire underwriters require that automotive vehicles be painted in spray booths designed for the purpose. But even if such requirements are not in force, it always

Fig. 28-20. Type of drive-through spray booth.

pays to use a spray booth. The initial cost is soon offset by better paint jobs and improved health of workers.

There are two basic types of spray booths: 1. Dry type. 2. Air washer type.

Some variations of the dry type booth are used almost exclusively by auto body refinishers while the air washer type is used in production work.

In the dry type spray booth, Fig. 28-20, contaminated air is drawn through baffles or removable filters and is expelled directly outside. In the watertight spray booth, air is drawn through a series of water curtains and baffles to remove solids from the overspray, before it is exhausted. Commercially constructed booths are desirable, but some auto refinishers construct their own booths by partitioning off a corner of the shop. A large exhaust fan is installed and air is drawn into the booth through filters such as are commonly used in hot air heating systems. The spray booth must be so designed that all joints are sealed and the filtered air intake must be of adequate area to filter all air being moved through the booth by means of the exhaust fan. The fan should be capable of maintaining air movement of 100 linear feet per minute throughout the booth.

PAINT DRYING EQUIPMENT

In order to hasten the drying of the finishes used in refinishing the automobile, various types of drying equipment are used. Such equipment ranges from a single bulb type

Fig. 28-21. New, bulb type, portable infrared panel used mostly for spot or panel drying. (Devilbiss Co.)

Fig. 28-22. Infrared traveling oven with pneumatically operated top, permitting use on standard size cars and vans as well. (Devilbiss Co.)

Lacquers dry primarily by evaporation of their solvents. Enamels dry because of two chemical changes, oxidation and polymerization. In the oxidizing process of drying, the enamel absorbs oxygen which causes the enamel to dry. In the case of polymerization, the synthetic resin in the enamel acts somewhat like an egg when heat is applied. It solidifies, becomes hard, and will not return to a liquid state, no matter how much heat is applied.

Polymerization speeds up drying beyond that which would take place with oxidation alone. It also makes the paint harder, improves water and chemical resistance, and enhances its durability and gloss.

Force drying temperatures of below 165 deg. F. dries the finish only by increasing oxidation, and does not start polymerization. The higher the temperature of the baking system, the greater the oxidation, and poly merization. With true baking temperatures around 300 deg. F., finishes can be dried in a few minutes.

unit, Fig. 13-11, to huge batteries of infrared lamps, as shown in Figs. 28-21, 28-22, and 28-23. In some operations, the drying

Fig. 28-23. Drive-through type of drying equipment.

equipment is installed in a spray booth. In large establishments, a baking tunnel type oven is placed at the end of the spray booth. As soon as the spraying is completed the vehicle is rolled forward into the drying room.

Paint baking equipment is used particularly when the vehicle is refinished with enamel.

There are two basic types of baking equipment: Radiant and convection. The latter bakes with hot air, circulated in well-insulated ovens into which the vehicle is pushed. The heat in such cases is usually produced by natural gas or oil.

Radiant units bake with electrically powered infrared lamps or ceramic heating units. The lamps use 125, 250 or 500 watt bulbs, Fig. 28-23. A shop turning out more than 10 cars per day, will usually find the tunnel type equipment economical. Smaller shops will use equipment shown in Figs. 28-21 and 28-22.

When an infrared baking unit is used, consideration must be given to the fact that darker colors absorb more heat than the lighter colors. Excessive heat may cause loss of gloss and discoloration, blistering and wrinkling. Baking time of different colors must therefore be kept in mind.

Before putting the car in the baking oven, 10 to 15 minutes should elapse to provide time for the solvents to "flash off." Heavy fills of putty and 10 or 12 coats of old surfacer have a tendency to cause blistering when placed in the bake oven.

Loss of gloss can be caused by applying

Fig. 28-24. Respirator used when spraying urethane paint.

insufficient enamel, porous old finish or undercoat, too much heat or too long a bake, too much reducer, insufficient ventilation. Windows of the vehicle should be left partly open during the baking process. This will provide better distribution of heat and reduce any tendency for the glass to break.

RESPIRATORS

Paint fumes are toxic, particularly if inhaled constantly. When spraying paint, or when working in an area where paint is being sprayed, a respirator should be worn. See Fig. 28-24. A respirator is a mask worn over the nose and mouth to prevent the inhalation of toxic pigment particles, harmful dust and vapors from various types of paints and lacquer. The hood type respirator which protects the eyes of the wearer is a popular type. The organic type respirator is equipped with replaceable cartridges that remove organic vapors by chemical absorption and also any dust particles that may be present.

Some respirators are satisfactory for removing dust only, not toxic fumes. Other respirators, Fig. 28-24, are designed for use when spraying urethane paint.

QUIZ - Chapter 28

1. A spray gun uses air to atomize the material being sprayed.
   True.
   False.
2. The spray gun with an air valve is known as a bleeder gun.
   True.
   False.
3. An external mix gun is usually used when refinishing an automobile.
   True.
   False.
4. The air cap is located at the front of the spray gun and directs the material stream into the compressed air to atomize it and form it into a spray.
   True.
   False.
5. What size fluid tip is usually used when refinishing an automobile? (Suction feed gun.)
   .041 in.
   .025 in.
   .100 in.
   .014 in.
6. A major advantage of a spray gun is that it is not necessary to clean it after each use.
   True.
   False.
7. If small holes in air cap become clogged, what should be used to clean them?
   Wooden match stick.
   Wire nail.
   Fine wire as used for attaching tags.
8. What type of lubricant should be used on fluid needle packing, air valve packing and trigger bearing screw?
   Light oil.

Transmission lubricant.
Lubriplate.
Wheel bearing grease.

9. In a pressure feed system, the spray gun can be held at any angle.
        True.
        False.

10. In a two-stage compressor, air is first compressed in which cylinder?
        Larger cylinder.
        Smaller cylinder.

11. Cooling fins of compressors should be kept clean.
        True.
        False.

12. A high quality air transformer will keep air pressure within what limits?
        3/4 lb. variation.
        2 lb. variation.
        5 lb. variation.

13. Air hose used in painting is usually what color?
        Red.
        Green.
        Black.

14. What is the inside diameter of fluid hose used when refinishing automobiles? (Large gun.)
        1/2 in.
        3/8 in.
        1/4 in.

Section view of spray gun--DeVilbiss type JGA.

Chapter 29

HOW TO
SPRAY PAINT

USING A SPRAY GUN

A production type spray gun, clean and in good condition is required to obtain proper atomization and application of paint in a minimum amount of time. Either a suction feed gun, or a pressure feed type may be used, Fig. 29-1.

For suction feed work a suitable air cap and fluid tip are needed. A one quart capacity suction feed cup attached directly to the spray gun is generally used.

Fig. 29-1. Using a suction feed gun to spray a car.

The fluid tip or nozzle normally used for suction feed guns will be .070 in. (1.78 mm). For faster application, a .086 in. (2.184 mm) tip is used. The air cap for the .070 in. (1.78 mm) tip will require 11.5 cu. ft. (.0325 m^3) of air per minute at a spraying pressure of 60 psi (413 kPa). For the .086 in. (2.184 mm) tip, an air cap consuming 13 cu. ft. (.368 m^3) of air at 60 psi (413 kPa) pressure is needed.

For pressure feed work, a fluid tip from .0425 in. to .046 in. (1.08 to 1.17 mm) should be used. A pressure feed cap consuming 14 cu. ft. (.396 m^3) of air will be needed.

Both suction and pressure feed spray guns have two manual adjustments, Fig. 28-10, provided by the spreader adjusting valve for side port control and the fluid adjusting valve. When the spreader adjusting valve is fully closed, it shuts off air to the horns on the air cap and a round spray pattern results. See Fig. 29-2. As this valve is gradu-

Fig. 29-2. When spreader adjusting valve is fully closed, a round pattern results as shown at the right. When valve is opened the pattern becomes oval as shown at the left.

ally opened, air is emitted from the horns on the air cap and the spray pattern is changed to an oval, Fig. 29-2. This adjustment allows the operator to select a spray pattern width to suit the job. For touch-up-work or spotting in a round pattern a small fan is used. For panel and large areas the gun is adjusted to a wide or oval pattern.

The fluid adjustment, Fig. 28-10, controls the amount of paint coming from the gun. When fully closed, no paint leaves the gun. When fully open, maximum paint flow is provided. This adjustment permits the operator to select a setting that will give the proper paint flow for the job. On spot work a minimum flow is used, and on panels or other large areas, maximum flow is used.

AIR PRESSURE

The air pressure used at the gun to atomize the paint will vary with the viscosity of the paint and to some extent the type, that is lacquer, enamel or acrylic. Gun air pressure

WRONG

Heavy Coat with sags, ripples or orange peel.

REASONS

Dirty air nozzle.
Gun too close.
Paint too Thin.
Low air pressure.
Stroke too slow.
Too much overlap.

WRONG

Thin Coat, rough, dry, no lustre.

REASONS

Wrong air nozzle.
Gun too far away.
Paint too heavy.
Too much air.
Stroke too fast.
Not enough overlap.

RIGHT

Medium Coat, good flow-out with hardly any orange peel and no sags.

REASONS

Gun clean and properly adjusted.
Gun distance okay.
Proper thinning.
Right amount of air.
Stroke okay.
Overlap 50%.

Fig. 29-3. Right and wrong ways of operating a spray gun.

is adjusted and controlled with the air regulator which is part of the air transformer, Fig. 28-18. The correct pressure to use is a matter of experience and is arrived at by a series of test patterns, Fig. 29-2. Not only is the shape of the pattern altered, but also its size. Varying the pattern is accomplished by the selection of the setting of the spreader adjustment valve. The spreader adjustment valve is a key to lower cost painting. Select the setting most suitable to the size and contour of the area being finished. Never have a pattern wider than the surface being refinished.

Too low an air pressure will result in under-atomized paint, Fig. 29-3, which will be rough or show a heavy orange peel. Atomizing pressure too high will result in a dry spray and may also cause an orange peel due to lack of proper flow-out in the material. As a matter of general practice the atomizing pressure at the gun will range from 30 lb. to 60 lb. A pressure feed gun will require less atomizing air pressure than a suction gun.

The first step in operating a spray gun is therefore to adjust the gun and air pressure until the desired pattern and atomization are obtained. Test the spray pattern on paper, or on a scrap panel. If the air cap or tip is not clean, or is worn, a defective pattern will result. Fig. 29-4. In general the height of the oval should be 5 to 6 in., and the width 2 in.

To correct the pattern distortions, clean the air cap and fluid tip thoroughly inside and out, using solvent, and a soft bristle brush.

"Spitting" is caused by dried-out packing around the material needle valve permitting air to get into fluid passageways. Loosen knurled nut on air valve and lubricate with machine oil. Spitting is also caused by dirt between fluid nozzle seat and body, loosely installed fluid nozzle, or by a defective swivel nut on syphon cup or material hose.

It is important, when spraying paint, that the gun be held at the correct distance from the surface of the work. For synthetic enamels, the correct distance is 8 to 10 in. or about the hand span of a normal size hand. For lacquers the correct distance is 6 to 8 in. If the gun is too close to the work, paint goes on too heavy and tends to sag. If the gun is too far from the work, there is ex-

Fig. 29-4. Detail A—Spray guns can be adjusted to either round or oval patterns. B—Top heavy patterns caused by horn holes partly clogged, obstruction on top of fluid tip, dirt on air cap seat or fluid tip seat. C—Heavy bottom pattern caused by horn holes partly clogged, obstruction on bottom side of fluid tip, dirt on air cap seat or fluid tip seat. D—Heavy right side pattern caused by right side horn holes partly clogged, dirt on right side of fluid tip, or twin jet air cap right jet clogged. E—Heavy left side pattern caused by left side horn holes partly clogged, dirt on left side of fluid tip, or on twin cap left jet clogged. F—Heavy center pattern due to too low setting of the spreader adjustment valve, with twin jet cap too low, an atomizing pressure or paint too thick, with pressure feed too high a paint pressure for the atomization air being used or the material flow is in excess of the normal capacity of the cap, too large a nozzle for the material being used, too small a nozzle. G—Split pattern due to air and paint not being properly balanced. Reduce width of spray pattern by means of spreader adjustment valve or increase fluid pressure.

cessive dusting and a sandy finish, Fig. 29-3.

It is important to remember that the gun should be held at the correct distance the entire length of the stroke and always perpendicular to the surface of the work, Fig. 29-5. When the gun is held at an angle to the

this . . .

. . . not this!

Fig. 29-5. To get even paint distribution and film thickness always hold gun perpendicular to the surface of the panel.

FIRST STROKE IS AIMED AT EDGE OF PANEL

START STROKE

PULL TRIGGER

AIMING POINT IS BOTTOM OF PREVIOUS STROKE

Fig. 29-6. In this method of spraying, the gun is triggered at edge of panel.

painted surface, more material is applied at one part of the spray pattern, less at the other. This results in streaks, sags, runs and wasted paint.

Always work for a wet coat. Use slow steady strokes across the surface from one side to the other. Never use a fanning motion. To insure smoother coverage, each stroke should overlap 50 percent.

When spraying a panel, the stroke may be started off to one side the surface of the work. The trigger is pulled when the gun is opposite the edge of the panel, Fig. 29-6. The

spray gun is then moved to the other side of the panel and the trigger is released at the edge of the panel, but the stroke is continued for a few inches before reversing direction for the next stroke. The triggering is part of the spraying technique. It maintains full coverage, without overspray. The quality of the paint job is improved and little paint is wasted.

Another method of painting a panel is to first "band-in" the ends of the panel, moving the gun vertically, Fig. 29-7. Then spray the face of the panel horizontally triggering the gun at the beginning and end of each stroke. After the edges have been "banded-in" the operator can begin each stroke and then pull the trigger. He can release the trigger before completing the stroke. Smooth, complete coating will result with a minimum waste from overspray. Incidentally, corners should be sprayed so that both edges of the corner are covered at the same time.

Fig. 29-7. In this method of spraying, the sides of the panel are first banded-in.

Some authorities estimate that 30 percent of the material atomized by the spray gun does not fall on the vehicle but on the inside of the spray booth. When the edges have been "banded-in" the habit of whipping the gun is more easily controlled. The banded surfaces act as a signal to "trigger" at exactly the correct moment of the stroke.

The stroke must be smooth and easy, allowing enough time for sufficient material to be applied, but fast enough so too much material is not applied and causes sags. "Whipping" the gun wastes energy and material. Strokes should overlap each other approximately 50 percent, Fig. 29-8.

When spraying a hood, top or other wide horizontal surface, always start at the near side and work to the far side. This is particularly important when lacquer is being sprayed. The reason is that any overspray will land on a dry surface. Overspray landing on a wet surface will result in a sandy

surface. If a pressure gun is not available, the suction gun can be tilted slightly to be as near a right angle to a painted surface as possible.

Fig. 29-8. Allowing a 50 percent overlap with each pass of the gun.

SPRAYING THE ENTIRE CAR

Two suggested area painting sequences are shown in Fig. 29-9. First paint the hidden edges, door jambs, inside the trunk lid, hood edges, etc., leaving the door slightly ajar to avoid sticking, and to permit proper drying. Then proceed with the exterior of the car, following the numbered sequence shown in either of the drawings in Fig. 29-9. Most painters prefer to do one-half of the top and complete it as they work around the car. When spraying door jambs, use air pressure of 20 psi (138 kPa). Then, increase pressure per paint manufacturer's instructions, usually 40 psi (276 kPa) for lacquers and acrylics and 60 psi (413 kPa) for synthetic enamel. Spray inside trunk lid, in back of bumper and bumper guards and under hood.

At no time should it be necessary to spray or lap into a semidry area, since that would cause air streaks on the finished paint job.

SPRAYING TEMPERATURES

There is an ideal temperature for spraying paint at which it will behave most satisfactorily through the gun and produce a paint job of high quality. If the material is too cold, it becomes thick and heavy bodied. When overheated, the viscosity drops and the material becomes more liquid. The correct temperature of the paint should be close to

Fig. 29-9. Two procedures for spraying a complete vehicle.

70 deg. F. (21.1 C). The temperature should be checked as the paint is put into the pressure pot or suction cup.

Always store painting materials and equipment at temperatures ranging between 70 and 85 deg. F. (21.1 and 29.4 C). If stored and applied at higher or lower temperatures, a poor quality paint job usually results. Remember: putting paint of correct temperature into a hot or cold container will affect temperature of material to be sprayed.

The vehicle to be sprayed should also be at from 70 to 85 deg. F. (21.1 to 29.4 C). Never attempt to paint a car that has been standing in the sun or in extreme cold.

On lacquer color only, to remove overspray or dry spray resulting from overlapping, spray over the entire car with lacquer thinner to which a little color has been added. Use care to avoid excessive wetting as this will cause runs. The thinner coat is applied to pick up overspray and put it back into the finish. It also helps to level any "orange peel" that may be on the surface. Less rubbing and polishing will be required.

SPECIAL NOTES ON REFINISHING

It is hardly possible to give detailed instructions for car refinishing that would be applicable to all jobs because the exact procedure will vary with the make of car and

type of refinishing material used and its condition. Therefore, when refinishing an automotive vehicle, keep in mind that the individual paint manufacturer's instructions should be carefully followed.

There are, however, a few basic procedures that are applicable to all jobs.

First of all, the surface must be smooth and free from minor imperfections of scratches and dents. The surface must then be treated to remove all traces of oil, dust and rust. Modern primer surfacers, while capable of filling in some fine scratches, are designed primarily to provide adhesion.

The next step after cleaning the surface is to spray the primer surfacer. The type of primer surfacer depends on the original finish and the type of material to be used for the color coat, that is, nitrocellulose lacquer, synthetic enamel, acrylic lacquer, acrylic enamel or urethane enamel. Applying heavy coats of primer surfacer in one pass of the gun is not recommended. Primer surfacers applied in that manner will usually have a surface hardness, but will not be dry close to the metal. Excessively heavy coats can lead to hard sanding, poor holding, pin holes and other film defects. It is better to apply thin wet coats of surfacer and allow a short solvent flash-off time between coats.

In spot spraying bare metal spots with primer surfacer, using a narrow fan-shaped spray from the gun, and building up the bare spot gradually, will usually produce good results.

After the primer surfacer has dried, putty can be applied to any rough areas. The time required for primer surfacer to dry will depend on the thickness of the coat, the type of thinner and atmospheric conditions.

The next step is to water sand the surface using No. 320 grit paper, Fig. 29-10. If, as

Fig. 29-10. Wet sanding a primer surfacer.

a result of sanding, the primer surfacer should be cut down to the metal, it will be necessary to respray the surface with another coat of primer surfacer. When sanding, do not bear down too hard but let the abrasive paper do the work. To eliminate sand scratches at any featheredge, use fine grit paper such as No. 400 to obtain a smooth surface. Some painters will use rubbing compound on the featheredge rather than fine sandpaper.

After sanding is completed, wash the sanded area with water to remove all traces of the primer surfacer which have been sanded from the surface. Then allow the surface to dry thoroughly. Blow out crevices and moldings with compressed air.

SPRAYING COLOR COAT

Just before spraying the color coat, all crevices should be blown and cleaned with compressed air and then carefully wiped with a tack rag to remove all traces of dust.

If the finish coat is nitrocellulose lacquer, the usual procedure is to spray three or four double coats, thinned in accordance with the

Fig. 29-11. Polishing to improve lustre.

manufacturer's instructions. Allow each coat to flash (thinner evaporate) before applying succeeding coats. Pressure at the gun usually is 40 to 45 psi (276 to 310 kPa).

Allow to dry at least four hours, preferably overnight, then hand rub with rubbing compound or machine polishing compound. Polish or dry buff with polishing disk or lamb's wool bonnet, Fig. 29-11. Allow 30 days for lacquer to harden before waxing.

If the finish is acrylic lacquer or acrylic enamel, many paint manufacturers recommend that after wiping with a tack rag, one or two coats of special sealer be applied. When that is dried, three or four wet double coats of acrylic, (thinned in accordance with manufacturer's instructions) are sprayed on. In hot weather a "retarder" may be added to the thinner to aid leveling and to prevent blushing (taking on white or grayish cast while drying). Allow each double coat to "flash" before applying succeeding coats. In spot repair of acrylic lacquer finishes, extend each color coat a little beyond previous coat to blend into surrounding finish. Next, spray a mist coat of retarder and thinner to increase loss and reduce compounding and level overspray roughness.

For most brands of acrylic, allow at least four hours for air drying or, preferably, overnight. If force dried with infrared or oven, heat the finished area at least 30 min. to 165 deg. F. (74 C). Then, process the repaired area with rubbing compound. Acrylic retains most of its original gloss and appearance for at least 18 months, so polishing is normally not needed. Wax may be applied after allowing 60 days for acrylic to harden. Acrylic may lose some of its original luster, if not thoroughly dry prior to compounding and polishing. If such after shrinkage occurs, the original luster can be restored by lightly buffing after two weeks or longer aging.

When the color coat is enamel, the usual

Fig. 29-12. Lifting. A swelling of wet film, caused by: recoating improperly cured enamel; improper drying of earlier coating; spraying over surface which has not been properly cleaned; using acrylic lacquer over enamel or acrylic enamel undercoats. Lifted material must be removed, then refinish.

Fig. 29-13. Bruises and chipping. Caused by stones, etc., striking the surface, NOT due to finish. Remedy: Sand out and refinish.

procedure after the primer surfacer has been applied, is to spray the area with one medium coat of primer sealer. After drying, the crevices are blown out with compressed air and the entire surface wiped clean with a tack rag. The finish enamel is then sprayed, making sure the enamel is thoroughly stirred and mixed with the correct amount of reducer. Spray a medium first coat and after drying spray a full second coat. The drying time of enamels vary greatly with different brands, and also with weather and atmospheric con-

Fig. 29-14. Peeling. Loss of adhesion is a film separation occurring between top coat and primer or top coat and old finish. Peeling is caused by improper bonding of finish coat to the surface being finished, which results from improper cleaning, poor preparation or incompatibility of one coat for the other. To repair, remove old finish from area larger than affected area. Properly clean and treat surface, then refinish. For metals other than steel, use recommended primers.

Fig. 29-15. Orange peel. Finish that looks like the peel of an orange may be caused by: too high air pressure; gun fanning before paint droplets have a chance to flow; color coats not reduced enough to permit proper atomization; wrong thinning or reducing; spray equipment not properly adjusted; gun held too far away; shop temperatures too high. To repair, use a fine compound on enamel, rub out orange peel surface. On lacquer, sand or use rubbing compound. Refinish.

Fig. 29-16. Fish eyes. Small, crater-like openings in finish are caused by spraying over silicone or improperly cleaned old finish. If finish is newly applied, wash off paint while wet. Thoroughly clean surfaces, then refinish.

ditions. Special reducers are available to aid in drying with different shop temperatures.

Some manufacturers recommend spraying one panel at a time, applying two full wet coats to each panel, one immediately following the other. Then move to the next panel. Metallic colors may require an additional coat, a mist coat.

Fig. 29-17. Wrinkling. A shriveling of the finish is caused by: excessively heavy enamel color coats; extremely high temperature or humidity conditions; if enamel is sprayed in hot sun, or if freshly painted surface is exposed to sunlight; if enamel finish coats are reduced with lacquer or acrylic lacquer thinner instead of enamel reducer; if air-dry enamels are baked or forced dried without using baking converter in color coats.

Fig. 29-18. Water spotting. Spotty appearance and dulling of gloss in spots will occur: if the finish is exposed to water before being completely dry; alternate exposure to sun and and rain will cause water spotting. To repair, use fine rubbing compound and rub lightly with a damp cloth. If polishing fails, refinish. To prevent recurrence, keep car out of rain and do not wash until paint is completely dry.

Pressure for spraying enamel is usually at or near 65 lbs., when a regular syphon gun is used. The greatest error in spraying enamel is putting on too much. A thick film of enamel is no more durable than a film of normal thickness. In some cases a thick film is even less durable. Two coats of a quality enamel will usually hide any color. Solid colors spray easiest by applying a good medi-

Fig. 29-19. Rust under finish usually appears as a raised section of the finish, or blistering. Usually caused by poor penetration and cleaning of surface. Remedy: Sand surface, treat surface with rust remover and refinish.

Fig. 29-20. Pitting. Usually caused by oil or moisture escaping through the air line. Remedy: Sand down to smooth surface and refinish. Overhaul compressor and separator to correct trouble.

Fig. 29-21. Blistering. Bubbly or swollen appearance is caused by: trapped solvents; painting over grease or oil; rust under surface; moisture in spray lines; prolonged exposure of film to high humidity. To repair, remove all blisters by sanding. If necessary, sand to bare metal. Refinish. To prevent blistering: clean and treat metal thoroughly; allow ample drying time between coatings; drain water from air lines; if temperature and humidity are high, use overly fast thinners.

um coat first. Allow this first coat to get tacky and then spray a full coat. Polychromatic colors will give best metallic effect by spraying on the full coat first, then applying a light coat.

Fig. 29-22. *Pin Point Blistering. This type of blistering is often confused with pitting because small broken blisters have the appearance of pits. These pin point blisters range in size from a pin point to a pin head. Remedy: Sand down to metal and refinish.*

Be sure to keep the gun at right angles to the panel and at the proper distance--about 10 in. If the gun is held too close, it will cause poor distribution of the enamel, and if too far away dry spray will result.

Examples of paint that have been applied to various types of poorly prepared surfaces are shown in Figs. 29-12 to 29-25.

Fig. 29-23. *Paint will have a mottled appearance if applied on surface which had been polished with silicone type polish. It is therefore imperative that all traces of such polish be removed from the surface before refinishing.*

TIPS ON SPRAYING COLOR COATS

To insure good adhesion and freedom from bleeding, a sealer should be applied to any primed surface before spraying on the finish coat. A sealer is especially necessary, when the finish coat is of a different material than the original coat. For example, when acrylic enamel is sprayed over acrylic lacquer, or vice versa.

When spraying acrylic lacquers at shop temperatures below 60 deg. F., crazing (mesh of fine cracks) may result. Crazing can be prevented by heating the area with an infra-red light and applying a sealer while the sur-

Fig. 29-24. *Checking. Deep cracks usually are caused by: spraying new finish over previously cracked finish; spraying too-thick finish coat over undercoats; and/or not properly dried; spraying top coats not sufficiently stirred; heavy application of finish coat with insufficient time between coats. To repair, sand down to smooth finish and, if necessary, sand down to bare metal. Avoid extreme temperatures. Spray uniform coats. Allow proper drying time between coats.*

Fig. 29-25. *Chalking is surface disintegration. Primarily due to weathering and sunlight and is characterized by dulling and powdering of the surface. Remedy: Apply paste cleaner, followed by polish. In extreme cases complete refinishing is necessary.*

Fig. 29-26. *Runs or sags. Failure of coating to adhere uniformly over surface may be caused by: slow drying thinner or reducer; over-reduced color coats; too little air pressure when applying color coats; color coats sprayed over wax, oil or grease; excessively heavy and wet finishing coats; refinish materials or work surface that is too hot or cold. To repair, use a fine camel hair brush to brush out sag. Then, recoat. When finish coat is completely dry, remove excess paint by sanding with a fine grit treated paper. Compound, polish or refinish as required.*

face is still warm. Also when the temperature is low, at least 24 hours drying time is required before the acrylic lacquer can be compounded.

When refinishing fiber glass bodies with acrylic lacquer: First, wash the area with water and detergent. Next, clean with a solvent. Then, sand and featheredge the area with an orbital sander, using 240 grit treated paper. Repair any damaged area with polyester body filler to build up the depth. For surfacing any minor imperfections, use lacquer type primer surfacer. After surface is dry, sand and seal with special sealer.

Special sealers are available for use with synthetic enamel over reds and maroons to prevent bleeding. Some of these sealers must not be baked and must dry at least one hour before applying the finish coat.

Give special attention to cleanliness when using acrylic enamel. Use a solvent after a water wash and before sanding.

Before priming zinc-coated metals, be sure to check with your supplier for recommendations.

When refinishing fiber glass with acrylic enamel, you can obtain better adherence by cleaning the entire repair area with solvent. Then, sand and featheredge the area. Repair any damage with polyester type body filler.

For surfacing minor imperfections, use a lacquer type primer surfacer. After the surface is dry and has been sanded, use an acrylic enamel sealer. When top coating prepared fiber glass, allow extra time for flash between coats to avoid trapping of solvent.

When applying solid or nonmetallic acrylic enamel colors, see that air pressure at the gun does not exceed 50 psi. Spray one full wet coat and allow flash off at least 10 minutes before spraying second full wet coat.

When spraying metallic colors with acrylic enamel, spray one medium wet coat. Allow flash off for at least 10 minutes, then spray second coat. If a mottled appearance occurs after second coat, apply a mist coat to produce a uniform appearance.

URETHANE ACRYLIC ENAMEL

When preparing the surface for urethane acrylic enamel, follow the same procedure as for acrylic enamel. Follow the manufacturer's instructions for reducing. The spraying procedure is the same as for acrylic enamel. Under normal conditions, allow three hours drying time before masking. Clean equipment immediately after use. Decals may be applied to urethane acrylic enamel surface approximately four hours to one week from taping. Be sure to use an acredited respirator when spraying urethane paints.

WATER BASE ACRYLIC PAINT

Starting with production of 1975 models, Vegas built at the Southgate Assembly plant were painted with a water based enamel top coat and a water based enamel interior. As in the past, these vehicles are identified by the letter "W" prefixing the GM code number on the body identification plate.

The term "water base" concerns only the production application of the paint. The new water base acrylic is repairable in service with conventional arcylic lacquer. For proper adhesion of acrylic lacquer to water base acrylic, scuff sanding and the application of a sealer are absolutely essential. Therefore, the water base acrylic (according to Chevrolet) is currently not spot repairable.

Repairs to water base acrylic requiring the application of color must be carried to the nearest break line. Failure to follow the repair procedure will result in paint peeling and adhesion problems.

The Chevrolet procedure for color coating water base acrylic is as follows:

Clean the complete panel with a paint finish cleaning solvent. Scuff sand, dry, with 400 grit paper. Reclean and apply the best sealer available for sealing acrylic lacquer repair system. Apply acrylic lacquer to panel for accurate color match. Allow lacquer to dry thoroughly. Then, rub out and polish the finish.

USE CORRECT AIR PRESSURE

In most cases, the correct air pressure for spraying paint is indicated on the paint can by the manufacturer. If not, the following general recommendations should prove satisfactory:

Acrylic lacquer for overall finishing,
40-45 psi (276-310 kPa).
Acrylic lacquer for spot repair,
30-35 psi (207-241 kPa).
Alkyd enamels for overall finishing,
50-70 psi (345-483 kPa).
Acrylic enamel for complete refinishing,
50-70 psi (345-483 kPa).
Acrylic enamel for spot repair,
45-65 psi (310-448 kPa).

REFINISHING FLEXIBLE EXTERIOR PARTS

The refinishing of flexible exterior parts such as bumpers, bumper fillers and side shields creates some unusual problems. Special refinishing materials and special procedures are needed to provide the necessary adhesion and flexibility.

Some manufacturers provide a special additive for their acrylic lacquer. Others formulate a special urethane enamel, designed for use on urethane parts.

When refinishing any urethane part with acrylic lacquer, the usual procedure is to mix the special additive with the lacquer.

First, prepare the surface by washing with special solvent. Then, scuff sand with No. 320 coated paper. Again wash the surface with special cleaner. Mix the acrylic lacquer and the additive according to instructions. Spray it on the vehicle in the normal manner. Allow ample time for drying between each of four coats. Compounding should not be necessary. Recommended gun pressure is 40 to 45 psi.

When refinishing urethane parts with urethane enamel: First, clean surface with solvent. Then, hand sand with No. 240 grit treated paper. Again clean with special solvent.

For urethane parts which have not been finished, follow the same procedure except, prior to the application of the color coats, prime the surface with a special wash primer. For color application, spray two full wet coats. Allow 10 minutes between coats. Apply a third coat, if needed. Follow the paint manufacturer's instructions regarding the use of a reducer.

CAUTION: Manufacturer's emphasize the need for using a vapor/particulate respirator when spraying urethane enamel.

CLEAR COAT FINISH

Clear coat is an extremely glossy "wet" coat finish. In car factory production, it consists of primary coat, two coats of enamel of the desired color and two coats of clear enamel. According to Ford, because of the toxicity of air dry enamel (which requires polyisocyanate as a drying agent), only acrylic lacquer should be used in making repairs.

Clear acrylic lacquer is a transparent material which, when sprayed over a metallic or solid color coat, provides a high gloss. The gloss level, then, is influenced by the number of lacquer clear coats applied.

The repair color coat and clear coat must be sprayed on the vehicle with extreme care. Unlike conventional exterior paint that can be sanded if a run or sag occurs, the color coat must be free of all imperfections before the clear coats are applied. Any dirt particles, mottling, sand scratches or sags left in the color coat will be magnified when the clear coats are applied.

FILM THICKNESS

Some paint manufacturers now specify the thickness of the applied paint. Thickness affects the gloss, tendency towards sagging and durability of the paint. Thickness of the paint varies with the type and manufacturer, as well as conditions under which it is applied (air pressure, spraying technique, etc.).

For example, Sherwin-Williams' Kem Transport finishing enamel should not be sprayed to more than 2 mils (.002 in.) thickness. Films in excess of that thickness dry slowly and tend to wrinkle. The same company's specification for clear coat is 1.5 mils (.0015 in.) maximum thickness for application of two medium wet coats. Also, Ditzler states that the maximum thickness for two coats of their Durethane aircraft/fleet finishes is 2.0 mils (.007 in.).

Specialized equipment is available for measuring paint thickness.

LOWER BODY SIDE STONE PROTECTION

To protect the lower body side from being marred by flying stones, some cars (Ford, for example) are protected by a sprayed-on vinyl coating. See Fig. 29-27. A small dent in the sheet metal that did not mar the vinyl surface can, in most cases, be corrected. It calls for careful bumping methods while avoiding damage to the vinyl coating.

FRONT OF VEHICLE

SHADED AREAS DESIGNATE THE APPLICATION OF STONE PECKING PROTECTION MATERIAL FOR ALL UNITED STATES AND CANADIAN BUILT VEHICLES (REAR OF FRONT FENDER, ROCKER PANEL, DOOR, AND QUARTER PANEL).

Fig. 29-27. Location of vinyl coating used as a protection against stone abrasion. (Ford)

Noticeable scratches or gouges not over 1 1/2 in. (38 mm) long, or dents when ironed out, can be repaired by using special polyfiller. Proceed as follows:

Wipe area with silicone and wax remover. Use a heat gun or lamp to soften vinyl coating of damaged area until it can be scraped off with a putty knife. Next, repair sheet metal. Then, following instructions on label of polyfiller can, blend this special filler with surrounding vinyl coating. Allow polyfiller to completely cure. Then, carefully sand this area to remove any high spots or knife marks. Prime and paint.

In the case of large area repairs or replacement of sheet metal, it will be necessary to install pressure sensitive, clear urethane film. Proceed as follows:

First, wipe surface with silicone and wax remover. Then, use heat gun to soften vinyl coating until it is pliable. Scrape off vinyl with a putty knife. If necessary, use an orbital sander to remove this coating. Make necessary repairs to damaged area. Paint damaged area or new sheet metal with usual

Fig. 29-28. Align masking tape with character line to assist in the accurate application of urethane film.

procedure, restoring it to original color and finish condition. Allow time for paint to cure before installing urethane film.

Pressure sensitive film requires proper surface preparation. Determine length of urethane film required to cover area by measuring panel surfaces and flanges. Allow about 1 in. (25.4 mm) extra at each end for wrapping around flanges and for handling. Use a sharp knife or razor blade to cut off film. DO NOT REMOVE PROTECTIVE COATING; CUT WITH FILM SIDE UP.

Carefully prepare surface of car to insure good adhesion and long life of film. Wash with proper solvent to remove all traces of foreign matter (gasoline, oil, tar, etc.). Then, use a tack rag. NOTE: Sheet metal and film must be at a temperature of 60 deg. F. (15.6 C) to obtain satisfactory adhesion.

If film is to be applied adjacent to a molding, use molding as a guideline. However, if a sheet metal character is to be guideline, apply a strip of masking tape along guideline to assist in proper film alignment, Fig. 29-28.

Apply film carefully. Its adhesion to a painted surface makes it difficult to remove and reposition. Urethane film may be installed by either the "wet" or "dry" method. The wet method is for flat surfaces. The dry method usually is used for compound curvatures.

The wet procedure is as follows:

First, wipe area with silicone and wax remover. Make sure flanges are clean. Carefully peel back protective backing from urethane film. DO NOT touch adhesive side in any area that will be used on car since fingerprints and dirt will be retained on adhesive.

Using a 50/50 mixture of clean water and isopropyl alcohol, spray sheet metal area. This will greatly assist in correct alignment and application of urethane film.

Carefully position film (side-to-side) and, aligning upper edge to guideline, finger tack this edge to sheet metal. Using a plastic squeegee, run down film to sheet metal, which will force out any air or liquid. If some air or liquid becomes trapped, use squeegee to carefully pull urethane film loose. Then, re-squeegee. Do not secure ends or bottom edges at this time.

If there are any small blisters, puncture them with a pin, expel air and re-squeegee film down. Using a razor blade or sharp knife, trim excess film at ends and bottom edge to allow about 1/2 in. (13 mm) to wrap around flanges.

Use heat gun sparingly to dry edges of film at ends and bottom. If a flange or edge has compound angles, carefully trim or slit film to allow good wraparound to conform to flange. Apply heat as needed to provide good adhesion. The slight, initial haziness will disappear when final adhesion levels are attained.

The dry method of applying urethane film to compound surfaces proceeds more quickly:

First, prepare the surface carefully to remove all traces of foreign matter. Wipe the area with silicone and wax remover, making sure that all the flanges are clean.

Next, carefully position the film (side-to-side) and align upper edge to guideline. Finger tack this edge to the sheet metal as shown in Fig. 29-29. Then, using a plastic squeegee, run down film to sheet metal.

Fig. 29-29. Tack upper edge of urethane film in place, aligning it with edge of guideline.

1. Spray pattern should always be larger than surface being refinished.
   True.
   False.
2. When atomizing pressure is too high a dry spray results.
   True.
   False.
3. As a matter of general practice what will be the range of the atomizing pressure?
   30 to 60 lbs. (207 to 413 kPa)
   75 to 90 lbs. (517 to 620 kPa)
   15 to 25 lbs. (103 to 172 kPa)
4. When spraying synthetic enamels, what is the correct distance between the gun and the work?
   8 to 10 in. (20.3 to 25.4 cm)
   6 to 8 in. (15.2 to 20.3 cm)
   10 to 12 in. (25.4 to 30.5 cm)
5. If a panel is not banded-in, where should the trigger be pulled when painting the panel?
   At the edge of the panel.
   Just before the edge of the panel.
   Just after the gun passes the edge of the panel.
6. When spraying a hood, where should the spraying be started?
   At the near side.
   At the far side.
   At the center.
7. What is considered the best temperature for spraying a car?
   70 deg. F. (21.1 C)
   65 deg. F. (18.3 C)
   80 deg. F. (26.7 C)
   60 deg. F. (15.6 C)
8. When refinishing with acrylic lacquer, how many coats should be applied?
   Single heavy coat.
   Three or four wet double coats.
   One heavy and one mist coat.
9. Is a special respirator needed when spraying urethane enamel?
   Yes.
   No.

Chapter 30

CUSTOMIZING
AUTO BODIES

Customizing or altering the lines of automobile bodies can be easily accomplished by using epoxy resins and fiber glass. Such work can range from a simple job of filling in joints between two metal panels, to providing new fender lines, and even a complete new body.

A simple job is to remove chrome trim and use epoxy resin to fill the holes used for the clips that held the chrome trim in place. The procedure for such work is similar to that explained in Chapter 13 for filling in dents. Filling in seams between panels is done in the same manner.

When altering the lines of an auto body, the basic procedure is to first build up a frame work of wire mesh. The epoxy resin and fiber glass are then applied over this form. When dry, the surface is sanded smooth, and painted.

The purpose of the wire mesh is to provide a form for the resin. Instead of wire mesh, some body men use stiff cardboard, which is taped in position on the auto body. However, wire mesh is generally preferred as it is more easily formed to the desired shape, and will retain that shape more easily than cardboard. The wire mesh is formed to the desired shape, and is welded or soldered in position on the automobile. If desired, self-tapping screws can be used to hold the wire form in place, instead of welding.

When "hooding" headlights or wherever a form is required in duplicate for the other side of the vehicle, it is essential that the two forms be identical. An excellent method is to first make a master (male) form. This must be the exact shape desired. Its outer surface must be smoothed, sealed and covered with a parting agent.

To seal the surface it is simply sprayed with a clear lacquer. When that is dry, it is coated with a parting agent, or mold release, which is usually a wax emulsion. The next step is to lay on a couple of laminations or layers of fiber glass material. When this has hardened, the mold which has been formed (female mold) is completed and is lifted off the male mold. This may be used to make as many identical lamp hoods, tail fins, wind scoops, etc. as desired.

Making female mold models, which are then used as master molds, is the preferred method. However, many body men when customizing, will simply build a wire form of the shape desired, and fasten the form in position. The wire form is then covered with fiber glass material. Sufficient fiber glass is used to permit considerable sanding so that the two forms on each side of the body can be duplicated.

The fiber glass is cut to the desired shape, and is dipped in the solution of resin and hardener, as described in the chapter on filling dents. The glass is then positioned on the form. When dry it is sanded smooth. Heat lamps can be used to speed the drying.

As previously mentioned, lamps may be hooded, air scoops formed, and tail fins altered by this method. In addition, complete auto bodies can be built.

BUILDING COMPLETE BODY

Briefly the method of building a complete auto body is to first build a form of wood, wire and plaster of paris. The plaster of paris is sanded to produce the exact form desired. This is known as the male form, from which a female form is made which in turn is used to produce the final body.

Fig. 30-1, shows the first step of making

Fig. 30-1. Skeleton frame built up of plywood used as basis for building body of fiber glass.

Fig. 30-2. Here the skeleton frame is covered with chicken wire prior to the application of fiber glass.

Fig. 30-3. The completed body after application of fiber glass and preliminary sanding.

a form. This consists of a series of plywood panels, the edge shapes of which conform to the shape of the desired auto body. This must be well made and strongly braced so that it will support the weight of plaster of paris and the stresses when the form is sanded.

This wooden form is in turn covered with wire netting, Fig. 30-2. This is covered with plaster of paris, Fig. 30-3. After the plaster of paris has dried, it is carefully sanded to produce the exact form, curves and contour desired. When sanding the plaster of paris be sure to wear a respirator as the air will be filled with powdered plaster of paris.

Fig. 30-4. Custom Ford body of plastic.

Fig. 30-5. Special body designed for land speedster.

The next step is to seal the plaster of paris by spraying it with clear lacquer. Two coats should be used to be sure that the pores of the plaster of paris are sealed.

When the lacquer sealer has dried, it is covered with the mold release, or parting agent. This is necessary so the fiber glass body (when completed) can be lifted from the form. The parting agent is usually in the form of a wax emulsion. After the mold release has been applied, the form is ready for the fiber glass, or if preferred a female form can be made. The female form is another form made from the male form. The easiest

Fig. 30-6. Note special customizing features on this Ford Mustang. It has flared fenders, special louvers, front air dam, and rear spoiler.

material to use is fiber glass. Simply lay on a couple of laminations of fiber glass after it has been dipped in the epoxy resin mixture. When it has hardened, the female form is completed. The inside of this form is coated with a mold release and then fiber glass sheets are pressed into position in the female form. After it has hardened, the fiber glass body is lifted out and fitted to the vehicle chassis.

The amount of materials needed will depend, of course, on the size of the body being made. One manufacturer estimates it takes from 12 to 15 gallons of resin and 20 to 30 sq. yds. of fiber glass cloth, and about 10 yds. of matte. Two laminations (with the long weave at right angles) are generally sufficient for the female mold. One gallon of resin will saturate 30 to 40 sq. ft. of cloth, and 15 to 20 sq. ft. of matte. Matte is about twice the thickness of cloth. Use a layer of cloth and then a layer of matte and then a final layer of cloth for the auto body.

After the body is completed, add more glass underneath in the form of ribs or strips to reenforce corners and other areas which are subject to greater stress.

Doors can be fabricated by making wooden frames and covering them with wire mesh,

Fig. 30-7. Highly modernized body.

then fiber glass. Hinges can be attached by laminating them in position with several strips of fiber glass cloth. Accessories also can be mounted in a similar manner.

Brackets for mounting the body onto the chassis can be attached to the body by means of several layers of fiber glass cloth. The body can be supported along its sides and at the front and rear to chassis cross members. Such points should be considered when making the original plans. The location of the fire wall behind the engine is particularly important.

To stimulate the design of fiber glass bodies, Figs. 30-4, 30-5, 30-6, 30-7 and Fig. 30-8, are presented.

The fiber glass cloth method of making repairs can be used extensively when repairing auto bodies, particularly when it is impossible to obtain replacement panels for repairing antique cars and foreign cars where replacement parts are not available in the U. S.

For additional details on the fixing of the epoxy resin and the application of fiber glass cloth the reader is referred to Chapter 13.

QUIZ - Chapter 30

1. When altering the lines of an auto body, the basic procedure is to first build up a frame work of wire mesh.
   True.
   False.
2. A parting agent is used so that the female mold can be easily lifted from the male mold.
   True.
   False.
3. Describe briefly how a form for a complete fiber glass auto body is made.

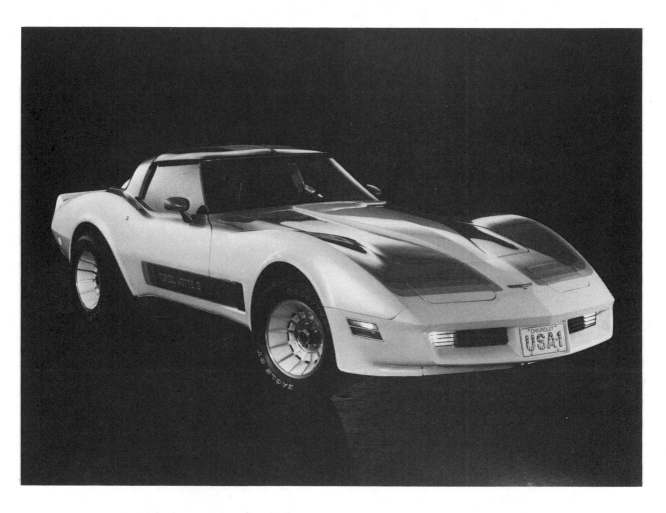

Fig. 30-8. Custom painted, turbocharged Corvette has an almost all aluminum engine.

Chapter 31

CUSTOM PAINTING

Custom painting is a term used to describe refinishing and/or decorating an automobile in a personalized manner, Fig. 31-1. Custom painting generally involves pictorial effects, such as landscapes, and many variations of geometrical forms and designs.

Customized effects are obtained by the use of spray guns and masking tape, plus the skill of an artist. In addition, special decorative tapes can be used to produce many dramatic effects.

While almost any type of paint can be used for custom painting, the most popular choice is acrylic lacquer. This finishing material may be applied with the conventional spray gun, a touch up gun, an air brush or by spraying paint from a pressurized can. Each method

has certain advantages, depending largely on the design and the area to be covered.

In custom painting, the conventional spray gun is used primarily for spraying large areas with primer coats, base paints and mist coats. The touch up gun is similar to the conventional spray gun in operation. However, it is lighter and has a smaller capacity since it is designed for short term use. The touch up gun is used extensively for spraying small areas, general touch up work, stenciling and for small area detail work.

The air brush is flexible. It is used for fine detailing, fish scaling and similar work. Pressurized paint spray cans are convenient for small or occasional work.

Custom painting, like conventional painting,

Fig. 31-1. Commercial vehicle with flame design customizing.

starts with a careful preparation of the surface: First, sand off the original paint. Then, if the surface does not have any dents or other defects, wipe it with a rust preventive solution. Follow up with another solvent that eliminates any oil film or traces of silicone polish. Then, apply the primer coat. When dry, apply a second primer coat. When dry, give the surface a wet sanding with 500 grit paper.

When the finish is completely dry, carefully wash away all residue from the sanding operation. Wipe the surface with a lintless cloth, then spray on the base color.

Masking is a most important part of custom painting. Masking materials include, tape, masking paper and stencils.

Masking tape, Fig. 31-2, is available in varying widths, including 1/8, 1/4, 3/8, 3/4

Fig.31-2. Using masking tape to produce a special design.

and 1 in. rolls. Widths greater than 1 in. are available, but are seldom used in custom painting.

The 1/8 in. wide tape, Fig. 31-3, is used extensively for outlining sharp turns and when an "endless line" design is required. There is also very narrow colored tape available that may be used for pin striping effects and also for endless line designs.

The stencil is actually a form of masking. It is cut from stiff paper or cardboard in the desired outline or form, Fig. 31-4. Then, the stencil is masked in place in the desired area while the paint is being sprayed.

One frequently used custom painting technique is called "endless line," Fig. 31-3.

Fig. 31-3. Applying endless line tape as a means of customizing.

After the surface has been prepared in the usual manner, the 1/8 in. wide endless tape is applied in the desired design. Then, spray the surface with several coats of acrylic lacquer. Allow each coat to dry thoroughly, then wet sand with 400 grit paper. Wash the surface and blow off with clean air.

Another design for custom painting is known as "the flame," Fig. 31-1. The flame-like design is produced through the use of stencils and paint. The stencils are easy to make: Draw the design on stiff paper or thin cardboard, such as office file folders. Then, cut out the design and apply it to the body panel. If desired, the flame pattern can be edged or fogged with an air brush. A conventional spray gun can be used if sufficient masking has been provided.

When using any stencil, the most important thing is to hold it firmly and smoothly on the surface being customized.

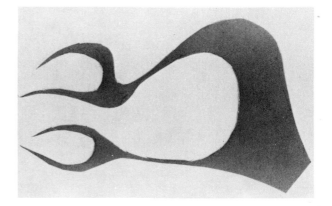

Fig. 31-4. A special stencil is cut to form a flame design.

"Spider webbing" is an unusual custom painting effect that is fairly easy to produce. No stencil is used. Basically, spider webbing is produced by forcing the acrylic lacquer from the spray gun in the form of fibrous threads. First, apply the base color in the usual manner. Do not thin the acrylic lacquer, and apply it with heavier than normal air pressure. Usually, 35 to 40 psi is required.

Then, adjust the spray gun to produce a heavy, stringy stream, and hold the gun about four feet from the panel being sprayed. By varying the adjustment of the gun, thinner or thicker webbing will be produced. After the webbing is dry, apply several coats of clear acrylic lacquer. Then, sand the surface with 400 grit paper.

One of the most popular custom painting methods is "shading" (also known as "card masking"), Fig. 31-5. It is created by over-spraying the surrounding panel. Careful masking of the working surface is extremely important, since most of the material being sprayed will fall on the masking, not on the working area.

Fig. 31-5. A card fan used to produce a zig zag design.

To produce "shading," arrange a number of cards in the form of a fan. The outer edges may be even or staggered, as desired. Hold the fan a few inches from the working surface, and apply color in a quick, light fog around the edge of the masked surface. Most of the color will fall on the masked surface, and the overspray creates a shading effect. Adjust air pressure and atomization to obtain the desired pattern. Allow sufficient time for drying before proceeding with the clear coats.

Special stencils or templates are used to produce the effects of shell, swirl and quilt, Fig. 31-6. The effects are obtained by overspray in the same manner as shading. The template is placed in the work area and

Fig. 31-6. Some popular forms of customizing stencils.

sprayed. After flash drying, the template is moved to the next position.

For especially fine work, an air brush is used by some painters, Fig. 31-7. An artist's design is shown in Fig. 31-8.

Fig. 31-7. Air brush used for especially fine detail work.

PROTECTIVE STRIPING

Protection against scratches and nicks from other cars in parking lots can be provided by special decorative striping. Latest striping materials are easy to apply and will not come loose.

Fig. 31-8. Special custom painting design painted by an artist.

When applying protective vinyl moldings, consider these important tips from the 3M Company:

1. Do not install molding on cold bodies nor on unclean or waxed bodies. The car body should be at least at 70 deg. F.

2. Clean the body with solvent, then wipe dry.

3. Install masking tape as an aid in applying the molding in a straight line.

4. Do not cut the molding through the door opening or on car body paint. Instead, use a clean backup surface to protect the paint.

5. Remove the backing and immediately apply the molding at the widest point of the car body.

6. Use firm pressure of about 10 psi with a roller or by hand to seat the molding in place. See Fig. 31-9.

QUIZ - Chapter 31

1. What is the most popular type of paint used for custom painting jobs?

Acrylic lacquer.

Acrylic enamel.

Synthetic enamel.

2. Shading is a customizing technique also known as "card masking."

True.

False.

3. Spider webbing is accomplished by using a special stencil and an air brush.

Yes.

No.

4. Shell, swirl and quilt effects are obtained by using special stencils and overspraying the surrounding panels.

Yes.

No.

5. To cut protective moldings to length, cut through the door opening.

True.

False.

Fig. 31-9. Applying special protective striping by sighting to a fixed point. Another method is to first apply masking tape.

Chapter 32
WHEEL ALIGNMENT

As the result of collisions, the alignment of the front wheels is often changed and it is, therefore, important that auto body repairmen understand the fundamentals of front wheel alignment.

No attempt will be made in these pages to describe the use of the various types of equipment used in measuring the alignment of automobile front wheels because there is great variation in the design of such equipment. The reader is, therefore, referred to the instruction book which accompanies such equipment.

Fig. 32-1. *Illustrating positive and negative caster.*

Front wheel alignment and front end service are the keys to good steering control, safe handling and maximum tire life. Correct alignment calls for the use of reliable accurate equipment to aid in making critical checks and precise adjustments of caster, camber and toe-in.

However, correct alignment of the steering angles is so interrelated with good working condition of steering and suspension parts that many preliminary checks and adjustments are required along with any needed repairs and/or parts replacement. Among the more common causes of steering and suspension troubles are: Worn ball joints or tie rod ends; unbalanced wheels; bent wheels; weak or inoperative shock absorbers; unlike tread patterns or different degrees of tread wear on the front tires; improperly adjusted steering gear. Trouble shooting details are given in the accompanying list at the end of this chapter.

CASTER

Caster is the steering angle that utilizes the weight and momentum of the vehicle to lead the front wheels in a straight path, and is illustrated in Fig. 32-1. It is measured in degrees, and is the backward or forward tilt of the ball joint (or king pin) axis from the vertical axis of the front wheels. It tends to stabilized steering in a straight direction by placing the weight of the vehicle either ahead or behind the area of the tire-to-road contact. POSITIVE caster is the angular amount the steering axis is tilted at the top toward the rear of the car. NEGATIVE caster is the amount the steering axis is tilted toward the front of the car. Caster can be adjusted to the manufacturer's specifications by means of shims, strut rods, or eccentric bolts, bushings, pins or oversize bolt holes.

CAMBER

Camber, as shown in Fig. 32-2, is the outward tilt of the wheels at the top. It is also measured in degrees, and is closely associated with steering axis inclination,

Fig. 32-2. *Camber and ball joint inclination.*

which is the inward tilt of the steering knuckle. These two steering angles share a common side (the vertical axis of the wheel) and form what is known as the included angle. Its purpose is to place the turning point of the wheel at the center of the tire-to-road contact area. Camber can be adjusted by means of shims, eccentric bolts, bushings pins or oversize bolt holes. A typical adjustment is shown in Fig. 32-3.

TOE-IN

Toe-in, as shown in Fig. 32-4, is the amount in inches that the front wheels are "pigeon-toed," or closer together in front than at the rear, as measured at hub height (with one or two exceptions). Its purpose is to prevent slipping and scuffing of the tires on the road. The small amount of toe-in serves to keep the front wheels running parallel by offsetting the forces that tend to spread them apart. Toe-in is adjusted by turning the tie-rod ends which are also known as the steering connecting rod ends, to

shorten or lengthen the tie rod. On some cars, as shown in Fig. 32-5, the adjustments are made by means of sleeves on the connecting rods.

Toe-out on turns, as shown in Fig. 32-6, refers to the correct relative position of the front wheels on turns. Since the outside wheel on turns is approximately five feet further away from the point about which the car is turning, it must swing through a greater arc than the inside wheel. To accomplish this, the steering arms are designed to angle several degrees inside of the parallel position. This serves to speed the action of the arm on the inside of the turn as it moves toward the center line of the wheel spindle. The effect on the outside wheel is to slow it down to obtain true rolling contact of the tires rather than slipping and scuffing. The amount of toe-out on turns is not adjustable

Fig. 32-3. *A popular method of adjusting camber is by means of shims.*

Fig. 32-4. *Front wheels are toed-in when dimension B is less than dimension A.*

SECTOR SHAFT (PITMAN ARM)   STEERING ARM-TO-IDLER ARM ROD   IDLER ARM AND BRACKET

SLEEVE   SPINDLE CONNECTING RODS   CONNECTING ROD END   G1147-

Fig. 32-5. Layout of steering linkage on Ford cars. Note sleeves which are adjustable for toe-in.

TOE-OUT

FRONT OF CAR

Fig. 32-6. Note the wheels toe-out on turns.

but is controlled by the angle of the steering arm. Should these become bent, they should be replaced. In no case should heat be used to straighten steering arms or any other steering parts which are heat treated.

Fig. 32-7. Special pulling equipment is needed to correct wheel alignment on MacPherson type front suspension. (Blackhawk Collision Repair Div., Applied Power, Inc.)

MACPHERSON FRONT SUSPENSION

Many imported cars now have MacPherson type front suspension. There is no provision for adjusting wheel alignment with this type of suspension. Therefore, bending is necessary when correction is required. Special equipment is available for making such corrections, Fig. 32-7.

TROUBLE SHOOTING

Causes of steering difficulties include:

HARD STEERING
    Lack of lubrication.
    Under-inflated tires.
    Maladjustment of steering gear.
    Incorrect front wheel alignment.
    Bent frame.
    Sagged front spring.

LOOSE STEERING
    Maladjustment of steering gear.
    Defective front wheel bearings.
    Worn steering knuckle ball joints.
    Worn pitman shaft bushings.
    Worn steering linkage.
    Loose gear assembly at frame.
    Worn control arm bushings.

SHIMMY
    Unbalanced front wheels.
    Faulty front wheel bearings.
    Loose wheel nuts.
    Defective front brakes.
    Worn steering linkage.
    Defective shock absorbers.
    Bent wheels.

Low tire pressure.
Incorrect caster.
Incorrect toe-in.
Worn steering knuckle bushings.
Defective ball joints.
Worn control arm bushings.
Inoperative stabilizer.

WHEEL TRAMP
Unbalanced wheel assemblies.
Defective shock absorbers.
Inoperative stabilizer.

ROAD WANDER
Under-inflated tires.
Maladjustment of steering gear.
Defective front wheel bearings.
Worn steering linkage.
Worn steering knuckle bushings.
Worn ball joints.
Incorrect wheel alignment.
Shifted rear axle.
Worn steering gear.
Binding upper or lower control arm shaft.

CAR PULLS TO ONE SIDE
Low or uneven tire pressure.
Incorrect caster or camber.
Uneven car height at front.
Bent frame.
Shifted rear axle.
Incorrect toe-in.
Broken or weak rear springs.
Bent steering knuckle or knuckle support.
Inoperative shock absorber.
One brake dragging.

SIDE WEAR ON TIRES
Outside wear.
Excessive positive camber.
Inside: Excessive negative camber.
Outside and Inside: Under-inflated tires or
vehicle overloaded.

CENTER RIB WEAR OF TIRES
Over-inflation.

SHARP RIB EDGES ON TIRES
Inside: Excessive toe-in.

Outside: Excessive toe-out.
Inside on one tire, outside on opposite tire:
Bent arm or steering knuckle.

TIRE THUMP, TRAMP, SQUEAL
Damaged fabric.
Unbalanced condition.
Incorrect air pressure.
Incorrect wheel alignment.

ABRASIVE ROUGHNESS
Incorrect toe-in.
Driving on rough finished concrete.

HEEL AND TOE WEAR
High speed driving.
Excessive use of brakes.

UNIFORM SPOTTY WEAR
Lack of tire rotation.

UNEVEN SPOTTY WEAR
Unusual driving habits.
Worn or loose parts.
Incorrect wheel alignment.

QUIZ - Chapter 32

1. Caster is the amount the wheels are tilted
to the side.
   True.
   False.
2. Camber is the outward tilt of the wheels
at the top.
   True.
   False.
3. What method is usually used to adjust
toe-in?
   Shims.
   Threaded tie-rod ends.
4. List four causes of hard steering.
5. List five causes of why a car will pull to
one side.
6. Are adjustments provided for caster and
camber on cars with MacPherson front
suspension?
   Yes.
   No.

Chapter 33

AUTO BODY MAINTENANCE

FIXING DUST AND WATER LEAKS

Car owners frequently complain of dust and water leaks occurring in their automobiles. Such leakage is often difficult to locate, as it frequently occurs at joints between panels which are normally sealed with special sealers, when the vehicle is being manufactured. It is important when repairing an auto body that all such sealing material be replaced whenever it has been removed or disturbed.

Dust and water leaks also occur at doors, windows, deck lids, ventilators and windshields whenever windlace, weather stripping and similar material has become damaged, is loose, or otherwise defective.

LOCATING LEAKS

The three principal methods used to locate water and dust leaks are:
1. Spraying car with water.
2. Driving car on dusty road.
3. Directing beam of light on car.

Before making the actual test, it is generally advisable to remove interior trim from the general area of the leak. In that connection it is important to emphasize that the actual source or entrance of the dust or water is often quite remote from its appearance in the interior of the vehicle. It is, therefore, suggested that the following should be removed:
1. Cowl trim panel.
2. Quarter trim panel.
3. Rear seat back and seat cushion.
4. Luggage compartment floor mats, spare wheel and side trim panels.

Fig. 33-1. Using water from a hose to locate body leaks.

5. Center trim panel on four door sedans.
6. Scuff plates.
7. All floor mats.

After removing such trim the location of most leaks will be readily evident.

Entrance dust is usually indicated by a pointed shaft of dust or silt at the point of entrance. Seal all such points with an appropriate type of sealer. Then recheck to make sure that the difficulty has been corrected.

CHECKING LEAKS WITH WATER

After removing the interior trim in the general area of the leak, spray the vehicle with a stream of water, Fig. 33-1. While that is being done, one man should be inside the vehicle with the windows shut, to act as an observer and carefully note just where the water is entering.

Testing for water and dust leaks by using water is to be preferred, as water under pressure is always available.

Fig. 33-2. *Applying sealer to windshield to stop water leaks.*

Fig. 33-3. *Opening drain holes on lower edge of door. (Ford)*

DRIVING CAR TO LOCATE LEAKS

Another method of locating dust leaks is to drive the car over a dusty road. Keep the windows closed so that the observer will not be confused by any dirt which may enter through the windows. Dusty roads are not always available.

USING LIGHT TO LOCATE LEAKS

Simple leaks can often be located by moving a light around the car, while an observer remains inside the vehicle. This method is satisfactory only when the course of the leakage is straight. If the path is devious, as is usually the case, a light beam will not be able to pass through the "turns."

Some body men light a candle in the car. As the candle is held in different areas of the car, the reaction of the flame to drafts is noted. Sometimes it is possible to find a leak by this means.

PLUGS AND GROMMETS

There are many plugs and grommets used in the floor pan and dash panels of automotive vehicles to keep out dust and water from the interior of the vehicle. These areas should be carefully inspected to make sure that all the plugs and grommets are in place and in good condition.

WEATHER STRIP LEAKAGE

When the weather stripping on doors and deck lids becomes loose or damaged, dust and rain leakage results.

On most vehicles the weather stripping used on doors and deck lids is cemented in place. Should it become loose, or when replacement is required, all that is necessary is to recement it in place. Fig. 33-2 shows how special weather strip cement is applied around the edges of the windshield.

To check for correct positioning of the weather strip around door and deck lid weather stripping, place a feeler gauge or card about .020 in. thick between the weather strip and the door frame. Then with the door closed, withdraw the feeler gauge. The weather strip should be checked all around the door or deck lid, as the case may be, and if there is little or no resistance when withdrawing the feeler gauge, the weather strip should be moved closer to the edge of the door, or replaced completely. For details on the procedure for removal and installation of various types of weather stripping, the reader is referred to Chapter 18.

PREVENTING RUST

One of the major causes of rusted auto body panels is parking the car out of doors where rain, snow, fog and sun deteriorate the finish and rusting of the panels takes place.

Contributing largely to the rusting of the panels is the failure to keep drain holes open. Drain holes are located on the lower edge of the doors, rocker panels and quarter panels. The construction of the drain hole system varies with different manufacturers. The type used on recent model Ford cars is shown in Fig. 33-3. The General Motors setup is shown in Fig. 33-4. It is important that these holes are kept open so that any water that seeps down past the windows will not collect in the panels.

In the case of the construction shown in Fig. 33-3, the valves are located in the lowest points of the panel. The weight of the water will open the valve and allow the water to escape the panel. After the water has drained, the valve will close automatically and prevent entry of dust. If for any reason the door trim panel, rocker panel, scuff plate or luggage compartment trim panel has been removed, the metal should be inspected to make sure the drain holes are not obstructed.

On late model General Motor cars the door bottom drain hole sealing strips, Fig. 33-4, are attached to door inner panels over door bottom drain holes. These are designed to prevent entry of dust at these area, and also permit water to drain.

The sealing strips are retained by two retaining plugs, which are in integral part of the sealing strip. These new sealing strips are of vinyl construction, and should not require lubrication. The sealing strip is easily pried out for inspection.

On older type bodies of all makes, drain holes are usually not provided with automatic seals, and it is particularly important to check the drain holes regularly to be sure they are opened and not plugged with dirt.

BODY MAINTENANCE

Regular body maintenance preserves the appearance of the car and reduces the cost of maintenance during the life of the car. The following steps are suggested as a guide for regular body maintenance.

1. Vacuum the interior and wash the car regularly.

2. Check all openings for water leaks; seal where necessary.

3. Cement all loose weather strips which are still usable.

4. Replace weather strips which are unfit for service. Apply silicone lubricant to the weather stripping.

5. Replace all cracked, fogged, or chipped glass.

6. Align hood, doors and deck lid, if necessary.

7. Inspect windshield wiper blades and replace if necessary.

8. Tighten sill plate and garnish molding screws.

9. Clean the seats, door trim panels and head lining.

10. Touch up or paint chipped or scratched areas.

11. Drain holes located on the underside of doors, rocker panel and quarter panel should be cleared periodically.

RATTLE ELIMINATION

Most rattles are caused by loose bolts or screws. Foreign objects, such as nuts, bolts, or small pieces of body deadener in the door wells, pillars and quarter panels are often the source of rattles. Door wells can be checked by carefully striking the underside of the door with a rubber mallet. The impact made by the mallet will indicate if loose objects are in the door well. All bolts and screws securing the body to the frame should

Fig. 33-4. Drain hole sealing strips on Fisher bodies should be lubricated. (Chevrolet)

be tightened periodically. In the event tightening bolts and screws, located on such assemblies as doors, hood and deck lid does not eliminate the rattles, the trouble may be caused by misalignment. If this is the case, follow the adjustment and alignment procedures for those assemblies.

Rattles and squeaks are sometimes caused by weather stripping and antisqueak material that has slipped out of position. Apply additional cement or other adhesive and install the material in the proper location to eliminate this difficulty.

REAR COMPARTMENT LID DRAIN HOLES

Deck lids on Fisher body styles B-C-D-E are louvered to accommodate the flo-thru ventilation system. Water entering these louvers is channeled rearward between the deck lid inner and outer panels outside of the body through holes provided at the lower edge of the lid assembly. These holes are equipped with drain valves, Fig. 33-5. These drain valves must form a complete and flat peripheral seal around the drain holes. If for any reason a drain valve is removed or missing, it must be reinstalled properly or replaced. Torn, mutilated or deformed valves must be replaced.

© General Motors Corporation

Fig. 33-5. Details of rear compartment lid drain holes.

HOOD NOISES OR PANEL FLUTTER

Squeaks or grunting noises in the hood when driving over rough roads, do not necessarily indicate misalignment of hood and fenders. These noises may be caused by metal contacts at some point where clearance should exist, or by worn or dry hood bumpers.

If hood squeaks, check with 1/16 in. thick feeler gauge all around hood for clearance at fenders and cowl. If an edge of metal is making contact at any point where clearance should exist, a bright metal spot will usually be found. Such spots can be depressed by spring hammering to provide clearance.

A grunting noise in hood is usually caused by dry rubber bumpers or cowl ledge lacing. Lubricate all rubber bumpers on rails and cowl with silicone rubber lubricant. To correct case of squeaking or grunting, where hood top panel contacts ledge lacing, even when lubricated, cement 1/16 in. thick strip of felt to panel where lacing makes contact.

To prevent hood panel flutter, the rear end of the hood panel must have firm contact with the lacing attached to cowl ledge. It may be raised or lowered by adjustment.

EXTERIOR CLEANING

The outside finish should be washed frequently. Never wipe the painted surfaces with a dry cloth. Dusting the finish when it is dry tends to rub the dust and dirt into the finish and leaves a sandpaper effect on the surface. To keep finish bright and attractive and eliminate necessity of using polish, it is advisable to wash the car whenever it has accumulated a moderate amount of dirt and road salt.

CLEANING BRIGHT PARTS

The bright metal parts of the car if made of stainless steel require no special care. Periodic cleaning will preserve the beauty and the life of such material. Wash with clear water or if any parts are very dirty use a special cleaner for stainless steel.

Chrome plated parts rust or corrode because chemical agents present in road silt and traffic film seep through pores in plating and attack underlying base metal. A plating of nickel is applied underneath chrome to seal plating and protect base metal.

Deterioration of chrome plated parts can be avoided by keeping parts clean and by periodic application of a preservative which will aid in retarding seepage of destructive agents through plating. Plated parts should be washed with clear water only, using mild detergent when necessary. Avoid using scouring powders, cleaning compounds or stiff brushes.

INTERIOR CLEANING

Use a vacuum cleaner to remove dust and dirt from the upholstery or floor covering. Vinyl and woven plastic trim that is dusty can usually be cleaned with a damp cloth. Do not use cleaning materials containing kerosene, naphtha, toluol, xylol, lacquer thinners, cellulose acetate, butyl cellulose, carbon tetrachloride, body polish, battery acid, antifreeze, gasoline, motor oils, or other type lubricants.

HOW TO REMOVE SPOTS

In automobiles the seats are covered with what is called trim material. There are four general types of this material being used in current model vehicles. In order to remove spots most easily, it is important to know what is the best cleaner to be used for each type of material.

The four general types of material used to upholster the seats in automobile bodies are:

1. Fabrics - - either plain fabrics (broadcloth, gabardine, etc.), or pattern fabrics which are made with either natural or synthetic (nylon, orlon, rayon, viscose, etc.) fibers.

2. Genuine leather.

3. Coated fabrics (vinyl or nylon).

4. Polyurethane foam.

Dust or dirt particles that accumulate on the upholstery of a car should not be allowed to accumulate, but should be removed regularly.

Do not use a whisk broom on fabrics having a raised tapestry pattern since damage to fine threads may result. On polyurethane foam materials use only a soft bristle brush. Do not use a vacuum cleaner or a whisk broom.

REMOVING SPOTS

For best results stains should be removed as soon as possible after they are made, as the longer they remain in the fabric, the more difficult they are to remove.

Cleaning precaution: Do not use any of the following to clean upholstery fabrics: Colored gasoline or gasoline which may contain tetraethyl lead, acetone, lacquer thinners, enamel reducers, bleaches, hydrogen peroxide, chlorine.

TYPES OF CLEANERS

There are four basic types of cleaners commonly used for removing spots and stains from automotive upholstery materials.

1. Volatile cleaners, which are usually colorless and include such liquids as benzine, carbon tetrachloride.

2. Synthetic detergents.

3. Neutral soap.

4. Ammonia.

USING VOLATILE CLEANERS ON FABRICS

When using volatile cleaners, it is generally advisable to do the work out-of-doors and care must be exercised that there is no flame in the vicinity. Avoid inhaling the fumes of cleaners, as many are toxic. Also avoid prolonged contact with the skin and take special care to keep the cleaner away from the eyes and mouth.

Do not use too much cleaner. Apply the cleaner with a clean cloth. Remember the solvent is designed to dissolve the material forming the spot or stain, which is then absorbed by the cloth. Use only a minimum of pressure.

First brush away all loose particles of dirt or soil. Then dampen a clean cloth with the volatile cleaner. Open the cloth and allow a portion of the solvent to evaporate so that the cloth is just slightly damp.

Using a very light pressure and circular lifting motion, rub the stained area, starting at the outer edge and working toward the center until the entire area has been covered. When the cleaning cloth becomes dirty it should be discarded and a new one used.

Before proceeding, wait several minutes to allow most of the cleaner that is in the upholstery to evaporate. This will avoid the danger of a cleaner penetrating into the padding under the upholstery. Repeat the foregoing procedure until the spot has been removed.

If a ring should be formed when removing a stain, repeat the cleaning operation but start well beyond the area of the ring and again work toward the center. Old upholstery is often so full of dust it is almost impossible to treat a single spot without leaving a telltale ring. In such cases it is advisable to go over the entire seat area with a cloth dampened with cleaner.

USING SYNTHETIC DETERGENTS ON FABRICS

In addition to special synthetic detergents designed specifically for cleaning upholstery fabrics, many body shops use such materials as Tide, Lux, etc.

Make a solution of the synthetic detergent in lukewarm water. With a clean cloth or sponge dampened with the solution, apply to the surface of the upholstery using light pressure. Repeat several times, taking care that clean areas of the sponge or cloth are used each time. With a second clean cloth dampened with lukewarm water (no detergent) rub over the area to remove excess detergent. Follow with a clean dry cloth and wipe off the excess moisture.

Allow fabric to dry and if necessary repeat cleaning operation.

CLEANING LEATHER AND COATED FABRICS

Care of genuine leather and coated fabrics, including vinyl coated formed head lining is relatively easy. The surface should be wiped occasionally with a clean dry cloth. Whenever dirt accumulates the following cleaning procedure should be followed: Use lukewarm water and a neutral soap. Apply a thick suds to the surface worked up on a piece of clean cheesecloth. Use a damp cloth but no soap to remove all traces of soap. Then dry with a clean cloth.

Polishes and cleaners used for auto body finishes, volatile cleaners, furniture polishes, oils, varnishes or household cleaning and bleaching materials should never be used on leather and coated fabrics.

CLEANING POLYURETHANE FOAM

Normal soilage, such as dirt and fingerprints can be removed with a cleaning solution of approximately 2 oz. of white detergent powder mixed in a gallon of water. Immerse a clean cellulose sponge in cleaning solution. Wring the sponge out thoroughly leaving suds only; then clean soiled area carefully. Rinse off the clean area with a sponge and clean water. Do not soak the clean area. Soilage such as cements, sealers and grease can be removed by first cleaning the soiled area with a detergent solution as described previously. Do not rinse. Leaving suds on the soiled area, clean area with a

clean cloth that has been dipped in a good volatile upholstery cleaner and thoroughly rung out. Then clean soiled area with detergent suds and rinse as described before.

CLEANING FLOOR CARPETS

Thoroughly brush or vacuum the floor carpet. In many instances the floor carpet may require no further cleaning. If carpet is extremely soiled remove carpet from car and thoroughly vacuum to remove loose dirt; then with a foaming type upholstery cleaner, clean approximately one square foot of carpet at a time. After each area is cleaned, remove as much of the cleaner as possible using a vacuum cleaner. After cleaning the carpet use an air hose to fluff the carpet pile, then dry the carpet. After the carpet is completely dry, use an air hose again to fluff the carpet pile.

REMOVING SPECIFIC STAINS

Some types of stains and soilage, including blood, ink, chewing gum, etc., require special consideration for most satisfactory results. For these and other stains specific instructions are outlined in the following paragraphs. It must be expected, particularly where water treatment is specified, that some discoloration and finish disturbance may occur. By following the procedures outlined with normal care and caution, reasonably satisfactory results can be expected.

BATTERY ACIDS

Apply ordinary household ammonia water with a brush or cloth to the affected area, saturating it thoroughly. Permit the ammonia water to remain on the spot about a minute, so that it will have ample time to neutralize the acid. Then rinse the spot by rubbing with a clean cloth saturated with cold water.

BLOOD

Do not use hot water or soap and water on blood stains since this will set the stain.

Rub the stain with a clean cloth saturated with water until no more of the stain will come out. If this treatment does not remove all the stain, apply a small amount of household ammonia water to the stain with a cloth or brush. Let stand a moment, then continue to rub the stain with a clean cloth dipped in clear water. If the stain remains after the use of ammonia and water, a thick paste of corn starch and cold water may be applied to the stained area. Allow the paste to remain until it has dried. Then carefully brush off the dried corn starch. Several applications may be necessary.

CANDY

Candy stains, other than candy containing chocolate, can usually be removed by rubbing the affected area with a cloth soaked with hot water. If the stain is not completely removed, rub area lightly (after drying) using a cloth wet with a volatile cleaner.

Candy stains resulting from cream and fruit filled chocolates can be removed more easily by rubbing with a cloth soaked with lukewarm soapsuds (mild neutral soap) and scraping while wet with a dull knife. This treatment is followed by rubbing the spot with a cloth dipped in cold water.

Stains resulting from chocolate or milk chocolate can be removed by rubbing the stain with a cloth wet with lukewarm water. After the spot is dry, rub it lightly with a cloth dipped in volatile cleaner.

CHEWING GUM

Harden the gum with an ice cube and scrape off particles with a dull knife. If gum cannot be removed completely by this method, moisten it with a volatile cleaner and work it from the fabric with a dull knife, while the gum is still moist.

FRUIT, LIQUOR AND WINE

Practically all fruit stains can be removed by treatment with hot water. Wet the stain well by applying hot water to the spot with a clean cloth. Scrape all excess pulp, if present, off the fabric with a dull knife; then rub vigorously with a cloth wet with very hot water. If the stain is very old or deep, it may

be necessary to pour very hot water directly on the spot, following this treatment with the scraping and rubbing. Direct application of hot water to fabrics is not recommended since discoloration usually results.

If the above treatments do not remove stain, allow fabric to dry thoroughly; then rub lightly with a clean cloth dipped in a volatile cleaner. This is the only further treatment that is recommended.

Soap and water are not recommended since they will probably set the stain and cause a permanent discoloration. Drying the fabric by means of heat (such as the use of an iron) is not recommended.

GREASE AND OIL

If grease has been spilled on the material, as much as possible should be removed by scraping with a dull knife or spatula before further treatment is attempted. Grease and oil stains may be removed by rubbing lightly with a clean cloth saturated with a volatile cleaner. Be sure all motions are toward the center of the stained area to decrease the possibility of spreading the stain.

ICE CREAM

The same procedure is recommended for the removal of ice cream stains as described for removing fruit stains.

If the stain is persistent, rubbing the spot with a cloth wet with warm soapsuds (mild neutral soap) may be used to some advantage after the initial treatment with hot water. This soap treatment should be followed with a rinsing, by rubbing with a clean cloth wet with cold water. After this dries, rubbing lightly with a cloth wet with a volatile cleaner will help to clear up the last of the stain, by removing fatty or oily matter.

NAUSEA

Sponge with a clean cloth dipped in clear water. After most of the stain has been removed in this way, wash lightly with a soap (mild neutral) using a clean cloth and lukewarm water. Then rub with another clean cloth dipped in cold water. If any of the stain remains after this treatment, gently rub clean with a cloth moistened with a volatile cleaner. Another method is to use a cloth dampened with ammonia and rub until the spot has been cleaned.

SHOE POLISH AND DRESSINGS

On types of shoe dressing which contain starch or dextrine or some water soluble vehicle, allow the polish to dry; then brush the spot vigorously with a brush. This will probably be all the treatment that is necessary. If further treatment is required, moisten the spot with cold water and after it has dried repeat the brushing operation.

Paste or wax type shoe polishes may require using a volatile cleaner. Rub the stain gently with a cloth wet with a volatile cleaner until the polish is removed. Use a clean portion of the cloth for each rubbing operation, and rub the stained area from outside to center.

TAR

Moisten the spot lightly with a volatile cleaner and then remove as much of the tar as possible with a dull knife. Follow this operation by rubbing the spot lightly with a cloth wet with the cleaner until the stain is removed.

URINE

Sponge the stain with a clean cloth saturated with lukewarm soapsuds (mild neutral soap) and rinse well by rubbing the stain with a clean cloth dipped in cold water. Then saturate a clean cloth with a solution of one part household ammonia and five parts water. Apply the cloth to the stain and allow solution to remain on affected area for about a minute; then rinse by rubbing with a clean wet cloth.

LIPSTICK

The composition of different types of lipstick vary greatly, making the stains very

difficult to remove. In some instances a volatile cleaner may remove the stain. If some stain remains after repeated applications of the volatile cleaner, it is usually best to leave it rather than try other measures.

QUIZ - Chapter 33

1. Spraying a car with water is one method of locating water leaks.
    True.
    False.
2. On most vehicles the weather stripping is cemented in place.
    True.
    False.
3. Indicate the location of water drain holes.
    Lower edge of doors.
    Wheel housing.
    Rocker panels.
    Quarter panels.
    Deck lids.
4. Rattles and squeaks may be caused by weather stripping which has slipped from position.
    True.
    False.
5. Scouring powders should be used to clean chrome plate.
    True.
    False.
6. Gasoline is recommended for cleaning spots from upholstery.
    True.
    False.
7. Which of the following should be used to clean genuine leather upholstery.
    Gasoline.
    Neutral soap and water.
    Carbon tetrachloride.
8. Is household ammonia satisfactory for use when battery acid gets on upholstery?
    Yes.
    No.
9. What should be used to remove fruit stains?
    Hot water.
    Carbon tetrachloride.

Chapter 34
SAFETY IN THE AUTO BODY SHOP

Safety is everyone's responsibility. This is particularly true in the auto body shop where there are greater possibilities of accidents than in most any other department. This results from the use of combustibles, such as the highly flammable lacquers, enamels, thinners and other highly volatile chemicals, coupled with the use of welding equipment. Because of the nature of the work, the body shop floor is usually more cluttered than shops doing other types of repair work. Also, there is a greater possibility of cuts and bruises when handling dented and torn sheet metal.

One of the basic rules of safety in any shop is the proper and correct conduct of every individual. There can be no running, no practical jokes, no horseplay. Such conduct invariably results in accidents as well as distracting others in the shop from the work they are supposed to do.

As previously pointed out, there is great danger from fire because of the great use of combustibles. Paints and thinners should always be kept in closed containers. This will not only prevent fires but also will reduce loss due to evaporation.

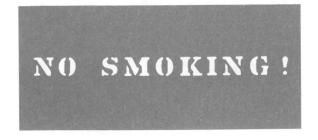

Fig. 34-1. No smoking signs should be posted throughout the shop.

Smoking and unprotected flames should never be permitted. "No Smoking" signs should be prominently displayed, Fig. 34-1.

Painting should always be done in a spray booth provided with exhaust fans and conforming to underwriters' requirements, Fig. 34-2. In addition, painters should always

Fig. 34-2. Since paint fumes are highly inflammable, all painting should be done in a properly ventilated paint booth.

wear respirators, Fig. 34-3, as the inhalation of fumes from lacquer and enamel will result in respiratory ailments.

All body shops should be provided with an ample number of fire extinguishers. Everyone should be familiar with their location, and the owner or manager of the shop should make it a personal responsibility to check the fire extinguishers regularly to be sure they are in operating condition. Remember that water cannot be used to extinguish a fire from lacquer, thinner, gasoline or grease. For such fires a carbon dioxide or foam type extinguisher is

Fig. 34-3. *Special respirators should be worn, especially when spraying urethane paints.*

specified. If nothing else is available, sand can be used.

As a further protection against fire, oil and paint rags, together with used abrasive paper, should be kept in suitable containers. Care must be taken so that spontaneous combustion does not occur.

Depending on the nature of the collision to a vehicle, the electrical wiring may be damaged so that there is a strong possibility of electrical shorts occurring. It is, therefore, always good policy to disconnect the starting battery as soon as any car is brought into a shop. In that way the possibility of fire is greatly reduced.

When using sanders or grinders, autobody mechanics should always wear goggles or a mask as protection for the eyes, Fig. 34-4.

Fig. 34-4. *Safety mask is worn by mechanic; oxyacetylene tanks are chained to prevent tipping.*

It is particularly important that the shop be well lighted, not only to avoid eye strain, but also to reduce the possibility of accidents resulting from tripping over parts on the floor which cannot be seen because of lack of proper illumination. Special attention should be paid to keeping the aisles clear and free from parts removed from vehicles undergoing repair. This is a difficult problem in auto body shops, as panels and other parts are often removed so that other parts can be more easily reached. In such cases, place removed parts against the wall or in some other out-of-the-way place.

An ample number of electric outlets should be provided so there is no reason to have extension cords snaking across the shop floor. Such a condition is a hazard to mechanics who may trip over a cord and be injured.

Keep floors clean and, particularly, free from grease and oil. Such spots are a fire hazard. They are also very slippery and could cause accidents to persons walking through the shop. Whenever oil or grease spills on the floor or drips from a vehicle, clean up immediately. Special compounds are available for absorbing oil and cleaning such spots.

Much auto body repair work is done with the car raised on jacks or stands. Therefore, make sure all equipment is in safe operating condition and capable of supporting various vehicles. If floor jacks are used, see that the handle does not protrude and trip someone.

USING TOOLS SAFELY

Files should never be used without protective handles, as there is always the danger of injury from the pointed tang. Neither should files be used as pry bars, or hammered. Files are made with hard temper and consequently are quite brittle and when hammered, small pieces may fly off and cause severe wounds or loss of eyesight. Hardened surfaces, such as the face of an anvil, should not be struck with a hammer as bits of steel may fly off and cause damage. Further in connection with hammers and sledges, care must always be exercised that the head is always securely attached to the handle. Loose hammer and sledge heads may fly off when the tool is used and anyone standing in the way will be struck and severly injured.

When the head of a chisel becomes swagged over, it should be discarded or reground to remove the swagged edges. This will prevent bits of steel from flying off and causing damage.

Whenever grinding or welding is done, mechanics should wear goggles to protect their eyes, Fig. 34-5. The grinding wheel should always be provided with a protective guard. The reason for the guard is that in the event of the grinding wheel flying apart due to centrifugal force, the danger to the operator will be minimized. Unless the grinding wheel is designed to take such strains, its side surfaces should not be used for grinding.

HEADBAND

CLEAR PLASTIC

Fig. 34-5. Different types of goggles and masks used in a body shop.

As there is always a possibility of a driving belt breaking or a rotating wheel bursting, it is always advisable to stand well away from the plane of rotating parts. In the event of any such breakage, pieces will be hurled with terrific force, and anyone standing in line with the rotating part may be severely injured.

When using a wrench, there is always less danger to the mechanic who pulls on the handle, rather than pushes on it. Should the wrench slip when pulling on it, there would be less danger of skinning the knuckles. Further in that connection, when the jaws of a wrench become worn or are sprung, the wrench should be discarded, as it will no longer fit the nut securely and will tend to slip.

Compressed air is an important "tool" in every shop. The air gun should never be pointed at anyone. The high pressure of the air can blow dust and dirt particles at such high speed that they will puncture the skin and get into the eyes.

Care must always be exercised, when working around any machinery, engine or motor that there is no chance of loose clothing being caught and entangled in rotating parts. Neckties should always be tucked within the shirt. If long sleeves are being worn, these should always be buttoned at the cuff. Caps without brims are considered safer than those with brims, because of the possibility of the protruding brim being caught in some rotating part.

In regard to safety precautions when using oxygen and acetylene for welding, there are many points to observe. Never allow oil or grease to contact oxygen under pressure. Do not lubricate welding and cutting apparatus. Never use oxygen as a substitute for compressed air, as a source of pressure, or for ventilation. Before starting to weld or cut, make sure that the flame, sparks, hot slag, or hot metal will not be likely to start a fire. Always wear goggles when working with a lighted torch, Fig. 34-5.

Be sure to keep a clear space between the cylinders and the work as you may find it necessary to reach and adjust the regulators quickly. Do not risk hand burns by lighting the torch with a match. Use a friction type lighter as it is safer and also easier. Never use acetylene pressure higher than 15 psi. Never release acetylene where it might cause a fire or an explosion. Always check equipment before starting to work. Never braze, weld, or use acetylene flame on gasoline or other fuel tanks. Acetylene and oxygen tanks should always be in a special carrier, or chained to a post to prevent falling.

QUIZ - Chapter 34

1. Paint and thinners should always be kept in closed containers.
    True.
    False.

2. What material can be used to extinguish lacquer, gasoline, grease and thinner fires?
    Water.
    Carbon dioxide.
3. Why should the starting battery be disconnected on vehicles after they have been in a collision?

4. Files may be used as pry bars.
    True.
    False.
5. It is always advisable to stand in the plane of rotating parts.
    True.
    False.

Safety in the auto body shop means clean floors, good ventilation, ample lighting, adequate tool storage space, equipment engineered to do the job and separate facilities for body work and paint spraying. (Blackhawk Collision Repair Div., Applied Power, Inc.)

ASBESTOS WARNING

Dust containing asbestos particles can cause cancer. Many wheel brake and clutch friction materials contain asbestos. Therefore, do not clean brake and clutch parts with a dry brush or compressed air. Use a vacuum source or flush with water. Also, wear an approved filter mask.

FIBERGLASS RESIN CAUTION

Use care when adding the hardener (catalyst) to fiberglass resin. If one drop of hardener gets in your eye, it will progressively destroy eye tissue and result in blindness. Wash the hardener from the eye within four seconds after the accident. Wear goggles when doing this work.

Chapter 35

CAREER OPPORTUNITIES

Many and varied jobs are performed in an automotive body and paint shop. Job titles range all the way from "apprentice," who may sweep the floor and help mask bodies prior to painting, to "owner," who runs the establishment, Fig. 35-1. In between, you have

Fig. 35-1. *Heading up a large auto body and paint shop are the owner and shop manager. Almost invariably, they have gained experience through years of work in the shop.*

metal straighteners, power equipment operators, painters, wheel alignment specialists, cost-of-repair estimators and shop manager.

In addition, auto body repairing and repainting also may lead to insurance adjusting or teaching the subject in a vocational school. Some experienced body workers and painters also have entered the field of selling auto body repair equipment and tools.

There has been a falling off in the number of automobile repair jobs of certain types

because of improvements in design and materials. However, collision repair work and repainting have increased, and the number of repair jobs per year will continue to rise in keeping with the steady increase in automotive registrations.

THE APPRENTICE

The apprentice in an auto body and paint shop usually starts with sweeping the floor. It may not be very exciting, but it affords a priceless opportunity for observing how the work progresses to restore a severely damaged wreck to a smoothly finished product.

The apprentice auto body mechanic is also called upon to bring needed tools and straightening equipment to the job. An alert apprentice soon will be able to anticipate the need for a special item. Cheerfully doing these simple jobs well could be the basis for advancement to more interesting work.

Generally three to four years of on-the-job training are required to become a fully qualified auto body mechanic. During this time, the tasks become more difficult and the apprentice is expected to accumulate hand tools while gaining experience.

THE AUTO BODY MECHANIC

The auto body mechanic must be capable of doing many jobs well: removing dents, Fig. 35-2, replacing badly damaged parts, welding torn metal, Fig. 35-3, cutting out body panels, installing filler and filing or sanding it smooth. Each vehicle in for repair presents a different problem. Therefore, a broad knowledge of automobile construction

Fig. 35-2. Hammer and dolly work is one of the basic skills that must be mastered by the auto body mechanic.

Fig. 35-4. After dents have been removed and filler material applied, the repair area is sanded smooth by the mechanic.

and repair techniques is required.

A lot of auto body work starts with simple dolly and dinging hammer work in straightening minor damage. This work is not difficult, but it requires skill and practice. Actually, the final appearance of the finished job depends largely on how well the hammer and dolly work was performed.

A good body mechanic with a dolly and hammer can straighten a panel so well that little or no filler will be required. This kind of craftsmanship cuts down on overall time on the job and it simplifies the work of the painter.

Sanding the surface of a panel is a very important part of refinishing the body of an automobile, Fig. 35-4. Final appearance of the completed job depends on how well the sanding was performed. While sanding is not difficult, care and experience are necessary to do a satisfactory job. A little carelessness or lack of attention can result in deep scratches and gouges in the surface. As a result, still more sanding will be required.

Sanding starts with the selection of the right type of abrasive paper and, as the job progresses, paper of finer grits will be required. The worker must know how much sanding is required on that particular surface. If too much material is removed, time is wasted. If too little material is removed, additional primer will be required or poor paint adherence may result.

POWER EQUIPMENT OPERATOR

Power equipment operators in an auto body shop are specialists who analyze the damage and make necessary corrections by bracing, pushing, pulling and spreading the damaged members. With today's power equipment, it is possible to straighten wrecked cars that formerly would have been passed on to the junk yard.

There are many different types of power equipment available, each with certain individual advantages. These units utilize hydraulic and/or pneumatic power to straighten bent and twisted automobiles.

To use power equipment successfully, the

Fig. 35-3. Arc welding and gas welding play an important part in the successful and profitable operation of an auto body shop.

Fig. 35-5. The power equipment operator's skillful use of pulling equipment saves time and effort in auto body shops so equipped.

body mechanic must know the basic structure of automobiles and where to apply the straightening power so the damage can be corrected, Fig. 35-5. In many cases, the power must be applied at several points and in different directions at the same time. Obviously, work of this scope requires care and skill in execution.

Power equipment work involves more than straightening sheet metal. In a wrecked car, the heavy frame members may be bent and can be only straightened with the proper application of power. Vehicles with the body bolted to a heavy frame require one type of treatment, while vehicles with "unitized" construction require still another treatment.

In addition, late model cars have heavy strengthening beams in the doors for protection of the passengers. This safety feature also complicates the repair of damaged doors, making the use of power equipment imperative.

STEERING ALIGNMENT SPECIALIST

Alignment specialists are needed in the auto body shop because the steering linkage often is damaged in a collision. While these parts usually are replaced rather than straightened, alignment work involves the correction of steering geometry (caster, camber, toe-in and toe-out on turns).

Alignment specialists align and balance wheels, using special alignment equipment and wheel balancing machines. They also repair steering mechanisms and suspension systems.

THE GLASS INSTALLER

Windshield and door glass replacement is also an auto body and paint shop function. Smaller establishments often send their glass work to specialists. Larger shops make it an important part of the services offered.

Windshield replacement usually involves two workers, an experienced glass installer and a helper.

New caulking materials have made the sealing job easier, but windshield work requires special handling techniques, some specialty tools and careful positioning of the glass in the body opening before the windshield is pressed into place.

Door glass replacement can be difficult at times, particularly when the door has not been accurately straightened. Window regulators often present a problem when damaged as the result of a collision. There is little uniformity in the design of regulators. Consequently, the glass installer must become familiar with a lot of different designs in order to do a satisfactory job of door glass replacement.

THE UPHOLSTERER

Automobile upholsterers (trimmers) repair worn and torn upholstery. Usually, this work includes not only the repair or replacement of surface materials, but also the repair of padding and springs. Other areas of work involve headlinings, seat covers, door panels, convertible tops and vinyl tops.

Upholsterers may work on both passenger cars and trucks. In many shops, the upholsterer must be skilled in the repair and/or adjustment of power seat and power window mechanisms and convertible top and tail gate mechanisms.

THE AUTO BODY PAINTER

Auto body painters are specialists. However, there is a lot more to painting than pointing the spray gun at a body panel and pressing the trigger.

A necessary and important preliminary job is masking parts and areas that are not to be painted. Masking is done by covering these surfaces with masking paper and masking tape. In a large shop, it is done by an apprentice or assistant painter. In smaller shops, the painter will do the job.

Care must be taken to see that the masking paper is securely taped to the surface and provides a sharp edge that limits the area to be painted.

Painting requires patience and practice. Many factors are involved in painting an automobile. The surface to be painted must be clean and free from oil and other foreign matter. The temperature of the vehicle and temperature of the paint should be within specified limits. Paint must be thoroughly mixed and the color accurately matched. The spray gun must be clean. Air pressure must be correct. The spray gun must be held the correct distance from the panel. Proper paint drying equipment must be used.

All these points, and many more, must be considered by the painter, along with a knowledge of primers, sealers, solvents and other painting materials.

In related areas, sign painters are needed on occasion to hand letter commercial vehicles, Fig. 35-6. Artists are employed to paint intricate scenes or designs on passenger cars, vans and recreational vehicles, Fig. 35-7.

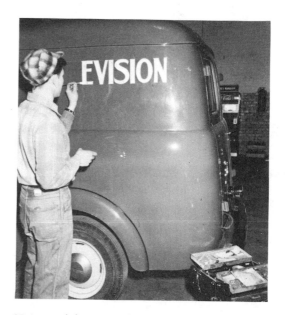

Fig. 35-6. Hand lettering of commercial vehicles takes the special skill of a sign painter.

While it is unusual to find women doing work in an auto body and paint shop (other than in the office), there is a growing number of women employees, particularly in the field of paint. Here, a woman's sensitivity to color is a great asset.

Fig. 35-7. Painting also involves an artist's "personal decoration" of a vehicle. (Dodge Div., Chrysler Corp.)

THE PARTS MANAGER

Parts managers in large auto body shops maintain a sizable stock of collision parts, especially when the shop is operated in conjunction with a new car dealership. See Fig. 35-8. While it is impossible to carry a complete inventory of parts, slower moving items can be ordered through warehouses on a one-day to one-week basis.

THE ESTIMATOR

One of the most important jobs in an auto body and paint shop is estimating the cost of repair. The estimator is the man or woman who examines the damaged automobile and tells how long it will take and how much it will cost to make the necessary repairs.

In virtually all other auto repair work (brake job, tune-up, transmission overhaul, etc.), the price of the necessary repairs can be obtained from a book. Not so in the case of a wreck job. No two auto body repair jobs are alike. In many cases, major damage is hidden and will have a large effect on the time required to complete the repairs.

The work of the estimator is important to the success of the auto body shop. If an estimator overestimates the cost of repairs, the job will go to another shop. If the estimate is too low, the shop will get the job but lose money.

When making an estimate, the estimator must know the capability of the shop, its workers and equipment. What is true for one shop is not true for another shop. In addition, the estimator must know the construction of the different types of automobiles.

In many cases, the estimator has gotten the necessary experience by working at the various jobs in the shop. In some shops, the owner does the estimating.

Fig. 35-8. Auto body collision parts service is a worthwhile related career opportunity. (Chrysler Service and Parts)

OWNER/MANAGER

The owner of an auto body and paint shop usually takes personal control of all business matters, and often assumes full charge of shop operation. In many body shops, even the supervisory work is performed by the owner. Only large shops have managers.

The supervisor (owner or manager) sees that sufficient work is scheduled to keep all workers busy and productive. Proper planning helps the workers complete each job on time. The supervisor hires enough workers to handle the volume of business at a profit, and sees that good and safe working conditions exist.

The shop owner handles all business relations with suppliers, associates and union representatives; sees that the company books are balanced; purchases all necessary equipment; establishes employee pay scales; decides what type advertising or promotion should be used to stimulate business.

THE INSURANCE ADJUSTER

Insurance adjusters do not work for auto body and paint shops; they work for insurance companies. Their job is to check the extent of damage on wrecked cars and decide how much the insurance company should pay for each repair job.

Insurance adjusters are among the highest paid workers in the field of auto body repair work. Adjusters must have vast and varied experience in body repair and paint work. They must have a thorough knowledge of the construction of all makes of automobiles and know the capabilities of all types of body repair and refinishing equipment.

AVAILABILITY OF EMPLOYMENT

With more cars on the road each year, there will always be work for the body and paint shop. Currently, there is in excess of 130,000,000 automotive vehicles in the United States. Every year, there are approximately 5,000,000 additional cars and trucks added to the list. Each passenger car, on the average, is driven in excess of 8600 miles annually. Male drivers average over 11,000 miles annually; female drivers average 5400 miles per year.

Almost any individual with experience as as auto body mechanic or painter, or one who has learned the basics in a vocational school,

has little difficulty in obtaining employment.

Skilled workers are in demand in independent shops, automobile and truck dealerships, trucking companies and bus lines. Work is available in every section of the country. Geographically, jobs are distributed about the same as population.

Salaries of auto body mechanics and painters vary in different areas, but generally are on a par with earnings of persons doing other mechanical work in the automotive field. In many areas, in fact, body mechanics and painters make above average wages, based on an hourly rate or on a commission of about half of the labor cost charged to the customer.

Many women are employed in the offices of auto body shops. Here, they handle business correspondence, attend to the billing and make sure that all parts used in the repair are included. They also order paint and parts that are needed. In many shops, women serve as cashiers, bookkeepers and act as pay clerks for the employees.

Vocational schools and the armed forces offer excellent opportunities to acquire necessary experience in auto body and paint work. Equally important are the training courses offered by various paint and equipment manufacturers.

Another area offering training in the automotive field is the Job Corp. The Job Corp is a training program for men and women between 16 and 21. For information on joining the Job Corp, contact the local State Employment Service, or the U.S. Department of Labor, Manpower Administration, Job Corp, Washington, D. C. 20210.

Using the pulling equipment pictured above is one of the many career opportunities available in the Auto Body field.

Chapter 36
GLOSSARY OF TERMS

ABRASIVE: A substance used for wearing away a surface by rubbing. Examples of abrasives as used in the automotive painting field are, aluminum oxide paper, silicon carbide paper.

ABRASIVE COATINGS: In closed coating paper no adhesive is exposed as the complete surface of the paper is covered with abrasive. In opening coating, adhesive is exposed between the grains of abrasive.

ACID CORE: Solder supplied in tubular wire form with the interior filled with acid flux in paste form.

ACRYLIC RESINS: Synthetic resins of excellent color and clarity used in both emulsion and solvent based paints. Available as a lacquer and also as an enamel.

ADHESION: How well a paint sticks to a surface to which it is applied. Surface preparation has considerable effect on adhesion.

AIR DRY: To dry paint at ordinary room temperatures.

ALUMINUM OXIDE: Hard and sharp abrasive made by fusing mineral bauxite at high temperatures.

ATOMIZE: The extent to which the air at the nozzle of the paint spray gun breaks up the paint and solvent into fine particles.

BAKELITE: A registered trademark identifying phenolic products used in varnish manufacture.

BINDER: The nonvolatile portion of a paint which serves to bind or cement the pigment particles together.

BLEEDING: Stain which works up or "bleeds" through succeeding coats of finish materials. Also when applied to hydraulic systems - the removal of air from the hydraulic fluid.

BLENDING: Mixing one color with another so colors mix or blend gradually.

BLISTERING: Formation of bubbles on surface of paint, usually caused by moisture behind film of paint.

BLOOM: Clouded appearance on finish coat.

BLUSHING: A finish coat is said to "blush" when it takes on a white or grayish cast during drying period. It is usually caused by the precipitation or separating of a portion of the solid content of the material, causing an opaque appearance.

BODY: Thickness of a fluid; that is, its viscosity.

BRONZING: The information of a metallic appearing haze on a paint film.

BUFFING COMPOUND: Soft abrasive in stick form bonded with wax.

BUTYL ACETATE: A lacquer solvent made from butyl alcohol by reaction with acetic acid.

CARBON TETRACHLORIDE: A nonflammable liquid with good solvent properties.

CARNAUBA WAX: A hard wax obtained from species of palm grown mostly in Brazil and used in some body polishing materials.

CAST: Inclination of one color to look like another. For example, sulphur is yellow with a greenish cast.

CAULKING COMPOUND: A semidrying or slow drying plastic material used to seal joints or fill crevices.

CELLULOSE: An inert substance, the chief component of the cell walls of plants. Nitrocellulose, used extensively in making lacquer, is prepared from cotton linters by treatment with chemicals.

CELLULOSE ACETATE: A binder made by chemical reaction of acetic acid on cellulose.

CELLULOSE NITRATE: A binder made by chemical reaction of nitric acid on cellulose (cotton linters). Also known as nitrocellulose and pyroxylin.

CHALKING: The decomposition of paint film into a powder on the surface.

CHECKING: The formation of short narrow cracks in the surface of a paint film. These cracks may assume many patterns, but the usual ones resemble the print of a bird's foot or small squares.

CHIPPING: Where small segments of top coat break away from the finish. Loss of adhesion.

CLEAR: A finish having no pigments or transparent pigments only.

COLOR RETENTION: When a paint product exposed to the elements shows no signs of changing color, it is said to have good color retention.

COMPATIBILITY: The ability of two or more materials to work together.

COMPRESSOR: A device used to compress air which in turn is used to spray paint.

COOL COLORS: Hues or colors in which blue predominates. The term "cool" is used because of association with ice, sky and water.

CORROSION: Break down of a metal caused by chemical action. Rusting for example.

COVERAGE: The area a given quantity of paint will cover; also how well paint conceals the surface being painted.

CRATERING: Formation of holes in the film. Usually caused by surface contamination.

CRAZING: Minute interlacing cracks on the surface of a finish.

CURING: The complete or final drying stage where a paint reaches complete strength and dryness as the result of chemical change.

DECALCOMANIA: Paint films in the form of pictures or letters which can be transferred from a temporary paper mounting to other surfaces.

DIE BACK: The loss of gloss in a finish coat usually caused in an acrylic or lacquer by continued thinner evaporation after the color has been polished.

DINGING HAMMER: A special hammer used for dinging or removal of dents from an auto panel.

DOLLY: A hand held metal tool or anvil designed to be held on one side of the dented panel while the other is struck with the dinging hammer.

DOUBLE COAT: A term used in acrylic and lacquer application. A single coat immediately followed by a second coat. (Often the second coat is sprayed in the opposite direction to the first - one horizontal and the other vertical.)

DRIER: A material added to paint to reduce drying time.

DRY SPRAY: The atomized paint that does not dissolve into the material being sprayed. Presents a rough dull appearance. Usually caused by too fast a reducer or thinner for the temperature, holding the gun too far from the surface so that too much of the solvent evaporates in the air, or too high an air pressure.

ENAMEL: Type of paint made by grinding or mixing pigments with varnishes or lacquers or acrylics.

EPOXY RESINS: Resins obtained by condensation reaction between phenols and epichlorohydrin.

ETHYL LACTATE: A solvent made by a reaction between ethyl alcohol and lactic acid.

FEATHEREDGE: When a paint surface is broken by stone bruises, grinding, etc., it usually leaves a sharp edge. This edge must be slanted or tapered with sandpaper or featheredging solvent. This taper edge of the paint is called the featheredge.

FIBERGLASS: Fine spun filaments of glass used as insulation and also in the repair of auto bodies.

FINISH COAT: Last coat applied of finish material.

FISH-EYES: Blemishes in the finish coat usually of a circular and opalescent character. Generally caused by failure to remove all traces of silicone polish prior to painting.

FLAKING: Detachment of small pieces of paint film.

FLASH OFF: Flash off is the rapid evaporation of thinner.

FLINT PAPER: Abrasive paper which is grayish white in color. Inexpensive but has short working life. Seldom used in auto body refinishing.

FLOW: The ability of particles of paint spray to merge together to form a smooth surface.

FOG COAT: A thin, highly atomized coat to obtain a fast flash off of the thinner and therefore, minimum penetration of the thinner into the old finish. Usually achieved by reducing the fluid speed while leaving air pressure at 45 lb. at the gun.

GARNET PAPER: Abrasive which is reddish in color, hard and sharp; comes from same source as semi-precious jewel by that name. It is more expensive than flint paper, but it lasts longer.

GLOSS: A term used to indicate the shine, luster or sheen of a dried paint film.

HEADLINING: The cloth or other material used to cover the inner surface of the car roof.

HUMIDITY: Amount of water vapor in the air.

INDUCTION BAKING: Using heat induced by electrostatic and electromagnetic means for baking finishes.

JIGSAW: A saw with a narrow blade, mechanically driven and used for cutting body panels.

LACQUER: Finishing material that dries by the evaporation of the thinner or solvent. There are many different types of lacquers, a popular type being that based on cellulose nitrate. Besides the cellulosic compound, lacquers contain resins, plasticizers, solvents and diluents.

MASKING PAPER: A special paper used to cover areas of body panels to protect them from paint spray.

MASKING TAPE: Adhesive coated paper tape used to mask or protect parts of surface from spray paint. Also used to attach masking paper to body panels.

METAL CONDITIONER: Special preparation to be applied to unfinished metal and designed to prevent the formation of rust and also slightly etch the surface.

METALLICS: A class of finishes or paints which include flakes of metal in addition to the pigment.

MINERAL SPIRITS: Petroleum product which has about the same evaporation rate as gum turpentine. Frequently used for cleaning spray guns.

MISCIBLE: Capable of being mixed.

MIST COAT: Over thinning the color and spraying very wet. Usually the final coat for flow with lacquer or acrylic polychromatic colors.

NEUTRAL FLAME: The flame of an oxy-acetylene torch so adjusted to eliminate all of the acetylene feather at the inner cone of the flame.

NITROCELLULOSE: See cellulose nitrate.

ORANGE PEEL: A nubby surface looking like the skin of an orange. It may or may not have a good gloss. Caused by poor flow because of too fast a reducer or lack of atomization.

ORBITAL SANDER: Power sanding tool that operates in an elliptical or oval pattern.

ORIGINAL FINISH: The paint applied at the factory by the vehicle manufacturer.

OVERLAP: That part of the spray band that goes on top of the previous swath of paint. Also that part of the spray that overlaps a previously painted area.

OVERSPRAY: An overlap of dry spray gun particles on areas where they are not wanted.

OXIDATION: Combination of oxygen from the air with the paint film. This process dries and continues to harden enamel for several weeks. The chalking (surface powder) of a paint film, that takes place in the aging of the film, is also a form of oxidation.

PAINT FILM: The thickness of the paint on the surface.

PAINT REMOVER: A mixture of active solvents used to remove paint and varnish coatings.

PEELING: Detachment of a paint film in relatively large pieces. Paint applied to a damp, or greasy surface usually peels.

PHENOLIC RESIN: Resin based essentially on reaction between phenol and formaldehyde.

PIGMENT: Material in the form of fine powders. Used to impart color, opacity and other effects to paint.

PINHOLING: Holes that form in the top coat or undercoat.

PLASTIC FILLER: Special compounds used to fill dents and cracks in automotile panels.

POLYCHROMATIC: Metallic effect imparted by adding aluminum powder in flake form to color coats.

POLYESTER BODY PUTTY: Sprayable material designed to fill hairline cracks, pin holes, etc., in metal or fiber glass.

PRIME COAT: Primer or primer surfacer applied to bare metal to obtain adhesion.

PUTTY: A heavy-body material used to fill flaws that are too large to be filled by primer surfacer.

REDUCER: Solvent combination used to thin enamel is usually referred to as reducer.

RESPIRATOR: A device designed to filter particles out of the air so that they do not reach the lungs.

RETARDER: A very rich, slow drying solvent that slows down the rate of evaporation.

RUBBING COMPOUND: An abrasive used to smooth and polish the paint film.

SAGS: A paint film that drips or runs.

SAND SCRATCHES: The marks made in metal or old finish by abrasives. Also those showing in the finish coat due to lack of fill or sealing.

SANDERS: Power driven tool used to sand auto bodies. Some sanders give a rotary motion to the abrasive, while others give a reciprocating motion.

SEALER: A liquid coating composition, usually transparent, for sealing porous surfaces to prevent previous coatings from bleeding through.

SHROUD: Sheet metal used to contain or direct air blast from cooling fan.

SILICON CARBIDE: Abrasive crystals are shiny black and iridescent; very hard. Made by fusing silica and coke in an electric furnace.

SILICONE: An ingredient in waxes and polishes which makes them sleek to the touch and improving the appearance of the finish coat. Must be removed before new paint is applied.

SINGLE COAT: Usually just referred to as a coat of paint. Once over the surface to be painted with each stroke overlapping the previous coat 50 percent.

SKIRT: That portion of the fender that extends down along the side of the wheel.

SLIDE HAMMER: Special tool on which the hammerhead is slid along a rod and against a stop, so that it will pull against the object to which the rod has been hooked or otherwise fastened.

SOLDER: A mixture of tin and lead, having low melting point and used to fill dents and cracks in auto body panels.

SOLIDS: That part of the paint that does not evaporate, but stays on the surface.

SOLVENT: A liquid capable of dissolving a material.

SPECIFIC GRAVITY: The weight of a given volume of a liquid compared to the same volume of water at the same temperature.

SPOON: A tool used in much the same manner as a dolly (i.e. an anvil) but so designed it can be used in areas where there is little clearance and there would be no room for a dolly. Also used to pry panels back into position.

SPRAY GUN: A device to mix paint and compressed air so that the mixture is ejected in a controlled pattern and highly atomized.

STRIKER PLATE: That portion of a door lock which is mounted on the body pillar and which is struck or engaged by the latch or lock extension when the door is closed.

SUN ROOF: Adjustable roof panel that slides backward and forward on guide racks.

SURFACE DRYING: Drying of a finishing material on top while the lower portion remains more or less soft.

SYNTHETIC RESIN: An artificial resin or plastic produced by systematic exploitation of chemical reaction of organic substances.

TACK COAT: The first coat with enamel. This is a full coat and is allowed to dry until it is quite sticky. From 10 to 30 minutes, depending on drying conditions and reducer used.

TACK RAG: A cloth impregnated with varnish and used to remove abrasive dust from surface just before applying finishing material.

TEMPLATE: A form or pattern made especially so that other parts can be formed exactly to the same shape.

THINNER: The solvent combination used to thin lacquers and acrylics to spraying viscosity is usually called thinner.

TOLUOL (TOLUENE): Lacquer diluent made normally by coal tar distillation.

TONE: A graduation of color, either in hue, a tint, or a shade; as a gray tone.

TOOTH: Roughened or absorbent quality of a surface which affects adhesion and application of coating.

UNDERCOAT: Second coat in three coat work, or first coat in repainting.

UNITIZED BODY: Automobile construction that has the frame built into the body.

URETHANE: A crystalline compound used in certain automotive acrylic enamels.

WARM COLORS: Colors in which red-orange predominate.

WATER SPOTTING: Water droplets mar the finish before the finish has become completely dry.

WATERSHIELD: Deflector built into door.

WEATHERING: The change or failure in paint caused by exposure to weather.

WINDOW REGULATOR: Mechanism in door which provides a means of cranking window up and down.

WINDOW STABILIZER: Device inside door used to support glass at belt line.

WINDOW STOP: Device inside door used to limit maximum glass height and depth.

WINDSHIELD HEADER BAR: That area immediately above the windshield to which the windshield header molding is attached.

WINDLACE: Special trim of a rope-like nature placed around the edge of the door frame as a decoration and also to reduce drafts.

WRINKLING: Skinning of a heavy coat of paint before the underpart of the film has properly dried.

Checking and adjusting wheel alignment is an important finishing step to frame and body straightening operations.   (Bear)

Chapter 37
USEFUL TABLES
AND CHARTS

DECIMAL EQUIVALENT OF THE NUMBERS OF TWIST DRILL AND STEEL WIRE GAUGE

No.	Size of No. in Decimals	No.	Size of No. in Decimals	No.	Size of No. in Decimals	No.	Size of No. in Decimals	No.	Size of No. in Decimals
1	.2280	17	.1730	33	.1130	49	.0730	65	.0350
2	.2210	18	.1695	34	.1110	50	.0700	66	.0330
3	.2130	19	.1660	35	.1100	51	.0670	67	.0320
4	.2090	20	.1610	36	.1065	52	.0635	68	.0310
5	.2055	21	.1590	37	.1040	53	.0595	69	.0292
6	.2040	22	.1570	38	.1015	54	.0550	70	.0280
7	.2010	23	.1540	39	.0995	55	.0520	71	.0260
8	.1990	24	.1520	40	.0980	56	.0465	72	.0250
9	.1960	25	.1495	41	.0960	57	.0430	73	.0240
10	.1935	26	.1470	42	.0935	58	.0420	74	.0225
11	.1910	27	.1440	43	.0890	59	.0410	75	.0210
12	.1890	28	.1405	44	.0860	60	.0400	76	.0200
13	.1850	29	.1360	45	.0820	61	.0390	77	.0180
14	.1820	30	.1285	46	.0810	62	.0380	78	.0160
15	.1800	31	.1200	47	.0785	63	.0370	79	.0145
16	.1770	32	.1160	48	.0760	64	.0360	80	.0135

LUBRICANTS FOR CUTTING TOOLS

Material	Turning	Chucking	Drilling Milling	Reaming	Tapping
Tool Steel	Dry or Oil	Oil or Soda Water	Oil	Lard Oil	Oil
Soft Steel	Dry or Soda Water	Soda Water	Oil or Soda Water	Lard Oil	Oil
Wrought Iron	Dry or Soda Water	Soda Water	Oil or Soda Water	Lard Oil	Oil
Cast Iron	Dry	Dry	Dry	Dry	Oil
Brass	Dry	Dry	Dry	Dry	Oil
Copper	Dry	Oil	Oil	Mixture	Oil
Babbitt	Dry	Dry	Dry	Dry	Oil
Glass		Turpentine or Kerosene			

Mixture is 1/3 Crude Petroleum, 2/3 Lard Oil; when two lubricants are mentioned, the first is preferable.

HIGH TEMPERATURES JUDGED BY COLOR
AND COLORS FOR TEMPERING

Degrees Centigrade	Degrees Fahrenheit	High Temperatures Judged by color	Degrees Centigrade	Degrees Fahrenheit	Colors for Tempering
400	752	Red heat, visible in the dark	221.1	430	Very pale yellow
474	885	Red heat, visible in the twilight	226.7	440	Light yellow
525	975	Red heat, visible in the daylight	232.2	450	Pale straw-yellow
581	1077	Red heat, visible in the sunlight	237.8	460	Straw-yellow
700	1292	Dark red	243.3	470	Deep straw-yellow
800	1472	Dull cherry-red	248.9	480	Dark yellow
900	1652	Cherry-red	254.4	490	Yellow-brown
1000	1832	Bright cherry-red	260.0	500	Brown-yellow
1100	2012	Orange-red	265.6	510	Spotted red-brown
1200	2192	Orange-yellow	271.1	520	Brown-purple
1300	2372	Yellow-white	276.7	530	Light purple
1400	2552	White welding heat	282.2	540	Full purple
1500	2732	Brilliant white	287.8	550	Dark purple
1600	2912	Dazzling white (bluish-white)	293.3	560	Full blue
			298.9	570	Dark blue

FIGURING PULLEY SIZES AND RPM

To Find:

RPM of Driven Pulley	Multiply diameter of driving pulley by its rpm and divide by diameter of driven pulley.
Diameter of Driven Pulley	Multiply diameter of driving pulley by its rpm and divide by rpm of driven pulley.
RPM of Driving Pulley	Multiply diameter of driven pulley by its rpm and divide by diameter of driving pulley.
Diameter of Driving Pulley	Multiply diameter of driven pulley by its rpm and divide by rpm of driving pulley.

MELTING POINT OF METALS

Metal	Degrees Fahrenheit
Aluminum	1220.4
Copper	1981.4
Iron	2795.0
Lead	621.2
Platinum	3224.0
Silver	1761.0
Solder (50-50)	*415.0
Solder (63% tin--37% lead)	360.0
Solder (40% tin--60% lead)	*459.0
Tin	449.4
Tungsten	6120.0
Zinc	787.2

*First melting point 360º.

METRIC CONVERSION FACTORS

TO CONVERT	INTO	MULTIPLY BY
Centimetres	Inches	0.3937
Feet	Metres	0.3048
Inches	Centimetres	2.540
Metres	Feet	3.281
Sq. Centimetres	Sq. Inches	0.1550
Sq. Feet	Sq. Metres	0.093
Sq. Inches	Sq. Centimetre	6.452
Cu. Centimetres	Cu. Inches	0.06102
Cu. Inches	Litres	0.0164
Cu. Feet	Cu. Metres	0.0283
Gallons U.S.	Litres	3.785
Ounces	Grams	28.35
Pounds	Kilograms	0.4536
Kilograms	Pounds	2.205
Miles per hour	Kilometres per hour	1.609

TO CONVERT ENGLISH MEASUREMENTS TO METRIC

Multiply	by	to get equivalent number of:
LENGTH		
Inch	25.4	millimetres (mm)
Foot	0.304 8	metres (m)
Yard	0.914 4	metres
Mile	1.609	kilometres (km)
AREA		
Inch²	645.2	millimetres² (mm²)
	6.45	centimetres² (cm²)
Foot²	0.092 9	metres² (m²)
Yard²	0.836 1	metres²
VOLUME		
Inch³	16 387.	mm³
	16.387	cm³
	0.016 4	litres (l)
Quart	0.946 4	litres
Gallon	3.785 4	litres
Yard³	0.764 6	metres³ (m³)
MASS		
Pound	0.453 6	kilograms (kg)
Ton	907.18	kilogram
Ton	0.907	tonne (t)
FORCE		
Kilogram (force)	9.807	newtons (N)
Ounce	0.278 0	newtons
Pound	4.448	newtons

Multiply	by	to get equivalent number of:
ACCELERATION		
Foot/sec²	0.304 8	metre/sec² (m/s²)
Inch/sec²	0.025 4	metre/sec²
TORQUE		
Pound-inch	0.112 98	newton-metres (N.m)
Pound-foot	1.355 8	newton-metres
POWER		
Horsepower	0.746	kilowatts (kW)
PRESSURE OR STRESS		
Inches of mercury	3.38	kilopascals (kPa)
Pounds/sq. in.	6.895	kilopascals
ENERGY OR WORK		
BTU	1 055.	joules (J)
Foot-pound	1.355 8	joules
Kilowatt-hour	3 600 000 or 3.6×10^6	joules (J = W.s)
LIGHT		
Footcandle	10.764	lumens/metre² (lm/m²)
FUEL PERFORMANCE		
Miles/gal	0.425 1	kilometres/litre (km/l)
Gal/mile	2.352 7	litres/kilometre (l/km)
VELOCITY		
Miles/hour	1.609 3	kilometres/hr. (km/h)

TEMPERATURE

Degree Fahrenheit (°F-32) ÷ 1.8 = degree Celsius (°C)

THE METRIC SYSTEM OF MEASUREMENT
MEASURES OF LENGTH

1 Millimetre (mm) =	0.03937079 inch, or about 1/25 inch
10 Millimetres = 1 Centimetre (cm) =	0.3937079 inch
10 Centimetres = 1 Decimetre (dm) =	3.937079 inches
10 Decimetres = 1 Metre (m) =	39.37079 inches, 3.2808992 feet, or 1.09361 yards
10 Metres = 1 Decameter (Dm) =	32.808992 feet
10 Decametres = 1 Hectometre (Hm) =	19.927817 rods
10 Hectometres = 1 Kilometre (Km) =	1093.61 yards, or 0.6213824 mile
10 Kilometres = 1 Myriametre (Mm) =	6.213824 miles

1 inch = 2.54 cm, 1 foot = 0.3048 m, 1 yard = 0.9144 m, 1 rod = 0.5029 Dm, 1 mile = 1.6093 Km

ACKNOWLEDGMENTS

This book contains material obtained from many different sources. The author and publisher wish to express their deep appreciation for the splendid cooperation of individuals and organizations that has made this book possible. Special credit is due:

AC Spark Plug Div., General Motors Corp., Flint, MI
Acme Quality Paints, Inc., Detroit, MI
Airco Welding Products,
  Div. of Air Reduction Co., Inc., New York, NY
American Lacquer Solvent Co., Phoenixville, PA
American Motors Corp., Detroit, MI
Ammco Tools, Inc., North Chicago, IL
Automotive Finishes, Inc., Dearborn, MI
Bear, Wheel Service Div.,
  Applied Power, Inc., Rock Island, IL
Bee Line Co., Davenport, IA
Behr Manning Div., Norton Co., Troy, NY
Binks Mfg. Co., Franklin Park, IL
Black and Decker Mfg. Co., Towson, MD
Blackhawk, Collision Repair Div.,
  Applied Power, Inc., Milwaukee, WI
Bonney Tool Div., The Triangle Corp., Orangeburg, SC
Buick Motor Div., General Motors Corp., Flint, MI
Cadillac Motor Car Div., General Motors Corp., Detroit, MI
Carborundum Co., Niagara Falls, NY
Car Fastener Co., Cambridge, MA
Chevrolet Motor Div., General Motors Corp., Detroit, MI
Chicago Pneumatic Tool Co., New York, NY
Chrysler Corp., Detroit, MI
Chrysler-Plymouth Div., Chrysler Corp., Detroit, MI
Clayton Mfg. Co., El Monte, CA
DeVilbiss Co., Toledo, OH
Ditzler Automotive Finishes, PPG Industries, Detroit, MI
Dodge Div. Chrysler Corp., Detroit, MI
E.I. DuPont deNemours & Co., Wilmington, DE
Fisher Body Div., General Motors Corp., Warren, MI
FMC - Automotive Service Equipment Div., Conway, AR
Ford Motor Co., Dearborn, MI

Hein - Werner Corp., Waukesha, WI
Ingersoll-Rand Co., Des Plaines, IL
K-D Mfg. Co., Lancaster, PA
Kelite Corp., Los Angeles, CA
Kester Solder Co., Litton Systems, Inc., Chicago, IL
Lincoln Electric Co., Cleveland, OH
Lincoln-Mercury Div., Ford Motor Co., Dearborn, MI
Lubriplate Div., Fiske Brothers Refinishing Co., Newark, NJ
Magnus Chemical Co., Garwood, NJ
Marquette, Performance/Safety Test Div.,
  Applied Power, Inc., St. Paul, MN
Martin Senour Co., Chicago, IL
Mystic Tape Borden Inc., Northfield, IL
Nason Automotive Finishes, S. San Francisco, CA
Norton Co., Worcester, MA
Oakite Products, Inc., New York, NY
Oldsmobile Div., General Motors Corp., Lansing, MI
Owatonna Tool Co., Owatonna, MN
Paasche Air Brush Co., Chicago, IL
Permacel, New Brunswick, NJ
Pontiac Motor Div., General Motors Corp., Pontiac, MI
H. K. Porter Co., Inc., Sommerville, MA
Rinshed-Mason Products, Inmont Corp., Detroit, MI
Sherwin-Williams Co., Cleveland, OH
Skil Corp., Chicago, IL
Snap-on Tools Corp., Kenosha, WI
Sommer and Maca Glass Machinery Co., Chicago, IL
Steck Mfg. Co., Dayton, OH
Taylor & Art, Inc., Oakland, CA
Technical Tape Corp., New Rochelle, NY
3M Co., Automotive Trades Div., St. Paul, MN
Union Carbide Corp., New York, NY
Weaver Div., Dura Corp., Paris, KY

INDEX

sander, using, 28
Disks, sanding, selecting, 31
Dolly blocks, 14
Dolly, using, 18, 19, 20
Door,
adjustment, 103, 104, 107, 108
arm rest assemblies, 121
emergency opening procedure, 120
glass, 132, 133, 134, 135, 136
hardware service, 110
handles, 110, 111, 115, 119
lock assembly, 112, 115
lock strikers, 104, 108, 109
panel replacement, 94
reinforcing beams, 36
service, 132
trim assemblies, 121, 124
ventilator, 134, 135
weatherstrip, 129, 130, 131, 234
window assembly, 115, 132, 133, 134
Drain holes, 234, 235
Drying equipment, paint, 204
Dual acting tail gate, 157, 158, 159, 160

E

Electric arc cutting, 76
Electric arc welding, 62, 67, 68
Electric door locks, 119
Electric sun roof, 155, 156
Employment opportunities, 250
Enamel, 178, 180, 181
Energy absorbing bumper, 36
Estimator, career opportunity, 249
Extended method, installing adhesive
caulked glass, 143, 144, 145
Extension cables, 28
Exterior cleaning, 236
External mix spray gun, 195

F

Fabric roofs, 162, 163
Fender, 11
adjustments, 99
file, 16, 21
panel removal, 82
Fenders, replacing, 82, 83
Fiber glass bodies, repairing, 91, 92, 93
File holder, 16
Filing tips, 21
Filler preparation, fiber glass, 92
Filling dents, 86
Filling rusted areas, 89
Flashbacks, welding, 65
Flexible ABS parts, 185
Floor carpets, cleaning, 238
Fluid needle adjustment, 196
Fluid tip, 196
Four-way seats, 150
Frame damage, 45
repairing, 47, 48, 49

types of, 45
Frame gauges, using, 45, 46
Frame misalignment, checking, 45, 46
Frame straightening equipment, 47
Front door regulator, 114, 138, 139
Front door windows, 115, 132, 133, 134
Front end masking, 176
Front end sheet metalwork, 10

G

Glass installer, career opportunity, 247
Glass polishing, 148
Glass, window, service, 116, 132, 138
Glossary of terms, 252
Grease removers, 180
Grease stains, removing, 239
Grinding disk, attaching, 34
Grits, abrasive, 32
Grommets, 234

H

Hammer, 14, 18, 19, 20
dinging, using, 18, 19
impact, cutting, 78
marks, sanding, 34
pick, using, 21
slide, 42
Hand tools, 14, 18
Handle, door, 110, 111, 115, 118
Hard ABS parts, 185
Hardware, door, 110
Headlining assembly, 125
Headlining, removing, 125, 126
Headlining, replacing, 126, 127, 128
Heat shields, 17
High temperature color code, 258
Hinges, door, 103, 104, 105
Holder, file, 16
Hood alignment, 99, 101
Hood noises, 236
Hose size, spray gun, 202
Hoses, welding, 63

I

Impact hammer, cutting, 78
Installing abrasive disk, 33
Insurance adjuster, career opportunity, 250
Interior cleaning, 236
Interior trim removal, 121, 122, 123, 124
Internal mix spray gun, 194, 195

J

Jigsaws, power, cutting, 77

K

Kits, tool, 17
Korek straightening system, 42, 51, 52, 53

L

Lacquer, 178, 180, 181
Lap and shoulder belts, 39
Latch and striker pin adjustment, 109
Leaks,
checking with water, 233